Mystic Awareness For The Modern Mind

Dr. PILLAI G. K.

Originals
(an imprint of Low Price Publications)
Delhi-110052

Distributed By
D.K. Publishers Distributors (P) Ltd.
4834/24, Ansari Road, Darya Ganj,
New Delhi-110002
Phones: 3278584, 3278368, 3261465,
e-mail: dkpd@del3.vsnl.net.in
visit us at: www.dkpd.com

First Published 2001

ISBN 81-7536-233-2

Published By
Originals
(an imprint of Low Price Publications)
A-6, Nimri Commercial Centre,
Near Ashok Vihar Phase-IV,
Delhi-110052
Phones: 7401672, 7452453
e-mail: lpp@nde.vsnl.net.in
visit us at: www.lppindia.com

Printed At:
D K Fine Art Press P Ltd.
Delhi-110052

PRINTED IN INDIA

CONTENTS

INTRODUCTION

I sing
In praise of the cosmic order,
that is designed to subsist,
from eternity to eternity,
i seek the truth of reality,
underlying the wonderful design
that gives sweet, white milk,
from the udder of a black cow.

(ATHARVA VEDA)

Nature shows us only the tail of the lion. But i have no doubt that the tail belongs to him; even though he cannot at once reveal himself because of the enormous size.

(ALBERT EINSTEIN)

Let us live in tune with the universal soul,
renouncing ego, hatred & desire,
every particle in the universe proclaims,
he unity of existence
of all in that supreme reality.
Let us seek the most blissful experience,
of eternal existence
in the infallible wisdom of super consciousness.

(RIG VEDA)

The title of the book briefly tells you what it is all about. It is a capsule of knowledge to extend the ordinary consciousness to a far superior and holistic level of perception. The sole purpose is to enable you to realize the unity underlying all kinds of existence. It would eventually give you a pathfinder to return to the dreamy state of innocence of the early childhood. In the absence of the concept of self, the infant feels no needs, desires or ambitions. But, with the fixation of body awareness, the childhood serenity gives way to innumerable miseries of the adult life. Mystics claim to reach such exalted state of undifferentiated awareness through meditation or other mind-altering means. This book shows how even ordinary mortals like you and me can enjoy the ecstasy of unlimited awareness simply by following the path of knowledge to self-realization.

The innocence of childhood can be restored when the mind is slowly unbound from body awareness. The loss of individual identity may make one feel rudderless in the vastness of undifferentiated existence. But true knowledge will ultimately remove the misconception of identity created by the pleasure-seeking neural network in the brain. You may not immediately get instant enlightenment or ready answers to all the mysteries of nature. But if you involve actively in the pursuit of the wisdom of existence, you will definitely gain the most enjoyable experience of self-realization. The creditable achievement is that all this enlightenment is attained solely by your own efforts,

We begin our exciting intellectual adventure with systematic exposure to the facts ascertained by scientific inquiries on universe, life and mind. The intention is to take you to a higher level of awareness to appreciate the unfolding rational worldview. The missing links in scientific knowledge are supplemented with certain rational insights in our great heritage of mystic wisdom. You can incorporate in the emergent worldview all the spiritual and cultural values that you may cherish to preserve. At the end of the voyage of discovery, you will get an exquisite experience of rational wisdom emerging spontaneously without any external mediation. In short, though no free spiritual lunch is offered, you will get plenty of delicious appetizers that will entice you to reach the wisdom embedded in your own mind. The truth of reality will reveal to you the utter futility of the competitive struggle to amass wealth by any means. Of course, all this can happen only when you accept that the self is only a reflection of the eternal existence of universal consciousness. The wisdom to know what life is all about would change our mundane material existence to an enjoyable spiritual experience.

In our evolutionary ascend from apes to intelligent humans; we have come across several inexplicable enigmas of nature. The entire humanity must have shared from the very beginning the quest for the true knowledge of where we are, what we are and how we become capable of seeking answers to such profound matters of identity. At one extreme, some people simply assume that we are the chosen ones blessed with all the intelligence and authority to control the destiny of the universe. Some others feel that humans are mere biological curiosities created by random blunders accumulated during the saga of evolution of life on a tiny planet! But no universally acceptable rational explanation is available to solve the mystery of the existence of the great cosmos consisting of several complex structures including the humans.

Now we have plenty of scientific knowledge to answer the first and second questions. But in spite of all modern tools that enhance our perception, the third question on the emergence of a conscious self is still beyond our comprehension. We do not find a convincing explanation for an intelligent life of very short duration in the enormity of cosmic time. In fact, all our struggles to achieve higher standards of life seem to further shorten the inevitable destiny of a hasty exit. The apparent futility of our intense efforts to secure a few decades of worthless existence creates immense despondency in sensitive minds. Unless some rational explanation is found for our short sojourn, we cannot enjoy the experience of even the limited existence. Some acceptable explanations would surely emerge at the end of our voyage of discovery in to the origin and evolution of universe and life.

We have just entered a new millennium, which is likely to become an important landmark in the evolution of the humankind. There are several exciting possibilities before us, which would not have appeared even in the wildest dreams of our ancestors. Our accumulated wealth of knowledge has already transformed us from timid primates to intellectual giants capable of exploring the very basis of creation. The astonishing technological innovations in the last few centuries extended our sensory faculties far beyond the limits of original design for sub serving the physical needs. With the enhanced power of perception and comprehension, we have already unraveled most of the secrets of nature at all levels. In the next couple of decades, we may get all the correct and complete knowledge of everything in the universe.

With the accurate application of knowledge, we have already overcome most of the physical barriers set up by nature. Faster modes of transportation and communication now ensure our instantaneous presence any where in the planet. Scientists claim to have broken the unassailable speed of light by accelerating light pulses 300 times more than its normal velocity of 186,000 miles per second. The entire planet is now an interactive web of human intelligence. We have decoded many of the genetic messages and sequences encrypted on the DNA. The emerging knowledge of the patterns of inheritance will soon find successful applications particularly in medicine. It will enable us to create exciting varieties of new life and improve the existing species. Our future adventures will definitely include interplanetary travel, human cloning and the synthesis of exotic life in the laboratory. With so many achievements in hand and many more on the anvil, life in the new millennium should be far more adventurous for the humankind.

But, beyond these impressive achievements, we find an appalling scenario of abject misery and destitution. We have been mercilessly misusing the precious gift of knowledge to create calamities of great magnitude like the two devastating world wars. Third World poverty continues unabated, despite the great strides we made in agriculture and medicine. We have been inventing more and more deadly weapons of mass destruction instead of using modern technology to mitigate the miseries in the less developed parts of the world. If the rich nations diverted a small fraction of their defense budgets, poverty and illiteracy could have been totally wiped out from the entire world. Our uncontrollable greed has already destroyed much of the delicate ecology that sustained the existence of a wide variety of life. The wonderful innovations in low cost technology could have been used to produce sufficient food and medicine for the poor and the needy. Unfortunately, even in modern times, our avarice does not show any signs of a possible decline. The fruits of science only created a few islands of prosperity, while the majority of humanity languish helplessly in utter deprivation.

Our sustained success in overcoming most of the challenges of nature is undoubtedly a creditable achievement of humanity. But what is deeply disturbing is the utter failure to control the ever- increasing competitive urges to amass material gains. We mastered many secrets of matter and life, but the mystery of the mind that creates avoidable miseries for all still eludes our rational wisdom. Science has already unraveled most of the structural and functional aspects of the brain that give rise to the wonderful phenomenon of mind. But even the best of human intelligence assisted by the most modern analytical tools fail to reveal the non-physical qualities of the intractable mind. It is of course the most unique evolutionary wonder capable of experiencing a vast variety of thoughts and emotions. The splendid mental abstractions like great works of art and brilliant mathematical theorems give the proof of its vast abilities and infinite reach.

Unfortunately, the same mind is also the source of all undesirable and self-centered actions. If we were genuinely broad-minded, the abundant wealth of natural resources would have been equitably distributed to make every one happy and contended. Even the so-called mindless animals seldom kill for pleasure or hoard more food than what is essentially required for their immediate or near future consumption. In fact, the absence of a mind that foolishly accumulates possessions beyond the normal capacity of consumption seems to be a real blessing for them. The animal communities enjoy peaceful co-existence, as they are not disturbed by the delusions of grandeur that haunt the human mind.

`It is in this context that we need correct and complete knowledge about the mind that presumably controls our thoughts and actions. We have to seek the real causes underlying our deliberate acts of wanton destruction of life and environment. The phenomenon of consciousness that creates the mind must have initially appeared in some primates when evolutionary changes enlarged the brain. Later on, social interactions and extensive use of tools and linguistic capabilities must have speeded up the emergence of an intelligent mind.

We find that some animals like chimpanzees are also capable of experiencing an abridged version of self-awareness. But they certainly lack the capacity of an intelligent human mind to relate the multitude of external events in a coherent manner. Our ability to experience vast ranges of emotions and thoughts is not found in any other variety of life on earth. Since the concept of self is not at all an evolutionary necessity for survival, we would have acquired this rare faculty probably for peaceful existence in a social milieu. Certain kinds of bees and ants also show instinctive altruism necessary for a successful community life. How ever, the great quality of compassionate wisdom appears to be an exclusive cultural invention of human mind without any genetic or environmental cause.

It is now established that the mind emerges from the innumerable electro-chemical processes in the brain. It consists of several systems and sub systems but functions as a totally integrated entity. The sensory inputs received in the brain are immediately processed with reference to the memory for identification. An integrated image of the input is then projected to the mind for experiencing the objective reality. In our traditional wisdom, we believe that human behavior is always guided by a perceptive mind. But the latest discoveries reveal that our conscious decisions are just passive acceptance of the choices already made by the hard working neurons. We are totally unaware of the serial and parallel computing processes that continuously go on in the brain to create reality. It implies that the quality of our conscious thoughts and actions can improve only if the unconscious brain processes are somehow re-engineered to include altruistic intentions also in the cerebral software. Then only our consciousness could reach a higher level to perceive the fundamental truth of the unity of all existence.

The amazing computing power of the brain is the outcome of millions of years of evolutionary efforts to enhance the chances of survival. The time-tested strategies developed by the neural circuits to overcome the challenges of nature may not readily accept the modern altruistic urges in the pre-installed software. Continuous impact of correct information inputs from scientific knowledge can perhaps override egocentric genetic dispositions in course of time. At higher levels of awareness, inherited illusions about one's own superior status by birth or faith disappear. The modified mind perceives the truth of reality that all creations in the universe emerge from the same basic energy. Then we realize the wisdom of compassionate co-existence.

It is true that even in the twenty-first century, we depend solely up on the highly improbable theological explanations for spiritual enlightenment. The astonishingly accurate revelations of scientific enquiries, has already rendered the absolute certainty of divine will less than convincing even to the layman. But in the absence of a rational alternative to replace the inherited faiths, millions of followers of religious worldviews still fall back upon the imassilable wisdom of the God. We find even reputed scientists seeking the spiritual solace of religious experiences. In fact, scientists generally prefer to avoid meddling with the matters of the mind that are not amenable to the accepted methodology of rational inquiries. But we cannot simply run away from the fact that the mind is also an integral part of the physical reality. The reality now reflected in our scientific knowledge should also include the correct information in respect of the emergence and the functioning of the mind. We can hope to achieve universal peace and happiness only when scientific knowledge removes our misconceptions about the non-physical features of the mind. In short, unless the mind is demystified, we will never unravel the riddle of existence.

Systematic enquiries into the mysteries of the mind began in about BC 2000 by the Indo-Aryan scholars. Their incisive insights are found in the various "Upanishads", which are attached to the compilations of ancient wisdom called "Vedas". The anonymous visionaries conceived the truth of reality as "Brahman" which is the all pervading and undifferentiated energy of consciousness. According to the Vedas, "Brahman" is beyond all qualities, forms, and description but encompasses all entities in its ambit. They called it the "Supreme Self" or "Super Consciousness". It is presumably present in all forms of biological life and even in ordinary matter. We perceive the external reality and our own existence through the consciousness arising in the brain. Mystics claim that with the realization of the fundamental unity of all existence in universal consciousness, we align ourselves with the supreme self. They found the ultimate goal of perpetual peace and happiness in the realization of universal consciousness.

A sage called "Ashtavakra", who lived around BC 500, expanded and extrapolated the vedic vision of consciousness. He attributed all forms of existence to consciousness that manifests the external world in our perception. Undoubtedly, his ideas were far ahead of the then prevalent religious practices of Hinduism. Hindu theology is based on the assumption that an almighty God created, maintained and destroyed life and universe. His unconventional insights must have upset the powerful religious institutions that controlled all scholarly activities of the period. His verses of wisdom contain several excellent metaphors that drive home the full import of his esoteric concepts. The ignorant masses of ancient times, would have been more than shocked by the revelations in his crazy ideas.

An accurate analysis of the nature of consciousness emerges from Ashtavakra's dialogues with a venerable king called "Janaka". According to him, what we perceive is just a transient illusion of various forms of existence through the medium of consciousness. He did not equate universal consciousness to an almighty creator. The idea of a God is totally redundant if we accept consciousness as the Supreme Reality manifesting the entire world in our perception. If we accept this undeniable reality, the only goal of life is to integrate the self with the eternal wisdom of consciousness. The self then extends awareness to a higher level to perceive the unity of all existence in consciousness.

Once we reach the goal of self-realization, life will no longer be a miserable burden of mundane existence. With the true knowledge to guide us, we begin to enjoy the exquisite experience of oneness with all beings. The mind gets slowly detached from body awareness, possessions and personal relationships to experience the most blissful state of existence in consciousness. We cannot reach such extended awareness through meditation, yoga or rituals. Only the firm conviction that universal consciousness is the truth of reality can remove all illusions related to our separate existence in nature. Individual identities and the phenomenal world itself are seen as transient images that gradually disappear when the true knowledge of consciousness enlightens the mind.

The sage also suggests some fundamental changes in lifestyle to make existence a worthwhile experience. When self-related desires disappear with the acquisition of true knowledge, we spontaneously accept with grace whatever we get to satisfy the essential needs of life. In undifferentiated awareness we feel unity of existence with all creatures, which gives us the compassionate wisdom to coexist happily without any competition for survival. In fact, all riddles of nature simply vanish with the acceptance of the wisdom of consciousness that dispels ignorance of reality from the mind forever.

Here, I must warn the reader of the hidden danger in blindly following the wisdom of consciousness without understanding its real meaning and intentions. It is not meant to be a convenient alibi for inaction or escape from worldly responsibilities. The idea should empower us to overcome egoistic greed that gives rise to all kinds of miseries. We can even practice the wisdom of consciousness without abandoning the security of personal faiths and identities. It can be assumed that your personal God is in fact consciousness that enlightens the entire world for our perception. The realization that consciousness is the only Supreme Reality gives us the unique experience of detachment from all bondages created by ignorance. If we accept super consciousness as the truth of reality, we can achieve the blissful state of innocence of childhood.

Simply accepting universal consciousness as the sole truth of reality does not resolve the enigma of the origin of the universe and life. I have attempted to formulate a rational explanation of existence by integrating scientific knowledge with mystic wisdom in a harmonious model of the universe. The model gives the probable scenario of initial conditions and all causal relationships underlying cosmic coincidences and the origin of life. It also indicates some new possibilities for the evolution of the variety and complexity of life on earth. The model is based entirely on scientifically ascertained facts without using any irrational assumptions. It is kept flexible to accommodate even future discoveries that may demolish all our present understanding of universe and life. The model accepts, irrespective of different origins, all rational ideas that successfully withstood the test of scientific proof and the challenges of time.

Finally, when you recapitulate the collective wisdom of the worldview at the end of the voyage, you will find the spontaneous emergence of some rational conclusions from your own mind. It is the accumulated wisdom of humanity giving you the solutions to the puzzle of existence. They emerge as your own firm convictions derived from the carefully assimilated facts of reality that enhanced your awareness. The ultimate reward from all your intellectual pursuits is the realization that an intelligent, primordial energy is present in all forms of matter. When we achieve total unity with that universal energy, no need or urge will be felt for a separate identity and lifestyle. With the dissolution of the egocentric worldview, we will understand that the true meaning of existence is the symphony of super consciousness. Our existence becomes harmonious extension of cosmic consciousness if we choose to live in peace with all forms of life. The culmination of your search for super consciousness is the acceptance of this truth of reality that can transform your perception to a holistic appreciation of existence.

As we step deep into the third millennium, we will find more of everything in store for us everywhere. There will be more people, more accurate knowledge and astonishing technologies. But we will also find more greed for material possessions and consequential multitude of miseries than ever before. We will need many more rational solutions for the intractable problems of the mind that arise from the insecurities of modern life. In this book, I am not presenting any readymade solution or ultimate answers but just pointing out the proper path to a correct worldview for a better life. At the end of it all, I hope you will share my view that self-realization based on true knowledge alone can give us enduring peace and happiness. When our inherited and acquired ignorance is removed, ordinary consciousness will reach the higher level to perceive the unity of all existence. That is the blissful state of awareness that I promise to all involved readers of this book. In that grand symphony of super consciousness, we lose the self but gain the enduring reward of enjoyable existence in eternity.

PATHFINDER

Two kinds of knowledge we seek
The lower one, to learn arts, science &
So on, & the higher one to lead us
To the ultimate goal of self-realization.

(THE MUNDAKA UPANISHAD)

You believe in a dice-playing god,
& i, in the perfect rule of law in a world of
something objectively existing, which i try
to catch in a wildly speculative way.
The great initial success of quantum theory
cannot convert me to believe in that
fundamental game of dice.

(ALBERT EINSTEIN)

At the highest level of awareness
no senses, mind or action can interrupt
the undifferentiated consciousness,
In which we find unity of existence of all
beings. Only blissful serenity prevails
the mind, That realizes the ultimate truth
of reality.

(KATHA UPANISHAD)

Information For Knowledge

For the past 10,000 years or so, we have been acquiring knowledge about all kinds of natural phenomena including human life. The intellectual pursuits of about 250 generations created a wonderful heritage of knowledge on a wide variety of subjects. Initially, knowledge of seasons and natural forces would have helped our ancestors to survive in a hostile habitat. Later on, it was used to create and sustain great civilizations. Our inherited wisdom reflects the understanding about the natural phenomena and their casual relationships in different stages of civilization. In ancient times, knowledge was not available to all individuals in a community. It was usually confined to the exclusive domain of a few select individuals who took full advantage of its unlimited powers to manipulate both man and nature.

The learned ones among our ancestors might have gradually become the creamy layer of the society. They would have guided the rest of the population, with suitable institutional framework for ensuring peace and harmony in the community. The public must have entirely relied upon them to steer the society through various kinds of natural and man made calamities. The society must have revered the cognizant as God's own chosen men capable of conveying all the correct solutions to the innumerable challenges of nature. The majority invariably remained ill informed for various reasons like lack of opportunities, intellectual deficiencies and so on.

But, in the modern society, no individual or group can claim monopoly over any kind of knowledge. Widespread awareness of democratic rights and increasing literacy levels liberated intellectual activities from the stranglehold of the traditional custodians of knowledge. The great discoveries of science expanded the reach of the perception and comprehension of even the layman. The wisdom of humanity began to gradually permeate to all segments of society. In fact, in the democratic system of governance, the correct choice of representatives depends upon the level of literacy of the entire population. Actually, dissemination of knowledge is now the primary responsibility of any civilized country striving to raise the overall standard of life of the citizens.

Admittedly, the need of the time is an appropriate technology to convert all rational knowledge into a universally acceptable worldview available to all persons at minimum cost. The technological breakthroughs achieved with the electronic processing of information will make it possible to design policies and programs based on rational wisdom rather than traditional faiths. It can also reduce social tensions created by unfair competition for material gains. A rational worldview incorporating all our scientific knowledge and inherited wisdom would give us a genuine pathfinder to achieve peace and happiness.

Worldview For The Common Man

Ideally, a rational worldview should contain correct and complete information about everything in the universe. It should give us the true picture of all natural phenomena and their causal relationship. The information should preferably contain only the facts verified by scientific methods or logically coherent thoughts. They should be widely accepted by all segments of society. In brief, a correct worldview should be the summary of all the current rational knowledge available to us. It should also indicate the desirable directions for future explorations into the realm of the unknown.

Such a worldview should, as far as possible, be neutral to the conflicting interests and opinions emanating from different cultural and religious viewpoints. It should also desist from espousing any particular cause or creed. Rationality should be the sole criterion for accepting an explanation of a phenomenon. The decision to accept or reject any conclusions should eventually be left to the choice of the individual. Since all are not equally equipped to make intelligent choices, the worldview should point out the best available choice among the conflicting alternatives. Some degree of arbitrariness is, of course, unavoidable in such decisions. But the objective should be to help the individual to relate his abilities realistically to the external world for achieving maximum satisfaction from life. In short, the correct worldview should guide us like an unbiased observer conducting the traffic of life in a confused world of conflicting facts, faiths and opinions.

It is true that accepting a rational worldview or even acknowledging the need for one depends entirely upon the choice of an individual. A totally egocentric individual may not have any concern other than for his immediate personal needs. Such a person may not bother about acquiring true knowledge or a correct worldview. But most of us are not so insensitive to the world around us. Our quest for seeking the true knowledge is the greatest gift that makes life purposeful and enjoyable. Most of us do accept the fact that unless the wisdom of the true perspective is acquired, life would be an extremely miserable burden of ignorance. We generally seek rational solutions for the confusing complexities of the modern life. Even conflicts at global level arise out of inadequate appreciation of some simple basic facts of life. Incorrect ideas can easily influence the vast multitude of ignorant masses. The public opinion so created gets crystallized into rigid attitudes and irreconcilable national viewpoints. A rational worldview alone can guide individuals and the society to reach more fulfilling and harmonious standard of life.

Inherited Ignorance

Our search for the cause of natural phenomena must have begun with the emergence of self-awareness. Initially, the quest would have been confined to seeking the correct solutions to facilitate survival in hostile environments. But gradually, the irrepressible human curiosity sought deeper knowledge on a wide variety of subjects unrelated to the basic needs of life. With the advent of agricultural settlements, and plenty of leisure for intellectual pursuits, some gifted persons must have discovered more about the rules and regularities in the various occurrences in nature. The empowered humans created great civilizations and conquered the vagaries of nature that no other species could accomplish. The evolution of human intellect began with the building up of the wealth of inheritance of knowledge that was transmitted to future generations for further refinement to reach higher levels of competence. It would probably explain the fact that despite several debilitating environmental disasters, humankind survived to master the world while millions of other species perished.

From time immemorial, seekers of knowledge have been positing insightful worldviews based on speculative reflections and observations of various natural occurrences. With the passage of time, the emerging scientific knowledge reduced most of the worldviews to mere historical relics of archaic thoughts. It is true that the few religious explanations that survived the avalanche of rational knowledge still have millions of credulous believers all over the world. In fact, even by conservative estimates, more than 95% of humanity follows some faith or the other. For them, the ultimate truth of reality is the Holy Scriptures presumably containing the irrefutable divine wisdom. They will not accept any rational worldview even after scientific evidences clearly falsify the basic premises of such irrational faiths.

But the modern mindset may not readily accept all the currently popular religious explanations of existence. The main problem with the rational worldview is that it is devoid of the cultural and spiritual contents that we need to make the short life meaningful. Moreover, a harmonious worldview has not yet emerged from the vast database of science that lies scattered in disparate disciplines. What we desperately want now is a universally acceptable framework of thoughts that can combine the best of our inherited wisdom with the infallible truth of scientific knowledge. In the first few chapters of this book, I am presenting a comprehensive description of universe, matter and life mostly based on the facts ascertained by scientific inquiries. It is an extremely flexible conceptual framework that can incorporate the knowledge breakthroughs of all times. The gaps and deficiencies in the scientific knowledge are also highlighted and some alternative explanations are also offered from mystic wisdom.

Beginning Of Knowledge Era

We can trace the modern Scientific Worldview to the sustained investigations of the western scholars during the last half millennium. Their inquiries using empirical methodology based on reductionism revealed many unknown features of nature. Surprisingly, It all happened in the very short span of a few centuries. The East has also made significant contributions to the cause of knowledge through metaphysical speculations and observations of natural phenomena. In ancient times, the great civilizations of the East like the Chinese, the Indo-Aryan and Babylonian immensely enhanced our treasure of knowledge. Their holistic approach did not produce the kind of spectacular visible results that gave Western science instant mastery over matter and life. The industrial revolution that emerged from the technological innovations convinced the common man about the infallibility of scientific knowledge. It has been established beyond doubt that for making visible progress in the material world, true knowledge is much more dependable than metaphysical speculations. In fact, the West gained mastery over the rest of the world with minimum manpower supported by the tremendous advantage of the efficient tools of destruction.

The discovery of the satellites of Jupiter by Galileo heralded the arrival of the era of modern scientific inquiries in the West. He was the first to use a telescope to support his model of the universe. He posited that acceleration creates force and derived the equivalence principle that the mass of an object measured by its weight on earth, is identical to the mass inferred from its collision with other objects anywhere in the universe. This proposition led to the understanding of the nature of gravitational attraction and also to the theories of relativity.

The second great scientific event was the discovery of the force of gravity by Isaac Newton in 1680. Newton's contributions range from the Law of Gravitation to the Laws of Motion of objects under mechanical force. He also invented a new branch of mathematics called 'Differential Calculus' that was extremely useful in understanding the orbits of planets. The differential calculus invented by Newton was used in several other scientific discoveries. The electrical charges and their properties were discovered by the end of the 18th Century. Newton was the first scientist to formulate a complete worldview entirely, based on the accumulated knowledge of the period. He also guided the expansion of scientific enquiries by suggesting a comprehensive agenda for future research in various areas.

Modern chemistry began the conquest of the world of matter sometime toward the end of the 18th Century with the great idea that all matter is made up of atoms. John Dalton conceived the idea of atoms, elements and compounds and created the notion of atomic weight. Another revolutionary concept was the principle of conservation of energy, which postulated that no energy is lost in its transformation from one form to another. It was also established that heat, light, magnetism and electricity are all different interchangeable manifestations of energy. The concept of entropy, which is more scientifically known as the second law of thermo-dynamics, also appeared around that time. It states the tendency for disorder invariably increases in isolated systems. Entropy gives the direction of change in a physical system with the passage of time and is accepted as the scientific basis for the direction of the arrow of time.

The impact of the wonderful discoveries in physics, chemistry and mathematics was also felt in the realm of biological sciences. In 1858, Charles Darwin established that evolution of life was driven by the interaction between the organism and environment that creates variations of fitness in the population. He also clearly indicated the possibility of an evolutionary link between human beings and apes. For the first time, it was boldly stated with irrefutable fossil evidence that humans are only a highly evolved species of primates. The stories of creation propagated in various religious worldviews from time immemorial were rationally refuted and falsified. During this time Louis Pasteur also made the momentous discovery that infectious diseases are caused by invisible organisms called bacteria and not by divine wrath for worldly misdeeds. In fact, it marked the advent of a very bad time for the faith healers who could not survive the avalanche of remedies discovered by the modern medical science.

In 1860, James Maxwell proposed a unified theory of forces in a mathematical equation for describing both electricity and magnetism. His wave theory explains all kinds of electromagnetic radiations. He also posited that there is a medium called 'Lumeniferous Aether' that fills all the empty space. With the conception of a medium of ether, he tried to explain the independent existence of photons. Later on, it was revealed that even the empty space or a vacuum could also act as a medium. The age of global communications began with the generation of invisible Maxwell waves in the radio-frequency range. Another new kind of radiation called X-rays was also discovered during this period.

A milestone in the development of the scientific worldview in the 19th century was the discovery of the electron by J.J.Thomson. Maxwell's theory of the indivisibility of the atom was the basic premise of all scientific enquiries. But the new knowledge of the existence of electrons further revolutionized our concept of elementary particles of matter giving rise to speculations about the possibility of discovering other particles in the atom. There was tremendous progress in mathematics and chemistry also during this period. The new knowledge was immediately, converted to technological innovations that gave the western nations a crucial competitive economic edge. The process of colonization of the less developed regions of the world by the technically advanced European countries was completed much before the dawn of the 20th century.

One of the most important events in modern science is the formulation of the theory of relativity by Albert Einstein. He convincingly explained that energy could be converted into mass and vice-versa. He also conceived that nothing could travel faster than light and stipulated that there is no absolute position and time as they can be expressed only in terms of relativity. For the first time, it was scientifically accepted that we live in a four-dimensional world including time in addition to the three-dimensional space. Most of the predictions of the theory of relativity have been confirmed either by experiments or by observations. We got a clear explanation of space, time, mass and energy from the theories of relativity that also conceived the possibility of the beginning of the universe with a big bang.

The unquestioned certainty of the laws of classical physics was thoroughly shaken by the great discovery of quantum theory. It emerged from the study of radiation of energy. Max Planck suggested in 1900 that radiation of a particular frequency exists as 'Quanta' or tiny packets of energy. In 1910, Ernest Rutherford made a startling discovery that all atoms are made out of a number of negatively charged electrons and a positively charged central nucleus. Shortly thereafter, Niels Bohr in 1930 discovered the connection between the structure of the atom and the quantum nature of energy. He found that electrons travel around the nucleus in restricted space of orbits with well-defined energy, as if they are planets orbiting a star. This discovery laid the foundation for the altered worldview that radiation exists in both wavelike and corpuscular modes. Later, it was proved that electrons, actually, exist in dual states. Heisenberg posted the notion of quantum uncertainty that accepts the impossibility of measuring simultaneously the position and speed of a particle. Heisenberg and Schrodinger formalized Bohr's assumptions in matrix mechanics and wave mechanics respectively. Paul Derrick demonstrated that both the descriptions are equivalent to each other and the theory is now known as 'Quantum Mechanics.'

In quantum mechanics, we have a more accurate worldview incorporating the behavior of subatomic particles that shows a universe of probabilities rather than certainties. It gives us an entirely different picture of reality at the most elementary level of matter. For the first time, the direct causal relationship of physical phenomena was questioned and even falsified. Heisenberg's uncertainty principle has also changed the philosophical foundation of the then prevalent rational worldview formulated in terms of classical physics. Quantum theory is the greatest discovery after relativity but we are yet to achieve unification of both by including gravity in quantum mechanics.

Biological sciences also continued to make great strides during this period. With the help of the microscope, biologists investigated structure of the cell and found that chromosomes carried the inheritable characteristics of an organism. Genes were discovered at this time and Darwin's theory of evolution was finally accepted as the main theoretical framework of modern genetics. In 1953, Watson and Crick discovered the structural features of the DNA molecule. They also demonstrated how genetic information was transmitted through the DNA molecule. The science of biotechnology changed our traditional ideas about inherited instincts that motivate human behavior. Our biological quest has recently succeeded in decoding some areas of the human genome. We now know certain sequences and contents of the genetic instructions that will enable us to unravel more secrets of life in a few years. The genetic instructions will improve us to create disease resistant varieties of animals and plants. Ultimately super intelligent humans will reach the level of competence to compete with nature and even excel some of the creative abilities of nature.

The brief outline of the disclosures of science during the last few centuries gives a totally different picture of universe and life. Scientific enquiries have almost successfully uncovered the correct and complete state reality. Technological innovations in transportation, communication and medicine convincingly demonstrated the infallibility of scientific knowledge and its practical utility for humanity. It is now established beyond any doubt that ultimately the rationality of science will prevail over all popular misconceptions spread by theological worldviews. With increasing literacy, we are slowly but surely moving towards universally acceptable rational worldview that would hopefully reveal to all the true meaning and purpose of existence.

Ultimate Answers Unveiled

Our current level of scientific knowledge is presented in the three parts of this book. The first part gives a brief review of the explanations of the creation of the universe, its present status and the probable end. It is evident that science has not yet succeeded in creating a correct and complete model of the universe. Several inconsistencies and inexplicable coincidences in the scientific worldview give rise to serious reservations about their total acceptability. From the multitude of models, it is not easy to reach the true facts of the origin and organization of the universe. Some new astonishing future discoveries might also reveal an entirely different picture of the universe. Our future encounter with alien intelligence might also give us new information about the origin and organization of universe. We may find all sorts of surprises cropping up when we delve deep into the mysteries of the universe with advanced satellites and for reaching probing devices.

The second part of the book is all about the puzzling phenomenon of life. It begins with the origin of life on earth and the complex pathways of evolution that created the vast variety of existing and extinct species. The current scientific explanations of life are presented from the starting point of the first live cell to the evolution of advance forms of life. We have a fairly accurate picture of evolutionary progress of life in the time frame of a couple of billion years. But, several coincidences and doubtful assumptions question the credibility of a purely evolutionary explanation. The recent discoveries in molecular biology show highly intriguing and autonomous behavior of proteins that simply baffle our comprehensions. Interdisciplinary approach in scientific inquiries might very soon give us a clearer picture of the development of the variety and complexity of life. If we find any new form of life on other planets, it will probably give us more accurate information about the genesis of life in the universe.

The third part discusses all the scientific discoveries about the brain and the mind. We have plenty of true knowledge about the structural and functional aspects of the brain that gives rise to the phenomenon of mind. We approach mind as a generic concept that includes consciousness, self-awareness, intelligence and even compassionate wisdom and creativity. The main purpose of our exhaustive analysis of the mind is to understand the underlying factors that control our conscious behavior. We search the physical and non-physical features of brain in the waking state and dream state to arrive at some rational conclusions about the emergence of mind and of its mysterious tendencies.

In the last part, all pieces of the puzzle are put together to create a coherent and intelligible worldview. Against the background of the scientific knowledge presented in the preceding three parts, we survey the explanations of universe and life in mystic and religious thoughts. It is followed by a summary of the worldview of Ashtavakra and a commentary based on the latest scientific discoveries about consciousness. The physical processes in the brain are closely examined to reveal the emergence of consciousness that create an illusion of reality out of the various energy inputs received by the sensory organs. Scientific studies show us that the mind is totally dependent upon the serial and parallel computing processes continuously carried out in the brain. We find that the idea of "free will", which attribute all intelligent choices to an autonomous self is probably a myth created by our misconception. Our scientific knowledge of the brain fully supports certain mystic ideas of self and universal consciousness.

In the last chapter I present a rational model of the universe and life. It is an attempt to converge all scientific knowledge covering the entire sequence of cosmic events that existed even before the big bang. The explanations given are capable of accommodating the essence of diverse faiths and opinions. The model is a pathfinder to reach at the truth of reality. It is fully consistent with the spiritual needs and aspirations of humanity. I hope it will resolve the uncertainties and misconceptions created by conflicting faiths and the incomplete conclusions of contemporary science.

All the major findings of the four parts are converged in the conclusions that give the rational explanation of existence. An imaginary dialogue between the individual self and the Supreme Self that represents the collective wisdom of humanity gives us the final answers that we sought in the beginning of the book. The truth of the reality unfolds when the self realizes the unity of all beings in consciousness and accepts the fact that individual self is just a transient illusion.

In the end, the epilogue gives some foresights into the great possibilities of our achievements in the near future. It is followed by a glossary that contains, in simple terms, the meaning of difficult concepts and technical words. It is followed by an exhaustive bibliography of relevant books and articles for further reading in this area of enquiry. The author hopes that this book will create sufficient intellectual excitement in the reader to pursue his own exploration into the realm of matter, mind and the meaning of existence. The bibliography is meant for more serious readers who are not satisfied with the frugal fare presented in this book.

before the big bang. The explanations given are capable of accommodating the essence of diverse faiths and opinions. The model is a pathfinder to reach at the truth of reality. It is fully consistent with the spiritual needs and aspirations of humanity. I hope it will resolve the uncertainties and misconceptions created by conflicting faiths and the incomplete conclusions of contemporary science.

All the major findings of the four parts are converged in the conclusions that give the rational explanation of existence. An imaginary dialogue between the individual self and the Supreme Self that represents the collective wisdom of humanity gives us the final answers that we sought in the beginning of the book. The truth of the reality unfolds when the self realizes the unity of all beings in consciousness and accepts the fact that individual self is just a transient illusion.

In the end, the epilogue gives some foresights into the great possibilities of our achievements in the near future. It is followed by a glossary that contains, in simple terms, the meaning of difficult concepts and technical words. It is followed by an exhaustive bibliography of relevant books and articles for further reading in this area of enquiry. The author hopes that this book will create sufficient intellectual excitement in the reader to pursue his own exploration into the realm of matter, mind and the meaning of existence. The bibliography is meant for more serious readers who are not satisfied with the frugal fare presented in this book.

PART ONE

WHERE ARE WE ?

'CONVERGENCE TO DIVERGENCE'

In the beginning there was nothing. No space to envelope the universe nor any receptacle to contain it. No life, death, day or night. The self-contained alone shined, Sleeping calmly in supreme contentedness.

(RIG VEDA 10.121.1)

You are neither earth nor water nor wind nor fire nor sky. Freedom is in the knowledge that you are the embodiment of pure conciousness & the witness of all existence

(ASHTAVAKRA GEETHA 1.3)

All i know is that i know nothing

(SOCRATES)

CHAPTER ONE

CREATIVE EXPLOSION

FIRST THE DIVINE AROSE
AS THE SEED OF ALL EXISTENCE.
PUTTING THE MIND AND HEART TOGETHER
YOU CAN SEE THE UNBREAKABLE LINK
BETWEEN THE EXISTENT AND NON-EXISTENT
ABIDING IN UNITY AND BLISSFUL HARMONY.
[RIG VEDA]

THE SUPREME SELF OR BRAHMAN IS THE ONLY IMPERISHABLE POSSESSING THE QUALITY OF SELF-KNOWLEDGE. THE CREATIVE FORCES EMANATING FROM HIM ARE MANIFESTED IN THE MATERIAL UNIVERSE.
[BHAGAWAD-GITA]

Captivating Canopy!

Before the invention of the telescope, the universe was all that the naked eye could see in a starlit sky. Innumerable luminous objects in the night sky must have presented the most awe-inspiring spectacle to the early humans. The immense beauty and the inexplicable nocturnal appearance of the heavenly bodies would have excited the creative imagination of our forefathers. Even the modern day followers of various faiths worship the cosmic canopy as the holy abode of the Gods and departed souls. In religious literature we find several interesting descriptions of the cosmos with an omnipotent God creating life and guiding the destiny of his faithful wards. The rebellious ones who dare to deviate from the righteous path are invariably consigned to the miseries of the hell. They are made to suffer perpetual torture while the good ones enjoy the bliss that heavenly existence.

It is incredible but true that we got a fairly accurate description of the universe only in the beginning of the twentieth century. Recent astronomical observations with powerful telescopes falsified most of our misconceptions about the universe and revealed innumerable galaxies with billions of stars and planets. Our scientific knowledge of the universe presently consists of tentative conclusions supported by observational proof and verifiable evidences. We have now acquired correct information about the origin and composition of matter ranging from the microcosm of elementary particles to the macrocosm of great galaxies.

Not only that, we have also successfully formulated a standard model that describes matter in a mathematical matrix. Short of creating a unified theory of everything, we have plenty of true knowledge about the natural phenomena in the visible parts of the universe. The tremendous progress of science in the last few centuries gives us the foretaste of the magnitude of revolutionary revelations awaiting us in this millennium. Even our present level of knowledge can explain the universe and life more accurately than the mythological stories of creation.

Early Speculations

The highly improbable stories of creation in the Holy Scriptures of various faiths did not appeal to many serious Western philosophers. Ignoring the threat of religious sanctions, they explored the true nature of the astonishing astronomical phenomena. The patterns and repetitions in the celestial symphony gave them some correct ideas about the mysteries of nature. Pythagoras suggested that it was some sort of divine harmony that united humanity with the cosmos. He described the universe in certain numerological and geometrical concepts. His mathematical explanations reduced the entire cosmos to 10 heavenly bodies. Later, Plato described the universe as an eternal and flawless objective entity. Like the Eastern mystics, he also relied upon a holistic vision of the universe of timeless forms that transcend defective human perception.

Aristotle, a disciple of Plato, proposed a pseudo-scientific model of geocentric universe in BC 340. For many centuries, the Western thinkers accepted it as the true description of the universe. He identified four specific causal relationships to underlying changes in forms causes and their consequential effects. In his view, all forms inevitably moved towards an ultimate goal that was perfect and predetermined. We can find the origin of reductionism of modern science in the explanations of causal relations exposed by Aristotle. He relied more upon the genuine sensory experiences to comprehend the true nature of reality than accepting the wisdom contain in speculative thoughts. Aristotle's' geocentric vision of the universe was retained in the model of universe proposed by Ptolemy. According to him, eight spheres surrounding the earth carry heavenly bodies. The fixed stars are kept in the outermost sphere. Even the church accepted Ptolemy's model as an accurate representation of the cosmos, which is in conformity with the description of the universe in the scriptures.

In AD 1514, Copernicus suggested for the first time that the sun was the center of the universe and that all the planets moved around it in circular orbits. In 1609, Galileo scientifically proved with the support of telescopic observations that the geocentric description of the universe was incorrect. Kepler proposed elliptical orbits for the planets that actually matched with astronomical observations. In the recent past with the help of more powerful telescopes, the science of cosmology began to explore the secrets of the universe more reliably than ever before. Later on, Issac Newton used differential equations to explain the universe. He compared the universe to a clock like mechanism where the future could be predicted by the forces working in the present.

In theological explanations, we find many fanciful accounts of the creation, present status of universe and its possible end. They have all been falsified by the observational data collected by cosmologists. Aristotle, in fact, assumed that humankind existed eternally without allowing room for any evolutionary changes. Christianity and Islam accept the idea of the creation of the universe at a definite point in time. In spite of the well-accepted law of gravity, the universe was considered static until 1929. Only the actual astronomical observations could take the erroneous notion of a static universe from the scientific worldview. Scientists of all disciplines now agree that the universe was created in a big bang about 15-20 billion years ago. But many believers still hold that the God made the universe and all the structures in its ambit.

Explosive Genesis

The scientific community generally admits that the universe came into being with the most violent of all explosions initiating the process of creation of matter, forces, time and space. George Gamow, a nuclear physicist of Russian origin, originally mooted the idea of a big bang in 1947. He conceived the universe as a tiny bubble with not even a vacuum outside. He proposed that the empty space at very high temperature was filled with radiation and with the increasing pressure of radiation the bubble expanded. Gamow's ideas were later on modified by other scientists who tried to explain the after events of the explosion in a rational manner.

The "steady-state" theory of the universe, which is based on the model of continuous creation, did not survive the great flood of scientific proof in favor of the big bang. If the steady-state model were correct, the sequence of creation would be taking place even now at least in some part of the universe. The fact is that the concept of a steady state, is philosophically more appealing and elegant than the crudity of the big bang. The detection of the red shift and the background microwave radiation now establish beyond doubt that the universe is inexplicably expanding at the same pace even about 15 billions years after the big bang.

There are many other conclusive evidences of the big bang like the abundance of the element helium in the universe. This element could not have been created without a tremendous cosmic explosion. Heavy hydrogen and lithium were also made in the first few minutes of creation when the temperature was more than 1 billion degrees centigrade. The low mass of neutrinos is yet another piece of evidence that confirms the occurrence of the big bang. The chain of events like the evolution of matter in space-time as envisaged in the theory of general relativity would be possible only if we accept the idea of the big bang.

Assuming that the universe was created in the big bang, the most intriguing enigma is the unknown initial conditions that preceded the explosion. Scientists describe the initial conditions as an infinite singularity of intense state of energy. But such strange concepts like "singularity or a quantum vacuum" are not familiar to the common man who cannot comprehend the state of energy with such unknown properties. It could have been a kind of unitary state of super energy of zero size with no matter or forces, but capable of creating all of them from the great potential embedded in it. The big bang is attributed to the breaking of symmetries, or an unbalancing of the perfectly matched opposite energies or some other inexplicable ripple in the primordial vacuum. No explanation can complete the picture of the creation without giving an acceptable idea of the initial conditions and the real cause of the bang.

The cyclic big bang theory is a variant of the real big bang. It describes the genesis as a process similar to the rhythmic heartbeat. The universe expanded with the initial explosion and then collapsed into a big crunch under gravitational pull. It would have then reached the initial point to create another explosion and expansion. This process must have been going on in a cyclical manner creating brand new universes by recycling the old ones. The branching universe tells us the possibility of new universes breaking off from an expanding mother universe. While this explains the explosion and subsequent expansion, no attempt is made to describe the initial conditions. The uniqueness of the initial conditions makes it amenable to all sorts of interpretations. The religious worldviews assume that the initial condition was the will of the God who created the universe and all forms of matter including the various forms of life. We cannot successfully rebut the holy assumptions of creation unless a rational explanation is found for the initial conditions and the cause of explosion.

Quantum Vacuum

An easy way to solve the mystery of initial conditions is to simply avoid it altogether. The simplistic assumption that everything was anyway nonexistent before the big bang solves the riddle of creation. Some scientists avoid the issue as an indescribable infinity. It is also conceived as a kind of quantum vacuum that had the potential to become the mother of all creations. Before the big bang, matter and forces were united in a sort of high-energy flux with quantum characteristics. In the absolute vacuum there was no space-time or matter and forces. Some tiny ripples must have arisen like bubbles appearing in boiling water. Each bubble had the potential to become a stable universe if the parameters were good enough to create matter and forces.

Many scientists prefer to compare the universe to an electron existing simultaneously in several energy states or in parallel quantum states as "multiverse". One of the bubbles could have lasted longer and got itself detached from the vacuum. It could have been a circular entity without space or time like a "super string". Some cosmologists genuinely believe that our universe actually co-exists with many other universes in a symphony of multiverse. It is also suggested that our universe is linked to many parallel universes by an infinite network of extremely tiny wormholes. The collective support of all the wormholes keeps the universe stable. The infinite expansion of the universe in all these scenarios is explained in terms of the tremendous energy unleashed at the time of big bang.

To the uninitiated common man, ideas like the multiverse and quantum vacuum are as weird as the improbable religious explanations. They are based on unverifiable assumptions to give a scientific aura to the unknown initial conditions. The coincidence of correct physical constants that existed to create a stable universe and life are conveniently left out or deliberately ignored as irrational. The multiverse model simply assumes that the physical constants of our universe are suitable for life only by pure chance and not by any intelligent design. If we accept the possibility of an infinite number of universes, no unscientific assumptions are required to explain initial conditions or the coincidences that culminated in the various structures. The universe could have been created simply by the interplay of physical forces without any intervention of any kind of super natural will. If we have to believed such weird science fiction about the act of creation, we might as well accept the role of the God described in various faiths.

Seed In The Black Hole?

Lee Smolin and Andrei Linde suggest that our stable universe is one of the universes that emerged out of billions of black holes. They assume that every black hole can create a singularity capable of producing a baby universe. With billions of baby universes sprouting from black holes, there is some probability of finding at least one stable universe in which life can subsist. They suggest that intelligent humans are the lucky winners of the lottery of a friendly and habitable universe. This model even implies some sort of evolutionary struggle for survival among the baby universes to gain the advantage of a space-time niche in the crowded super space. It also avoids the unpleasant necessity of any external designer for the correct choice of physical constants. If there are billions of potential universes, it can be safely assumed that at least one of them would have possessed all the requisite constants to create a stable universe.

A self-organizing universe is a convenient concept to circumvent all unscientific assumptions about creation. But in our anxiety to avoid a designer, we fall unfortunately into a bigger trap of an impossible number of universes. While it is true that this model solves the nagging problem of cosmic coincidences, the probability of a habitable and stable universe arising out of one of the black holes is about 10^{229}. Since the total number of stars in the observable universe is only 10^{22}, we find absolutely no chance of a black hole giving birth to a universe having all the precisely honed physical constants. A scientific explanation having such rare odds for the occurrence of a phenomenon is worse than the irrational assumption of the existence of an omnipotent designer.

Expanding To Eternity!

We are now about 15 billion years away from the big bang. But the universe is still expanding as if it is an infinitely stretchable balloon being continuously pumped with more space. The amazing cosmic phenomenon is the continuous expansion of the universe so at the same critical rate even 15 billion years after the big bang. It is difficult to believe that the momentum of the big blast would have powered the inflation for such a long period of time. The puzzle is how the gravitational pull and expansion energy can keep the universe well balanced to avoid a big crunch? At a faster rate of expansion, no galaxy would have formed nor any kind of life would have appeared in the cosmos. The common man can attribute such delicate cosmic balance only to the divine will, but scientists cannot afford the luxuries of such unscientific assumptions. They call such strange coincidence as the "flatness problem" related to the unknown value of Omega. It symbolizes the density of total matter in the universe. According to scientists, "Higgs Field" is the power that emerged from the quantum vacuum to liberate the universe from the hold of gravity and put it on course for eternal expansion. We are not clear about the concept of Higgs field that check mates the conventional scientific wisdom of the invincibility of gravitational force.

Alan Guth posited a cosmological inflation model of the universe in 1979. Other scientists later on improved it with several modifications. A rapid inflation period said to have occurred at the first 10^{-37} seconds of the explosion when the universe was probably a small fireball. The exponential expansion that followed is attributed to the phase transition that broke the symmetry of forces. The tremendous energy released in this process would have overcome the gravitational effect to set off the infinite inflation. It is assumed that during the initial inflation the universe doubled in size in short intervals. This explanation of inflation can accommodate the closeness of the rate of expansion to the critical rate. It can also account for the uniform temperature found in different regions of the universe. But the critical rate of inflation depends upon certain specific values of physical constants, which cannot be chosen automatically by an expanding universe. For getting such magic figures, we have to accept some unscientific explanations like the intelligent design or even divine intervention.

To make the inflationary model more convincing, Andrei Linde suggested the idea of slow symmetry breaking. The astronomical observation of uniform background microwave radiation as compared to the predictions of the inflationary model seems to have made it less convincing. Another explanation is based on chaotic inflation caused by quantum fluctuations in a spin field. This idea avoids phase transition and assumes that the energy of the field would have an anti-gravitational effect that could cause inflation in some regions. After the initial inflation, the energy levels would have automatically reached the critical rate of expansion. But the symmetry and uniformity found in the expanding universe cannot be explained by any of these models. It seems that all regions in the universe began to expand together, obeying the same physical laws. The infinite density at the initial stage would have ensured uniformity all over the inflating universe. Some early distortions would have arisen from factors like time but inflation theories fail to account for the presence of wrinkles in the background radiation that created cosmic structures like galaxies and stars. Such inexplicable wrinkles also point out the possibility of the role of an intelligent design in the creation of the universe.

Primordial Mould

Our scientific knowledge of the universe begins only from10^{-43} seconds after the big bang. Matter, forces and space-time might have emerged in rudimentary form out of the unknown initial conditions. It is now revealed that within seconds after the big bang, the temperature fell by millions of degrees and photons, electrons and neutrinos appeared in the expanding universe. Antiparticles and some protons and neutrons might have also come into existence at that point in time. After about one and half minutes, protons and neutrons would have combined to form the nuclei of heavy hydrogen. They could have further reacted to make helium nuclei and also nuclei of some light elements like lithium and beryllium.

For almost a million years, nothing spectacular happened other than the simple expansion and cooling of the universe. When the temperature came down to a few thousands of degrees, electrons and nuclei overcame the electromagnetic attraction to become complete atoms. In computer simulations of the beginning of the universe it has been found that galaxies were formed out of tiny ripples in the energy from the big bang fireball. Using a powerful parallel super computer, the ripples were measured, which confirmed the theoretical predictions. The cluster of proto-galactic fragments got merged over billion of years to create the galaxies that we now see in the universe.

In some denser regions of the universe, the rate of expansion must have been probably slower causing the re-collapse and rotation of galaxies. Hydrogen and helium gases in the galaxy formed thick clouds that collapsed under their own gravity to form the stars. The temperature inside the stars would have reached the high levels required for nuclear reactions. The internal pressure created by the conversion of hydrogen into helium might have prevented further collapse of the star and the fusion reaction would have continued with tremendous radiation, heat and light. The bigger stars might have used up their nuclear fuels at a faster rate and contracted further generating more heat. The additional heat might have converted helium into heavier elements like carbon and oxygen. The sequences of various reactions appear to have been chosen to create elements like carbon without which no life would have been possible on earth.

About 75% of the total amount of matter in the universe is hydrogen, which is the lightest element. The second lightest element, helium is estimated to be nearly about 23%. All the other elements put together constitute only about 1-2% of matter existing in the universe. Hydrogen and helium gases were formed in the hot furnace of the universe at its initial stages. But all the heavier elements were created in subsequent nuclear reactions inside the stars. When the bigger stars exploded as supernovas, some of the heavy elements were thrown into the interstellar space and later re-collapsed into new stars.

The European laboratories for particle Physics (CERN) simulated the conditions that deemed to have prevailed immediately after the big bang by smashing together heavy lead ions in a fireball. By generating collisions at temperatures 100,000 times more than that in the sun's center and huge energy densities, quarks were separated from protons and neutrons. The experiment proved the existence of a new state of matter in the form of quark-gluon plasma, which would have existed before they combined together to form other particles when the universe cooled down. In this state of matter, quarks moved freely without getting tied down by gluons to create protons and neutrons. By the year 2005, more experiments are likely to be conducted at a bigger scale to unfold the unknown facts about the process of creation of matter and forces after the big bang. But for now, we have a fairly consistent account of the creation of matter and forces in the universe at different points in time consistent with the continuous fall in temperature.

Unknown Destiny

The destiny of the universe is another puzzle eluding our comprehension. It is assumed that if the density of the total cosmic matter or omega is above unity, the expansion will be reversed. The "Red Shift" being observed now will turn into "blue shift" heralding the onset of contraction. The temperature will reach such high levels that all stars and galaxies will ultimately turn into a compressed fireball. This is the scenario of the closed universe. On the other hand, if the density of matter in the universe is below the critical point, it will go on expanding forever. With infinite expansion, the temperature will go on falling and according to the second law of thermodynamics the universe will gradually become the graveyard of dead stars and black holes. Ultimately, it will end up as a chilled gas of electrons and neutrinos wandering in the vast emptiness. This possibility is the case of the "Open Universe."

Some scientists proclaim with great confidence that the universe will go on expanding forever powered by an exotic force called "antigravity". This assertion is based on the astronomical observation that exploding stars in distant galaxies seem fainter than expected as if propelled by a mysterious force. In fact, this observation brought back the once discredited idea of a "cosmological constant" created by Einstein to accommodate the acceleration in the rate of expansion of the universe. But the model of accelerating expansion is slowly losing ground with the latest observation that the explosions of stars in distant galaxies are less bright than that of nearby galaxies on account of some other unknown cause. The faster brightening supernovas of far away galaxies could mean that the expansion of the universe would be reversed eventually in a big crunch. In a study called "the Boomerang result" reported in the journal "Nature", it is stated that the total mass and energy density of the universe is equal to critical density and what we have is a perfectly flat universe. The total matter in the universe, according to this report, is not enough to make it collapse.

The different scenarios of our probable destiny reveal that we have no clear idea about the end of the universe. It can be either a fiery crunch or a big chill. The actual mass of the dark matter, as and when found, will probably indicate the future of the universe including the intelligent life. Our present predictions are made on the basis of the four known forces and identified particles that created matter. It is possible that new discoveries may bring new facts to light, which would require drastic revision of our earlier predictions about the final outcome. Theoretically, we can find an escape route from any kind of eventuality by widening the microscopic wormholes that presumably connect parallel universes. It shows that ultimately intelligent life will somehow or the other find friendly universes to continue infinite existence.

The ultimate destiny of the universe will become clearer when our space probes give more information that are currently inaccessible. We have no immediate reason to worry about any impending disaster that could wipe out the entire universe. The end of the universe will come about only after several billion years. Much before that eventuality, the sun, which is the sole source of our energy and life, will ensure a fiery end of our planet. Earth will eventually vaporize when sun becomes a red giant in a few billion years. But, according to some recent studies, the earth will become a desert in about 500 million years. About 95% of life will become extinct in 300-400 million years and oceans will evaporate into space in another 500 million years. However, by that time, we may manage to find other hospitable planets to escape from the unavoidable holocaust. We have already located about 28 "Extra solar" planets that are at least theoretically habitable. Our advanced technology can probably carry us to distant life-friendly planets to escape the eventual inferno. We find that even scientific predictions of the beginning and end of the universe sound curiously similar to most of the theological prophecies of a fiery end of the cosmos.

Invisible Arrow Of Time

Time is an integral part of our existence, but it is also the most difficult concept to define or describe in a scientific manner. It is generally considered irreversible, although the possibility of time travel cannot be ruled out as simple science fiction. The puzzle of time going only in one direction has always fascinated scientists and philosophers. The physical laws of mechanics state that motion in a frictionless surface is time-reversible. The concept of the forward flow of time must have originated in cosmological events beginning with the big bang and subsequent inflations. But we do not know the direction of time if the universe eventually starts contracting into a big crunch. Our idea of time is limited by the capacity of sensory inputs to comprehend movements of objects and events in space.

All closed systems show entropy or increasing disorder with the passage of time. This phenomenon clearly indicates the presence of an arrow of time in all closed systems. But the basic question is whether it is time that is driving entropy or whether it is entropy that is creating the arrow of time. The universe is definitely moving toward increasing entropy and becoming less of coherent. We have only some vague ideas about the concept of time derived from the process of entropy.

In quantum theory also, time is relevant to measure the collapse of the wave function into an event in the forward direction. Some scientists assume that the arrow of time might have arisen with symmetry breaking and the consequential events followed in a time-bound sequence. In the absence of any acceptable definition of the arrow of time, we can only have some sort of subjective agreement emerging from the observations of the interaction of different natural phenomena.

Time remains supreme in its relentless forward march may be toward infinity if the universe continues to expand forever.

Black Holes Revisited!

Among the great mysteries of the cosmos, black holes attract maximum popular attention. It comes into existence when a massive star shrinks under its own gravity after exhausting all the nuclear fuel. The escape velocity required to get out of a black hole has to be more than the speed of light. The surface of the black hole is covered by a horizon that grabs everything in its vicinity and does not allow anything to get out of its hold. Each galaxy is estimated to contain at least one hundred million black holes. They are supposed to reach the state of singularity when the strength of the gravitational field reaches infinity.

Although the origin of the concept of black hole can be traced to the general theory of relativity, attempts have been made to apply quantum theory to overcome the difficulties in explaining the nature of singularity. The activity inside the black hole has been compared to the conditions prevailing before the big bang. It can begin an inflationary phase with a bang that can even create galaxies and stars. If we assume that every black hole in reality can expand and contract in a cycle, millions of universes may exist as there are billions of black holes in the universe. It is also possible that particles can "tunnel" out of it to escape the hold of its infinite gravity. The concept of the black hole is now made more exotic by more mysterious ideas like event horizon and quantum gravity.

Initially black holes were consigned to the realm of science fiction. But their existence is now confirmed from the observational data. In fact, the Hubble Space Telescope detected many of them in the middle of huge galaxies 50 million light years away from us. Using indirect methods, many characteristics of the black holes have also been identified. It is assumed to be like a huge cosmic hurricane centered on a tiny dot of light having the weight of millions of stars. With the installation of more powerful telescopes, we will get lot more information about these invisible spinning phenomena that is at present beyond our perception and comprehension.

Other Cosmic Curios

Scientists say that a rotating black hole, unlike a stationary black hole collapses as a ring of neutrons. If one falls through the ring, one can reach a parallel universe. We will not be compressed into a neutron as if we then fall in through a tunnel between universes. Such wormholes can be widened with enormous power to allow matter to pass through from a collapsing universe to a more hospitable one. Theoretically, it is possible to travel faster than the speed of light through such wormholes. In recent experiments, particle scientists claim that they have broken the barrier of speed set by light. The general theory of relativity predicted the possibility of wormholes since gravity is the outcome of the curvature of space. Scientists are now eagerly waiting to test the predictions based on theoretical wormhole configurations with new data from astronomical observations.

Antimatter is another interesting scientific concept posited by Dirac by modifying Einstein's equation of energy. Since elementary particles have mirror reflections or symmetries, it is theoretically possible to find antiparticles like antiproton and positron. Similarly, a state of matter can be envisaged with the opposite charge of ordinary matter. But if it came into contact with ordinary matter it would explode releasing tremendous amount of energy. The existence of Anti-hydrogen for 40 billionth of a second has already been confirmed. In fact scientists created nine atoms of anti-hydrogen in 1996 but could not hold on to them. If anti-hydrogen could be collected in stable containers like magnetic bottles it can be used as fuel in space vehicles. Our technology is at present inadequate to perform such a stupendous task of harnessing the energy released from the fusion of opposites for practical purposes.

Another cosmic puzzle is the invisible "Dark matter" that is supposed to exist everywhere in the universe. Since matter in the visible universe constitutes only a small fraction of the mass of the universe, it should account for all the missing mass. In fact, only about 1% of the critical density that is required for a flat universe is contributed by the known quantity of matter in the universe. Moreover, the simple gravitational attraction alone cannot keep the stars orbiting in spiral galaxies. The relative motions of clusters and super clusters of galaxies also indicate the inevitable presence of some unknown dark matter. The additional mass of the dark matter is absolutely essential to keep the universe flat and functional.

There are several speculations about the physical properties of the dark matter. Some scientists believe that it is just ordinary matter like white dwarfs, neutron stars or black holes but emits no light. Dark matter can be neutrinos but we do not know the mass of the neutrino to confirm this presumption. The dark matter can also be a not yet discovered elementary particle. The only certainty is that without its presence, no stable and steadily expanding universe would have existed with large structures like galaxies, stars and planets.

Quasars are strange cosmic phenomena discovered in the Sixties. They are very small but bright objects found at large distances of 10^{10} light years away. They appear to be very small, but the brightness coming from their radiation far exceeds that of even whole galaxies. The radiation from quasars can be at X-ray, optical or radio wavelengths. They can be even the nuclei of distant galaxies that are too far from ours. Another possibility is that they can be a massive black holes attracting gases from nearby stars. As the gas approach the black hole the intense heat must be producing the radiation. The disc-shaped structure around the black hole where matter is heated by collision and rapid motion before it gets sucked into the void is probably the cause of the quasar phenomenon. Since they are observed only in the distant galaxies, they may represent some cosmic phenomena in the early stages of the universe.

Gravity And Repulsion

Some people are now questioning the universally accepted dictum that gravity is the sole stabilizing influence in the cosmos. A new proposition of stellar repulsion force has been made recently but not yet scientifically accepted as a fact. Stars are said to exert the repulsive force and the planets have an attractive force of gravity. The interaction of these forces could create a third force of retraction that gives rise to orbital motion and rotation of planets. This new concept is meant to correct the deficiencies in the gravitational attraction that cannot explain fully the expansion and stability of the universe. It is claimed that the repulsive force of stellar bodies can account for all the observable phenomena in the universe. But astrological observation and mathematical verification are yet to confirm such interesting possibilities of new forces. Such ideas keep the universe going in spite of the serious flaws found in the total dependence on the force of gravity. Since gravity itself is facing tremendous difficulties in arriving at some compatibility with quantum theory, a new force may possibly achieve the much sought after integration, to create a unified theory. We are probably near the end of the search for a theory of everything that will explain gravity in quantum matrix revealing all secrets of the phenomenal world.

At the present level of knowledge, we have a fairly clear idea about the beginning of the universe with a big bang. Its subsequent inflation and the process of formation of stars and galaxies are also well-understood events. However, there are several cosmic phenomena like black holes and dark matter that our present level of knowledge cannot fathom. We are also totally at sea when we come across surprising series of coincidences in the creation of universe and its structures. Our problem is that scientific explanations are inadequate to give us a complete picture of the original evolution of the cosmos. Other explanations of creation are far more irrational but in the absence of a convincing alternative, they will continue to confuse the ignorant multitude that follow various faiths.

CHAPTER TWO

MATTER MOST UNCERTAIN

THE UNIVERSE BEGAN IN THE GOLDEN WOMB
THAT CONTAINED THE SEED OF ALL EXISTENCE.
OUR LIFE BE DEDICATED TO HIM
WHO HOLDS HEAVEN AND EARTH TOGETHER
IN HIS ETERNAL AND INFALLIBLE WISDOM.
[Atharva Veda 4.2.7]

IN THE BEGINNING WAS UTTER DARKNESS,
NOTHING EXISTED FOR WAS VISIBLE IN THE
PRIMORDIAL VOID.
AN OMNIPOTENT ENTITY ENCOMPASSED
THE ENTIRE UNIVERSE,
WHOSE INTENSE ACTIVITY CREATED THE MATERIAL
WORLD?
[Rig Veda 10.129.3]

Slaves Of Virtual Reality!

We have many misconceptions about the objectivity of our perception of the phenomenal world. It is actually experienced from the inputs of tiny packets of energy that continually bombard our sense organs. We have about twelve perceptual senses that include the major ones of sight, hearing, touch, taste and smell and some minor ones like balance, fullness and tension of muscles. We collect and process most of the sensory information without any conscious effort. We receive only selective information about external reality probably because of the constraints of the brain to handle all the wavelengths of energy. Nature seems to have evolved the brain just to allow us to see, hear and feel what is absolutely essential for survival and successful reproduction. Our perception misses out radio waves, infrared rays, and x-rays and so on that are probably not relevant to our existence. The information inputs are chosen to serve the purpose of survival rather than for any great metaphysical contemplation.

Our basic need for food and occasional outlet of reproductive urges do not require the knowledge of the composition of matter at the micro level. The human body is equipped to receive and process information pertaining to the various functions that nature wants us to perform. It is true that our requirements now far exceed sensory capacities originally designed for enhancing chances of survival. We cannot blame nature for the partial blindness and deafness that we seem to suffer in comparison with much inferior forms of life like bats, bees and snakes. Those poor creatures are denied access to the sights and sounds of nature that we enjoy in plenty with a mind that can experience vast range of emotions and thoughts.

The limited sensory inputs that we receive require further mediation by memory to create a coherent picture of reality. We actually see only an illusion projected by the cerebral processing of the sensory inputs and memories of past experiences. An object cannot be perceived directly with all its unknown dimensions and properties. Nature in her wisdom must have decided that for our purpose, an abridged version of reality would suffice.

We are now fully convinced about the bizarre existence of matter at the micro level. Powerful microscopes can now reveal the amazing behavior of invisible particles that do not follow the conventional physical laws. Biological cells consist of a complicated network of molecular pathways and synchronized and purposive activities of molecules like proteins. While performing the predetermined functions, they interact intelligently to preserve the total viability of the organism. In the human body, there are about 100 trillion semi-autonomous cells which function harmoniously as if they possess one mind propelled by a single motive.

Each cell is in some kind of constant communication with others and the body is fully aware of the needs of every part of the system. The specialized cells that create a marvelous immune system strive to prevent the entry of alien microorganisms. The 100 billion neurons in the human brain give rise to a unique intelligence network that can penetrate not only the visible but also the invisible world of matter. We have also developed the sense of aesthetics to appreciate the beauty of nature and our own skills and creativity. All these acquired capabilities are our own innovations over and above the original inheritance conferred by nature to facilitate survival and propagation. We shall now take a closer look at the intriguing world of matter at micro level that build up all the beautiful structures in the universe including the vast variety of life on earth.

Wonderland Of Quantum

Now we know for certain that the entire visible universe is an intricate display of matter in various sizes and shapes acted upon by forces. Molecules are the building blocks of matter. They consist of ninety-two different kinds of atoms. Inside the atom, electrons orbit a nucleus containing protons and neutrons. The electrons are held to the nucleus by the photons. Further down, we find elementary particles like quarks held together by gluons to make proton and neutrons. The electrons and quarks constitute the most fundamental particles of the material world. The forces are all variants of electro-magnetic waves of different wavelengths and frequency. Reductionism can now describe the universe in terms of space-time, matter and energy or electro-magnetism and gravitation. Simply stated, the universe is just an interplay of time-space, electro-magnetism and gravitation. We can further simplify the description to the basic time-space continuum having certain metric properties like electro-magnetism and gravitation.

The astonishing attribute of elementary particles is that they are capable of existing in dual states. The electron can simultaneously be a particle as well as a wave. But our scientific knowledge is not familiar with the concept of an object having dual existence or split personality. Even the ubiquitous photon, which is the tiniest particle of light, seems to enjoy the double role of a particle and wave. It can be focused at a single point as a particle or be spread out in space like a wave. The interspersed pattern of light shows that photons can behave like particles when they strike a barrier but in the normal course, they enjoy a wavelike existence.

Before the Quantum Revolution of 1925, we had a classical concept of matter that was consistent with direct observations and obeyed all laws of physics then known to us. In the early days, the Greek philosophers conceptualized the Universe as made of Water, Earth, Fire and Air. It was Democritus, who first proposed that atom is the smallest building block of matter. But at that time, it was not known how the smallest particle could create matter. The quantum theory has now given us the complete process of creation of matter from a few elementary particles. We can even theoretically create all kinds of matter by combining the elementary particles under suitable conditions for reaction.

In the evolution of the universe, directly observable matter emerged in the galactic and chemical eras. The conditions that prevailed in the first two eras of evolution (Planck and GUT) are still speculative for want of facilities to replicate the act of creation in any collider. Until about 300,000 years after the big bang, the universe just contained only plasma, a type of hot and opaque state of interacting radiation and particles. In this period quarks and other fundamental particles were formed. According to the standard model, there are two kinds of matter particles called "quarks" and "leptons" with their associated anti-matter siblings. The basic components of forces are the color force and the electro weak force. At the fundamental level, matter and forces consist of a lot of intriguing small-scale phenomena that are beyond our sensory perception. In quantum mechanics we come across the charming drama of the strange interactions of quarks and electrons.

Observer Is Reality

It seems that nature does not want us to learn all her secret deals in the quantum world. But our insatiable quest for knowledge has already broken many taboos and natural barriers. The Quantum Theory posited by Erwin Schrõdinger, Verner Heisenberg and several other physicists attempts to describe mathematically the behavior of matter at the most basic level. The energy that was once considered continuous is now conceived as discreet packets called 'Quanta'. The subatomic particles are conceptualized as having dual existence as particles and waves. They are supposed to obey the Schrodinger Wave

Equation that determines the probability of the occurrence of events. The mathematics underlying the formulation of the equation consists of a system known as 'Matrix Mechanics', created by Heisenberg. The Schrodinger Equation is called 'Wave Mechanics' as it formulates the wave function of elementary particles. The wave function is associated with every particle, as a wave of probability and not as a physical effect. This is the Copenhagen interpretation, which is now widely accepted by most physicists.

In this interpretation, an observer is absolutely necessary for any physical reality to occur. It is assumed that an electron or photon can exist in discreet material form only if an observer is present. Otherwise, they exist within the probabilistic descriptions given in the wave function. An independent reality as we know in the ordinary sense, cannot exist without the presence of an observer. The observer or the observing apparatus interact irreversibly with the wave function of the photon or electron, making it materialize as a single point in space and time. At the moment of interaction, the probabilistic existence of the photon or electron in alternative states is abandoned and it selects a single state. The observation process presumably collapses the wave function causing a disturbance in the reality of a dualistic and probabilistic existence before observation.

In fact, the basic assumption of quantum theory is that no objective reality can exist without the act of observation. Further, the same logic can be extended to generalize that no universe can exist without a human observer. The universe would have existed in dual modes probabilistically without the intervention of time and space. It means that a conscious mind is a necessity to materialize the objective reality. What our brain receives is a barrage of vibrations of energy inputs in different frequencies. The quanta of energy that impinge upon us continually are without any qualities. Our experiences of the external world are not real images directly received from outside. They are only the projections of our conscious observations of the quantum phenomena in the brain. The Universe doesn't for us exist without the observation of its projection in our brain. The reality arises only when the conscious mind collapses the probabilistic existence of the universe into a concrete state of structures.

If such outlandish ideas were not supported by flawless mathematical theorems and empirical proof, they would not have survived for long. But it was given us a fairly accurate theoretical framework with testable empirical predictions. Successful practical applications of quantum phenomena like laser devices give sufficient evidence of the infallibility of quantum theory. The wave function is the most basic reality that goes on evolving in time. The constant creation of waves gives new probabilities for finding the particle in space. It is not only deterministic but if specified, even the future movements of the waves can be predicted. But as soon as an observation is made, the reality becomes crystallized by collapsing the wave function.

An essential condition to collapse the wave function is the exclusion of the measuring apparatus from the wave function of the system. The measuring instrument should also be on a different physical level from the thing being measured. Practically it should be at a higher level to induce a fundamental change in an elementary particle like the electron. One quantum particle cannot collapse the wave function of another one nor can for a wave cause its own collapse. The wave function is something like a software simultaneously holding all the information about the present and future states of the system. The particle function is the hardware of a computer but both are complementary to each other for the occurrence of reality. The external world mineralizes in our perception by the interference of the act of observation.

Curiosity Kills The Cat!

Unfortunately we can only have thought experiments to test the propositions of quantum theory. Several interesting situations are conceived to verify the role of the observer in creating the reality. "Schrodinger's Cat", is a thought experiment that brings out the dilemma of uncertainty involved in the act of observation. Details of the experiment are available in standard textbooks on quantum theory. It is all about a cat in a box that can either be dead or alive by the possible release of some toxic material while opening the box. The fact is that until an observation is made, superposition of two wave functions exists for the outcome of a live or dead cat. To reach the actual reality, the wave function has to be collapsed by an observation by opening the box. In reality, what happens to the cat is not known before the observation is made. We can even assume that the reality would not have existed, if the observation did not collapse the wave function into a cognizable event of either a dead cat or a live one.

Our traditional wisdom cannot accept that mere information can modify the reality even at the micro level. The record of an event at such level would also require conscious observations to make it meaningful. A simple measuring device on its own cannot collapse the wave function. Even the mind cannot understand it, unless it is capable of distinguishing what is monitored by the brain. According to Wheeler, a community of investigators is the minimum necessary condition to extract meaning from a measuring apparatus.

The quantum model of matter is not a universally accepted explanation of reality. Many scientists are uncomfortable with the indeterminism of the quantum phenomena. They consider that particles and properties exist in reality independent of any act of observation. They feel that the exclusion of some unidentified factors known as 'hidden variables' presumably invalidates the quantum approach. But experimental evidences clearly indicate that the predictions of quantum theory hold good in reality. It is also argued that the wave function can never collapse as predicted in quantum mechanics. "Everett" feels that it simply splits apart to take account of all possible outcomes. This view known as "Many Worlds Interpretation" is more deterministic as each of the possible states really occurs in reality. Further, it assumes parallel universes and the possibility that everything that can happen, will always happen. The popularity of the "Many Worlds Interpretation" is attributed to the fact that it avoids any need for a conscious observer to create reality. It does not explain how our conscious mind gets a clear idea of reality with the infinite division of possibilities that simultaneously exist in the world. May be we fail to understand the mysteries of matter at micro level because we are not equipped genetically to enter the wonderland of quantum phenomena.

Naturally Double Minded

The way the brain evolved over time would give us some clues about the dualistic nature of our perception. The left hemisphere of the brain is concerned with the analytical and rational aspects of the physical reality. It probably resembles a particle like existence of matter for creating reality. The right hemisphere predominantly has a holistic function of dealing with bigger structures in their totality in the space-time background. The right side does not fully participate in our analytical perception that seeks to know the mathematical or causal relations underlying natural phenomena. In a way, it is more interested in the totality of perception of matter in space at the macro level. It may be true that without conscious participation, no reality exists at the micro world of electrons and quarks. For conscious participation, we need an experiencing self created by the known ingredients of matter.

We can even conceptualize that the purpose of evolution of the mind would have been to enable us to perceive the dualistic nature of matter. For a comfortable life in the universe, we may not require all the accurate knowledge about the behavior of subatomic particles. Nevertheless, the true knowledge of reality at the micro level gives us the satisfaction of unraveling the well-hidden secrets of nature even if it does not increase our chances of survival or improve reproductive fitness. We find that patients after a split-brain operation in which the corpus callosum is surgically removed, behave as if they possess two minds. We can very well survive even with two minds may be with some reduced levels of conceptual abilities. The puzzle is why nature chose to integrate the two parts of the brain to give us holistic as well as analytic vision of reality. We will find some tentative answers about it after we delve deep into the complexities of life and the mind.

A Final Theory Of Everything

The 'Standard Model' based on the quantum theory, presumably explains almost everything about matter. It is capable of reproducing nature within one part in a billion. But the model involves 19 numbers like the masses of the quarks, electrons etc which look arbitrary and without much scientific basis. But, since the values of fundamental constants are fixed externally, we cannot accept that the standard model explains everything that a good theory should. It is at best a descriptive account of a part of the natural phenomena without explaining the more intriguing mysteries of matter.

The standard model assumes that there is a mirror image of everything including the universe. For every particle, the standard model finds an anti-particle, which is its counterpart with the same mass but having an opposite charge. It also allows breaking of symmetry in what is called charge-parity (CP) violation. CP violation is the phenomenon that gave matter an upper hand over its adversary in the struggle for survival in the early seconds of the creation of the universe. The scientists are still looking for proof of CP violations in the decay of electrically neutral particles called KAONS and B-MESON. The difference in the decay time provides a measure of the amount of symmetry breaking and also the correctness of the standard model. Many more experiments will be required to establish that standard model explains the truth of realty beyond any doubt. In its present form, we cannot accept it as a final theory of everything.

A unified final theory of everything should rationally explain matter, forces, space-time and all the cosmic coincidences in one theorem. It is the ultimate goal of all scientists trying to understand the secrets of natural phenomena. In spite of the proliferation of models and theories, we do not have a convincing explanation of gravitational force and the initial conditions that preceded the big bang. Some of the theories can explain certain aspects of matter and forces. But combining all of them in a single canvas seems to be an impossible task at the current level of scientific knowledge. The basic problem is that the quantum theory formulated in a flat space cannot reconcile with the curved space of general relativity.

There are several promising new thoughts that try to integrate all individual theories into one comprehensive explanation of nature. The concept of super symmetry assumes that every force and particle has an undiscovered symmetric partner. Accordingly, gravity is having super gravity, although it is not clear what it really means. Super string theory is yet another promising contender to the throne of the ultimate theory of everything. Some of the new theories use additional dimensions for providing possible explanations. But in reality, we find only the three dimensional space. Even if a unified theory of everything is formulated successfully, we mat not get an explanation for the phenomenon of consciousness that falls outside the realm of classical physics and quantum dynamics.

Many scientists are questioning the purpose of formulating a final theory of everything. If the initial conditions before the big bang did not follow any known physical law, the efforts to search for a theory to explain the events following the creation is definitely not worth all the intellectual investments. Any theoretical explanation of elementary particles and forces will only describe certain hidden aspects of natural phenomena. The theory of everything that can be derived from our present knowledge of matter and forces cannot remove all our confusions about the cause of creation. A rational explanation of the present state of the universe can only give us the satisfaction of discovering the laws of nature underlying the reality of existence. It can give us the causal link between the big bang and the natural phenomena that now exists in the universe. For reaching the deeper levels of knowledge of creations, we need more convincing answers to the basic questions of why the universe exists as it is with conscious observers to ask such questions. We will take up this challenging task in the next chapter on cosmic coincidences.

CHAPTER THREE

CONUNDRUM OF COSMIC COINCIDENCES

FROM A QUARTER OF THE DIVINE ENERGY
THE UNIVERSE CAME INTO BEING.
THE EARTH AND OTHER PLANETS EVOLVED
AND SOULS MANIFESTED IN HUMANS.
BUT THE UNKNOWN THREE QUARTERS ARE
THE ASTONISHING SECRET OF THE SUPREME BEING.

[RIG VEDA]

THE SAME FIRE BURNS WITHIN THE EARTH
IN PLANETS AND WATERS, STONES AND ANIMALS
IT LIES DEEP WITHIN HUMANS AND
LIGHTS UP THE HEAVENS AND KEEPS THE EARTH
IN A WARM MANTLE OF ENERGY.
MAY THE SAME FIRE ENLIGHTEN ME
WITH THE TRUE KNOWLEDGE OF SELF.

[ATHARVA VEDA]

THOSE WHO KNOW DON'T SAY. THOSE WHO SAY
DON'T KNOW.

[Tao Te Ching]

Choice Or Coincidence

We have seen that presently the universe is delicately poised between the possibilities of a big crunch and infinite expansion. Such finely balanced existence is extremely difficult to explain only on the basis of the total density of matter in the universe. If at the beginning of the universe, the value of omega that represents the total density was slightly different, the universe would have either collapsed or would not have created stars and galaxies. Whatever is the value of omega, the fact that it is designed to sustain a stable universe is the most intriguing cosmic coincidence that defies all rational explanations.

The recent discovery of microwave background radiation clearly supports the big bang theory. But for some tiny wrinkles, this radiation is distributed uniformly in all directions. Since regions moving in opposite directions would not have been interacting since the big bang, the fact that radiation is uniform in all directions also needs some convincing explanation. Similarly, we find that the cause of the tremendous expansion of the universe when it was 10^{-36} to 10^{-34} seconds old cannot be explained by any variant of the inflation theory. The Grand Unified Theory (GUT) explains the expansion but we cannot test any of its predictions. Since it does not include gravity, we can only assume inexplicable coincidences keep the universe expanding sedately at a constant rate.

Moreover, it is seen from the background radiation that one whole galaxy is moving toward the constellation of Leo as if a great attractor is pulling it. We have no idea about the identity of the attractor or what force it is applying on the whole group of galaxy. Similarly, we have the mystery of antimatter, which is the exact equivalent of matter but with an opposite charge. When matter meets antimatter both are eliminated in an explosion. But in the universe we find only matter that created stable structures like stars. When all the matter was created out of the same primordial ball of radiation, the antimatter seems to have simply disappeared. The only reason for our being here today is the surplus of matter left after the annihilation of all antimatter probably at the very instant of the big bang. The surprising fact is that the very small amount of left over matter could create stars and galaxies and also maintain the momentum of expansion.

Apart from these coincidences, there are many other strange natural occurrences that make the scientists feel uncomfortable. Currently, we simply assume that coincidences are inherent in the phenomena and hence no rational explanation is required. It only shows our inability to find any convincing cause for the correct choice of physical constants. The entire world of matter could not have been created in the absence of the knowledge of proper values of the basic constants. Without the correct mass of elementary particles and the relative strengths of various forces, structures would not have materialized. A slight change in the numerical values of their relative strengths or ratios would have made a different scenario without any galaxies or stars.

Even in the early days of scientific inquiries, the inexplicable cosmic coincidences generated heated academic debates. Lawrence Anderson listed several properties of some ordinary inorganic substances, which created conditions favorable for the emergence of life. Later on, further discoveries brought to light many more coincidences that seems to have occurred specifically to facilitate the appearance of life. Some people hold that the correct values of constants reveal a basic design beyond our level of comprehension.

We start with the atom, which is the primary building block of matter. It is the ratio between the mass of an electron and that of the nucleus that decides the shape of the atom. If the electrons had little more mass, they would have combined with protons to make neutrons. Presently, this process happens only in neutron stars under very high pressure. Thanks to the correct choice of the relative mass of proton, neutron and electron that constitute an atom, a variety of complex molecules like DNA can be formed. With slight deviation in the mass no atom would have formed to create matter.

Neutrinos are interesting particles without any charge or mass. Wolfgang Pauli theoretically predicted the possibility of their presence and later on it was experimentally confirmed. They seemed to have controlled the production of helium immediately after the big bang, when the temperature was about 1 billion degrees centigrade. Since neutrinos remove neutrons by converting them into protons, they must have maintained the level of helium optimally at about 23%. If the percentage of helium was slightly more or less, the story of the cosmos and human life would have been different one.

Similarly, the ratios of the strength of electric, nuclear and gravitational forces that bind the atoms and control their motion are also fixed to create atoms and molecules. Had the force of gravity been stronger, the sun would have lasted only for a very short time. A different value for the strength of electrical or nuclear force would not have given rise to galaxies and stars. Inside the atom also, we find that the nuclei remains stable because of a delicate balance of the forces. If the nuclear forces were stronger, relative to electric force, there would have been no hydrogen to fuel the fusion reaction in the stars. On the other hand, weaker nuclear forces would have produced nothing but hydrogen. In both the scenarios, there would have been no possibility of carbon -based life emerging anywhere in cosmos.

Even in the production of higher elements in the furnace of the star, we find the culmination of a series of coincidences. All stars are not equally equipped to produce the entire range of ninety-two known elements. The basic bricks of life had been made in massive stars that died away a long ago even before the birth of our sun. Without the debris of the big stars, planets like earth would not have formed and there would have been no intelligent life.

The creation of a carbon atom, the basic brick of biological life, is yet another cosmic miracle. To make one carbon nucleus in the core we need three helium nuclei to crash together. But in star chemistry, such crashes do not occur automatically. It requires the formation of a beryllium nucleus from two helium nuclei. Later on it has to combine with one more helium nucleus to make an atom of carbon. But beryllium being very unstable, it cannot readily combine with another helium nucleus to create carbon. It is the resonance in the carbon nucleus that makes the beryllium and helium to react. The value of the resonance of carbon nucleus is found to be 7.65 MeV. If it were slightly different, there would have been no carbon-based life. Not only that, if one more helium nucleus was involved in the reaction it would have produced an oxygen nucleus. Any change in the numerical value of carbon resonance would have resulted in an entirely different scenario that would have clearly excluded the possibility of the emergence of intelligent observers.

In addition to the astonishing array of such fundamental physical constants, Paul Dirac discovered some interesting numerical coincidences. He speculated the possibility of some basic principles that underlie the numerical coincidences. He noted that gravitational and electric forces obeyed the inverse square law. The ratio of strength of electrical and gravitational forces between an electron and a proton is about 10^{39}. He also found that the size of the observable universe also exceeded the size of a proton by a factor that is around 10^{39}. The estimated number of atoms in the universe was also about 10^{78}, that is, the square of the previous number. He assumed that the numerical coincidences indicated some deep linkage in the universe that is presently unknown to us. But no rational explanation can be found for such numerical coincidences. We can only say that the designer not only played dice but also had an advanced degree in mathematics.

The coincidences in the fixation of the values of basic constants are responsible for the formation of bigger structures like stars and planets. The planetary system requires a particular ratio or relationship in the strength of gravity and values of other constants. Both gravity and electric force are subject to the inverse square law because of the three dimensional nature of space. If gravity obeyed the inverse cube law, planets would have strayed away from the orbit and no life would have appeared on earth. Finally, we find that the standard model also contains several constants, which are arbitrarily fixed by coincidence. The mass of the meson, baryon and lepton match theoretical predictions with experimental values. The question is how they have been fixed externally at the first instance without having the help of any theory to derive the values of constants. Can we assume that an external intelligence has done all the homework of searching and fixing necessary values of constants to make the universe a grand success! If we accept such irrational possibilities, we are not more advanced than the wonderstruck Stone Age man gazing at the illumination in the starlit sky.

Who Devised The Constants?

The undeniable fact is that in the modern times we need a rational explanation for the existence of a stable universe. We know that it would not have existed but for the choice of certain finely tuned basic constants. The physical constants that govern the composition and strength of matter and forces seem to have been fixed sometime immediately after the big bang. The fundamental question is whether we can access the process or principle underlying the choice of the correct constants that created a stable universe and life. The easiest explanation is to assign the responsibility for all such arduous tasks of calculation to an almighty God. He would have anyway known all the correct parameters to create a suitable place for us to live in. The majority of humans readily accept this explanation, as they believe in some God or the other. But it is not likely to convince the scientific community looking for causal relations and hard proof for all natural phenomena.

Even in scientific literature we come across several irrational anthropic reasoning's for explaining such coincidences. All forms of anthropic reasoning assume that the universe was created for the ultimate emergence of life. The modern form of anthropic reasoning suggested by Brandon Carter distinguishes between the "Weak" and the "Strong" versions. The weak form assumes that our existence as observers decides what our universe should be including the narrow range of constants for the carbon-bound life. We are here just because it is possible for us to be here. This line of reasoning is acceptable to most of the scientists.

We can further extend this logic to assume that we exist among a large number of universes or regions. The laws of physics and the parameters chosen for constants might be different for each universe. We fortunately find ourselves in a universe that is suitable for our existence and for explaining all coincidences. The coincidences are in fact inevitable conditions that make human life a necessary corollary. The problem with the weak reasoning is that it can never be falsified as there life is no way of finding out the truth of its premises. But strong anthropic reasoning takes the extreme stand that the fundamental laws of any universe must allow observers to exist. It means that the only purpose of the correct choice of constants is the emergence of observers. Such an egocentric views of the universe cannot be accepted as the truth of reality.

Another anthropic explanation is the participatory view of the universe that also implies the essential existence of the observer for bringing any universe into reality. The world is a shared experience, where observer participancy is absolutely necessary, to collapse the wave function. In "the many worlds" approach, our universe is considered similar to a quantum phenomenon. It assumes that a large number of universes evolve in parallel and show great diversity with the progress of time. Lee Smolin gives another explanation of a process of natural selection of favored universes. He argues that our universe could be a product of natural selection by overcoming the challenges from competing sibling universes. Our own universe and others were probably created out of black holes with slightly different values of physical constants.

None of the explanations, whether anthropic or theological can give us a rational basis for the choice of cosmic coincidences. Latest entrants only try to fill up the information gap with some pseudo-scientific concoctions. It is true that we have discovered many physical laws that are applicable to observable natural phenomena. But what we would like to know by all means is the actual process or circumstances that decided the choice of the values of constants. The thrill of discovering the laws of nature alone is not sufficient to sustain the quest for the more fundamental scientific knowledge about the identity of the author of the story of creation. Uncovering some regularities and causal links without knowing the original design will only point out the apathy of the scientists to probe deeper the ultimate truth of reality.

The anthropic reasoning looks like a convenient excuse for avoiding the unpleasant presence of an intelligent designer in the drama of creation. In fact, the weak anthropic principle does not offer any explanation at all. It simply says that our existence decides the nature of the universe. It does not add anything to our knowledge about the casual links or our own life in the universe. One day we will probably formulate a theory of everything that might, give us the mathematical basis of existence. Anthropic reasoning will then become redundant, as all coincidences could be attributed to that theory. Our ingenuity will then elevate us to the level of nature or God who conceived the theory at the first instance to create the cosmos. This final conquest will probably be the greatest achievement of humans. We will return to this puzzle in our concluding part to find some convincing ultimate answers. Let us now try to get some more ideas about the fascinating enigma of the origin and evolution of life on our planet.

PART TWO

WHAT ARE WE ?

'DIVERSITY TO COMPLEXITY'

The divine grace pervades in the harmonious
existence of all life in nature.
The gentle dawn wakes us up with
the sweet tidings of a new day.
The dazzling noon brings
peace & happiness.
The serene sunset
puts to rest the wearied body
in the lap of nature.
To wake us up to yet another day
of existence in the eternal
love of god.

(YAJUR VEDA)

✦

The supreme self is too close to be seen,
But not too far to be ignored,
His divine poetry is nature's splendour
beyond all decay & death.

(ATHARVA VEDA)

✦

CHAPTER FOUR

CHILDREN OF STARDUST

LIFE IS AN ACT OF OFFERING
TO ACHIEVE THE HIGHEST BLESSING
OF SELF REALIZATION.
LET THE DIVINE FIRE BURN BRIGHTLY
TO FILL OUR SOUL WITH COMPASSION
FOR THE ENTIRE HUMANITY.

[ATHARVA VEDA]

THE CELESTIAL REGION WAS CREATED FIRST WITH THE MOST POWERFUL SUN. THE EARTH IS THE PRECIOUS POSSESSION OF THE UNIVERSE BUT BOTH THE HEAVEN AND EARTH DISAPPER IN THE NIGHT.

[YAJUR VEDA]

Down To Earth

In Part One, we have seen that all the basic ingredients necessary to create life on our planet were made in the fusion reaction in the stars. A dying megastar throws out a wide variety of atomic nuclei into interstellar space. They readily combine with the electrons to create atoms. Some of them react further to become even heavy molecules of water and ammonia. Such heavy molecules have been found in some meteorites that managed to reach earth un-burnt. Under the influence of gravity, the interstellar clouds begin to collapse creating new stars and also some planets to orbit them. We can safely conclude that the great saga of life on earth began in the core of the stars amidst plenty of fireworks.

Our planet is created out of the condensed stardust containing a wide variety of atoms and molecules. In the beginning, the accumulated interstellar matter was in the form of an incandescent ball of fire. While cooling down it slowly created an atmosphere, which was crucial for eye to appear. It also had all the ideal conditions and ingredients to create a wide variety of biological matter. The force of gravity on the planet was just strong enough to retain water molecules in the atmosphere. Plenty of liquid water in the oceans created conditions necessary for making and retaining molecules that became the building blocks of life.

The earth is placed at an optimum distance from the sun to enjoy a warm but not scorching atmosphere that can sustain the delicate biological life. All the benign planetary conditions including the presence of a moon of convenient size look like pure coincidence created by physical forces. Of course, many people see the invisible hands of a designer in making a wonderful nest to hatch primeval life on earth. Trillions of planets in billions of galaxies may be ideally placed like earth with potential to create life. But our technology seems to be grossly inadequate to receive any signals from intelligent life elsewhere in the universe. Or, the aliens may not be intelligent enough to send messages across millions of light years.

Cerebral Giants From Chemical Soup

Our scientific enquiries now reveal that life on earth is just an insignificant but inevitable corollary of a series of cosmic events that began with the big bang. There is undeniable continuity between the creation of matter after the big bang and the ultimate appearance of life on earth. Biological matter is intrinsically not different from other forms of matter. We find that all living cells are made up of molecules consisting of atoms made in the stars. All that distinguishes the complex biological organisms from inanimate matter is a set of capabilities for performing functions like reproduction, metabolism and evolution by natural selection. The clusters of inanimate matter that do not possess these faculties nevertheless contain the same basic ingredients of atoms and molecules. A slightly different configuration in another context would have given the ordinary matter more cohesiveness and potential for purposive action that we see in live organisms.

In religious literature, life is generally attributed to the creative imagination or design of a supernatural force. But such assertions are simply based on the assumption that the amazing variety and complexity of life cannot be the outcome of a series of coincidences. The majority of humans do believe that life is the creation of God or an intelligent designer. But all the available scientific evidences indicate that life originated from inanimate matter placed under certain favorable physical conditions that prevailed on earth about four billion years ago.

We do not know the exact mechanism that created biological matter from the concoction of chemicals on the primordial earth. One view is that evolution of inorganic chemicals in the presence of some catalysts culminated in the formation of an organic cell. In the same manner, complex living organisms also evolved by adding more and more specialized organs for performing new functions. Of course, there are many holes in the evolutionary explanation of life, but nothing else seems to give us a rational account of the appearance of life on earth. The subsequent diversification of primeval life into a vast variety of species and subspecies also requires an acceptable explanation.

Mysterious Origin

We are still groping in the primordial darkness of singularity to explain the initial conditions that preceded the big bang. Similarly, no clear scientific explanation has so far emerged about the origin of life on earth. But unlike the unknown past of the cosmos, we have a fairly accurate idea about the initial state of the earth about 4.5 billion years ago. During the first one billion years or so, the surface of earth was too hot to give rise to any form of life. The constant fall of meteorites on the unprotected surface of earth must have also created violent convulsions unsuitable for the emergence of extremely delicate biological organisms.

The cooling process that ensued in the first few million years after the condensation of the interstellar dust produced plenty of gases and liquid water. It also gave the earth an atmosphere to begin a chain of chemical experiments that probably culminated in the creation of the first live cell. The optimum size of the earth had just enough gravitational pull to hold on to precious gases like hydrogen, methane, ammonia, water vapor and so on. Plenty of liquid water was available to preserve the fragile macromolecules from the deadly ultraviolet radiation. All this could happen only in a warm and hospitable atmosphere maintained by the ideal distance of the earth from the Sun. The proximity of an obliging moon also gave the earth friendly tides and an axis of rotation a small but benevolent tilt.

Such favorable conditions alone would not have created in the first live cell without a triggering event to convert the hot soup of chemicals into biological matter. It could have been the flash of lightning, volcanic eruption, or even seeding by a mother molecule from a meteorite. The idea of the flash of lightning as the starter of life has already been tested in laboratory simulations. Scientists found some simple organic molecules that are components of larger organic molecules like proteins and lipids in the tests imitating the primordial conditions on earth.

Another idea that is gaining ground is that the combined effect of ultraviolet rays and the continuous bolts of lightning striking the surface of the earth might have broken up the gases floating in the biosphere. Complex chemicals like amino acids created in the atmospheric reactions must have been carried to the oceans in the torrential rains. Water must have protected the newly born chemical molecules from any possible damage by ultraviolet radiation. It has been confirmed that formaldehyde and hydrogen cyanide could have been produced in this process. They are essential chemicals for making DNA bases that contain the genetic code of life.

Cradle Of Clay!

The appearance of life on earth is also attributed to the reactions of various chemicals in stagnant clay pools. Such pools remain warm during the day, but in the night they become cold. The quartz and clay in the pools can transfer long chains of molecules. In recent laboratory stimulations, it has been confirmed that in the presence of clay, chemicals can form small chains of nucleic acids like DNA. Clay can also remove water from small molecules so that they can form larger chains that are essential for life. The ions of clay can probably act as catalysts capable of exhorting the chemicals around them to initiate reactions. It is also possible that some clusters of molecules would have developed a hydrophobic exterior like a drop of oil. The internal chemistry of the globule would have developed differently from the environment surrounding it. The membrane that separated the internal and external world must have protected the organic molecules from the rigorous conditions of a hostile environment.

Some enzymes in such droplets could have made energy from carbohydrates. Initially, energy would have been created by simple fermentation reaction. Later on, some of the droplets would have retained pigments capable of using light to produce energy. Ultimately some would have learnt to reproduce their own internal chemistry to perpetuate the production of that particular variety of droplets. The formation of the RNA that has catalytic as well as self-replicating capabilities must have heralded the beginning of life on earth.

But what is really surprising is how the complex chemicals evolved the process of interlocking into closed cycles or hyper cycles with self-organizing and replicating tendencies. To reach such exalted levels of biological activities, inanimate matter requires strong compulsions to repeat predetermined functions. We cannot assume such qualities in inanimate matter without the mediation of an external force or design? Such occurrences can be considered only as natural phenomena since our present level of knowledge cannot give any rational explanation. We have only some probabilities to probe the real identity of the mechanism that created life from the simmering soup of primordial chemicals.

Flight Of The Genes!

Another possibility in that life would have originated in some other planet before it reached the earth. Meteorites would have carried simple organic life like bacteria to earth before it acquired the protective atmosphere. Astronomers have detected in distant galaxies the presence of circularly polarized light that creates a preferred handedness in organic molecules. Large quantities of left-handed amino acids are found in Murchison meteorite, which fell on earth in 1969. Since left-handed amino acids are found only in living organisms and the circularly polarized light that creates this molecule is not found on earth, we can deduce that life would have originated elsewhere in the universe.

Recently in the analysis of the samples from Tagish Lake meteorite showed the presence of organic molecules that would have played some role in the origin of life on earth. When we complete the analytic study of the 220-ton meteorite that fell in a Canadian lake on January 2000, we may get closer to the secret recipe that created life. Scientific evidence shows that bacteria can change into spores in adverse conditions. The suspended animation of spores is revoked when it enters a friendly atmosphere. The speculation that such spores would have spread the seeds of life all over the universe is not mere scientific fiction. Spores of life could have successfully endured the long interstellar travel to reach hospitable planets to begin life afresh. It must have happened with the first major collision about 250 million years ago or even with the one that put an end to the rule of dinosaurs.

Shortly, we may get pure signals from outer space when earth-based interferences are completely eliminated. They will indicate the presence or absence of any extra-terrestrial intelligence capable of sending signals to reach us on earth. Other forms of life on distant planets may be inferior varieties, incapable of intelligent exchange of ideas. In spite of all our scientific knowledge abot the various possibilities, we have to admit the fact that the origin of life still continues to be an intriguing puzzle.

Whatever transformed the inanimate matter into self-bound, self-perpetuating biological structures, the successful saga of evolution of life began in right earnest when the first bacterial cell emerged on earth. Two coils of RNA could have come together to form a stable double helix structure creating the first DNA. Scientists claim that the evolutionary time of about 500 million years after the formation of the planet would have been sufficient for the droplets to evolve into the self sustaining clusters of live molecules. The bacteria had all the essential qualities of life to distinguish itself from inanimate matter. We will, probably in the course of the next few decades, reach some definite conclusions about the origin of life.

WWW Of Bacteria

The exponential growth of bacteria, which was propelled by self-replication, must have depleted most of the available sources of energy on earth. This would have created severe competition among them for the scarce resources. The evolutionary compulsion to perpetuate the species at any cost would have probably begun with the acute struggle for survival among the bacteria in the initial stages of life. It would have led to the invention of novel energy pathways like the breaking down of sugar or fixing of nitrogen and finally in photosynthesizing energy from the plentiful supply of natural resources. The hard working communities of bacteria would have clustered together in suitable habitats for launching new forms of multi-cellular life.

In addition, they must have regulated the composition of the biosphere to keep it suitable for all forms of life to survive in a symbiotic existence. A large variety of new species of plants and animals began to evolve with the benign bacteria supporting even their internal chemistry and other functions. The waste products of photosynthesis and fermentation of sugar were also recycled by bacterial communities to maintain the requisite balance of being the eco-system.

Higher organisms appeared on earth almost two billion years after the simple bacterial form of life began the evolutionary voyage in to the complexities of existence. They practically knew all the correct ingredients necessary to create new variety of life. Even DNA in the nucleated cell of higher organisms seems to have originated from the fragments of DNA scattered all over the bacterial cell. The bacteria even created proteins capable of self-repairing the damages of the cell. They could also exchange genes containing vital information for survival in adverse circumstances.

While 99% of the species in the early days of life had already become extinct the great global bacterial web continues to control the various parameters of the biosphere through their multifarious activities. The evolutionary relationships of plants and animals clearly indicate the possibility of the simple bacteria in its several variants and incarnations forming a substratum of all higher forms of existence. It is the symbiotic co-existence of bacterial communities that evolved specialized organs in higher forms of life. The great achievement of life would not have been possible but for the bacterial patronage of our planet.

Nucleated Cells For New Life

An important milestone in the evolution of life on earth after 2.2 billion years of its birth was the appearance of the nucleated cell. It is the basic component of all plants and animals. What distinguishes it is the large number of DNAs coiled into chromosomes inside an enclosed nucleus. In bacteria, the pieces of DNA are scattered all over the cell without the protective cover of a membrane. The nucleated cell must have evolved out of the symbiotic relationship of various kinds of bacteria living together for a very long time. It would have emerged from the sustained invasion of aggressive small bacteria on large docile ones that would have initially tolerated the nuisance. When the invader was ultimately absorbed in the cell, it must have performed certain benign functions helping the survival of the host and guest. Another possibility is that some nucleated cells would have got a free lift to earth on a meteor and later on evolved into complex organisms. They must have been developed in some distant planet hospitable to life.

With the appearance of nucleated cells having excellent mobility and the ability to make food out of solar energy, life began to diversify into new varieties beyond conventional forms. The conglomeration of cellular societies offered better chances of survival as compared to the isolated single cells. The symbiotic association of cells facilitated differentiation of functions commensurate with the location and structure of individual cells. The information about the specific location and specialized function of each variety of cells gets transmitted to the offspring through the genetic messages in the DNA.

But the basic question is how the correct genetic message was initially encoded in the DNA of a cell. Further, we do not know how the allocation of the discreet functions to different groups of cells was mooted at the first instance. We cannot expect an individual cell to gain full knowledge about the overall functioning of a complex organism. Some sort of sentience or design seems to have been guiding the cell to carry forward the genetic instructions. The same phenomenon of sentience is seen both at the lowest level of bacteria and in a complex organism having trillions of specialized cells. Surely in some unknown processes at the cellular level, intelligent exchange of information takes place, which is beyond our comprehension.

Mouse To Mankind

There is no precise chronological record of the first appearance of plants and animals on land. While some of the fossil discoveries indicate that it happened about 1.2 billion years back, other evidences give only 700-400 million years. There is acceptable evidence to show that the rudimentary form of animal brain that propelled life to greater complexity appeared about 600 million years ago. The first water-born animal must have been a mass of specialized cells living together in large colonies of coral reef created with their calcium secretions. When they came to terra firma, they would have faced extremely harsh challenges from the new environment. The toughest challenge would have been for the organs specially adapted for aquatic life to get it rewired for the different conditions of the land.

The amphibians and newts are the evolutionary links between water and land animals. This is evident from the fact that even now they get metamorphosed from water-breathing tadpoles to frogs. The insects that came to land created a wide variety of new species. Even today, they far exceed all other species both in number and variety. Amphibians later evolved into reptiles and a large variety of them ruled the earth for a very long time. They reached the peak of evolution by creating many exciting varieties like dinosaurs. Fungus is another wonderful form of life that came to land about 300 million years ago and established a separate identity and definition of life by their unique features. Instead of making energy from photosynthesis, the fungus directly absorbs chemicals into its body. This process has been helpful for the plants in getting atmospheric nitrogen fixed free of cost. Several ecological disasters created suitable contexts for the evolution and even extinction of a vast variety of life. Human origins are now being traced to the period when the earth began to cool down about 70 million years ago. A long intermission interrupted the steady progress of life on earth after the collision of a huge meteorite that wiped out large varieties of species including the dinosaurs.

The prolonged cold spell caused by the impact of a meteor about 70 million years ago, put an end to the reign of the dominant species of the time. Among the few survivors of the catastrophe were some small tree shrews that ultimately evolved to become apes and humans. These puny primates called 'pro-simians' retained most of the characteristics of their insect eating ancestors. Certain features like clinging hands and feet and opposable thumbs seemed to have helped them to survive in the hostile jungle of life. To start, with they were only as big as rodents and lived mostly on fruits and insects. No wonder, the latest finding of human genome mapping reveals that we have almost the same range of genes like the mouse.

The great ecological disaster would have also triggered off a chain of quick evolutionary jumps among the surviving mammals. There was nothing resembling humans on earth even 60-70 million years ago. Mainly it was only two type of Rodent like mammals that managed to derive maximum mileage from the ecological disaster. One variety remained on surface of earth scavenging the left over resources. But the other variety called prosimians took to the trees and lived mostly on fruits and leaves. They are our ancestors who evolved through several stages and challenges to reach the highest level of existence.

The common ancestors of apes and monkeys emerged from the line of pro-simians, who colonized Eurasia, which was an island formed by Africa and Arabia. The line of Great Apes consisting of orangutans, chimpanzees and gorillas appeared about ten million years ago. Certain chimpanzee species in the African tropics developed a complex brain and started walking short distances on two legs. They must have used the expanding capacity of the brain for creative purposes like making tools out of stones. The first human descendent from the Southern Apes appeared about 2-3 million years ago in East Africa. They are called 'Homo habilis' and they further evolved into heavily built 'Homo-erectus' or the "upright ones." They migrated from Africa to Asia and Europe and survived the harsh environments that followed the ice age.

All these evolutionary advances eventually culminated in the emergence of the wonderful "Homo sapiens" or the wise ones. About 100,000 years ago the process of evolution seems to have completed in Asia and Africa but in Europe, it happened only about 40,000 years ago. This brief overview of the evolutionary history of life on our planet is based on fossil evidences and other data collected in various scientific inquiries. Of course, life has many more interesting features worth discussion, but they are not necessary for our limited purpose of getting the crrect answers to the questions of what we are? However, certain outstanding milestones in the progress of life require to be highlighted to understand the process of emergence of vast diversities from the bacterial web.

Can We Define Life?

The brief history of the evolution of life on earth brings out certain essential features that clearly distinguish life from inanimate matter. The important requirement of life is a well-defined boundary between the organism and the outside world. The barrier should not, create a completely closed system, which would prevent even limited interaction with the environment. It should also permit the inflow of energy giving matter in requisite form and quantities. A suitable mechanism to discharge waste products generated in the internal processes is also necessary to prevent its toxic effect, which would be fatal to the organism. Plants generally get energy through photosynthesis while animals make it from the chemical reaction of molecular bonds. The cycles of energy producing reactions should be adequate for the sustenance of the organism. The self-bound structure is designed to keep the system away from entropy or thermal equilibrium that increases internal disorder. The organism is meant to survive and reproduce for a certain period of time until irreparable damages interrupt forever the process of energy and waste management.

A lot of energy is required to carry out the multifarious activities in the trillions of cells of a live organism. It is the complex organic molecules called proteins that do all the major work related to sustenance and reproductive success. The production of protein is controlled and commanded by the sequentially coded instructions in the DNA. There are 23 pairs of chromosomes in humans and each of them contains thousands of genes. It is now ascertained that the human genome contains only about 30,000 to 40,000 genes. The genes with specific instructions to make particular varieties of proteins are much less in number.

The gene is a long string as DNA molecules wound into coils. The DNA has four varieties of nucleotides and their sequential arrangement contains the entire information required for the functions to be carried out in an organism. Nature needs only four chemical alphabets to write the story of life in about 32 billion letters. In the English language we need 26 alphabets for effective communication. Recently, scientists have unraveled the entire sequence of the chemical instructions encoded in the DNA. The genetic information available now gives us far more insights into the origin and evolution of life on earth. It shows that basic variation in the human genome is only about .2 % in a total of 3.2 billion letters. The genes contain the entire history of human evolution from the primordial first cell until a few hundred years ago. Genetically all are equal despite the difference in the color of the skin or mental abilities. The only genuine variation in humans is based on gender.

Some of the DNA messages are found responsible for the physical features and even intelligence of the organism. The cell produces a template of DNA called 'RNA' that synthesizes proteins in the right sequence and required amount for the effective functioning of the cell. The double helix structure of DNA allows it to unzip properly during the cell division. DNA is constantly under attack from radiation, pollutants and alien microbes like viruses. Mutations are the abnormalities inflicted on DNA by various factors that ultimately lead to the death of the cell. Some mutations create errors that cause uncontrollable growth of the cell as in the case of cancer. Normally, only mutations beneficial to be organisms are carried forward to the next generation probably to improve their chances of survival. The malignant ones are not very effective in getting themselves transmitted to the future generations.

The surprising secret of DNA is that only 10% of its messages are read and used by the cell leaving about 90% as junk or redundant. We have no idea whatsoever why so much of redundancy is built into the precious DNA space. It may be for meeting some emergency or simply the leftover of some outdated instructions that are no more useful to the organism. Some genes are found to be capable of jumping from one location to another as if an unknown force is propelling them. It is also a fact that the same DNA can produce a caterpillar and butterfly. The messages on DNA must be given different interpretations in different contexts and environments.

Some of the DNA messages remain inactive as if they were following some invisible instructions. We find certain dormant ones suddenly becoming active after long intervals of hibernation. In virus infections, foreign DNA gets introduced into the cell's genetic system. We have also ample proof of DNA recombination by bacteria, which uses its global genetic message pool for updating information. It is found that the bacteria can go on changing the genetic instructions in frequent intervals to the extent of more than 15% on a daily basis. DNA recombination proves beyond any doubt that at molecular level there is effective communication between the environment and the organism. The DNA must be receiving information inputs directly from the environment that helps in gene jumping and DNA recombination. Perhaps, it is some sort of rapid exchange of information at molecular level particularly in the neurons that must have created higher levels of awareness in humans.

The modern scientific definition of life indicates a walled organism capable of reproduction, self-repair and creation of all the energy for its multifarious functions. It should have genes consisting of DNA molecules to direct activities to secure survival and propagation of the organism even in adverse circumstances. According to evolutionists, the random mutations that effect changes in the DNA bases better equip the organisms for survival. But the fact is that mostly beneficial changes are incorporated and carried forward to the new generations. We cannot assume that the cell has all the correct information about the habitat to choose wisely all the desirable qualities that would enable the organism to survive. It is too much to expect such high level of intelligence in a simple cell. The capabilities of the cell must have been derived from DNA that is capable of exchanging information with the environment at some basic level.

Men Are From Mice And Women Are From Worms

Before the discovery of DNA, several unscientific assumptions were in vogue about the possible origins of life on earth. It is now confirmed that all forms of life share almost 90% of common features in the DNA. Such high percentage of genetic similarities conclusively proves the common origin of all life. It also shows the possibility of evolutionary pathways creating pumpkins and monkeys out of the same basic stock. In fact, we have only about 1 to 2% DNA differences with the apes who are our closest relations in the evolutionary chain.

The latest revelations of the sequencing of human genome show that we are genetically endowed only as much as the humble mouse. The racists are the most dejected lot to find no evidence of any genetic preference for a particular race. We now know that race is only a cultural concept rather than a scientific certainty. It is also confirmed that individual variations are based on about 2 million differences in genetic letters. More surprisingly, it is revealed that genes are not all that important in molding ones life. It is the proteins created by the body according to the directions in the genes that control the destiny of biological organisms. But even the signals from DNA or the activities of the proteins cannot make a human capable of thinking, feeling and acting with care and compassion. Humanness arises from the cultural and social factors that condition our thoughts and behavior in different contexts. DNA sequences show that there are some remarkable genetic differences of gender and not between the blacks and whites or an intellectual and an idiot. It is also now revealed that mutations of genes are mostly a in "Y" chromosome that belongs to the man. May be it gives scientific proof to the already accepted fact that the women are less amenable to changes and gentle persuasions? Even the nature would have found it difficult to modify her mind with humble suggestions to upgrade the software.

Human genome sequencing has given an estimated numbers of about 26,000 to 30,000 genes for us instead of the expected 80,000. Out of that, much less is involved in the making of proteins. Now it is clear that we have only a few hundred genes more than the mouse that has no intellectual pretensions.

And the lowly placed worm has just 10,000 genes less than the great humans. Of course, the files are still shorter by about 20,000 genes but the monkeys are much closer to the sentient beings.

It simply means that it is the monkey genes marauding in more civilized packages that conduct 98% of human affairs. No wonder that even the normal human behavior sometimes shows lot of monkey tricks. But the surprising fact is that marginal variations in the monkey genome can create an immensely unique and intelligent organism. The architect of all the wonderful variety of life is the genome of a single fertilized cell called 'ovum'. The single cell undergoes rapid cell division making millions of diverse kinds of cells capable of performing several specialized functions. The final outcome of the time-bound process of cell division is an offspring having a distinctly different identity, but retaining most of the basic characteristics of the parents. The parentage of all forms of life whether mice or men actually goes back to the first cell that contained essential features of existence in a primitive form.

Sex For Better Life!

Reproduction by simple cell division would have created a large number of copies of the same organism. The copies would have carried forward the characteristics of the parent cell including its harmful mutations. In this scenario, life would have remained at the level of bacteria without pushing the species on the evolutionary ladder. Nature must have invented a new method for reproduction to make new varieties of life that can survive any genetic deficiencies. In fact, bacteria still continue to create offspring in the same manner without gaining any appreciable evolutionary edge over other forms of life. Their advantage lies in the sheer number rather than the quality of existence.

The great diversity of life began with the unique invention of sexual reproduction. In sexual reproduction, a specialized egg containing exactly half the number of chromosomes is fertilized by a sperm cell, carrying the same number of complementary chromosomes. The actual process of sexual reproduction in which the egg and sperm get united is specially chosen for each species. They are fully consistent with the physical features and requirements of the species. The fertilized egg is kept in a suitable medium to grow by rapid cell division in a predetermined time schedule. The growth of the embryonic cell culminates ultimately in an offspring that inherits all the prominent physical features and other characteristics of the parents.

Sexual reproduction is an advanced evolutionary innovation to transmit the best features of the species to the offspring. It is also the most effective method devised by nature to ensure that only the fittest in the species survive to create progeny. A great deal of careful design is involved in the mechanism of sexual reproduction. Specific attention has to be paid to all minute details from the moment of conception until the offspring becomes totally independent. The preparation of a specialized egg and sperm having exactly half the number of chromosomes but having all the vital information is an ingenious task. A special medium that contains all essential nutrients to accelerate cell division is required for the balanced growth of the embryonic cell in to a fully equipped prototype. The physical separation of the offspring from the mother is yet another complicated process, which involves delicate handling to avoid any dangerous consequences for the mother and the child.

Even the feeding and training program of the offspring calls for meticulous planning consistent with the specific needs of each species. In brief, sexual reproduction is the vehicle that carried simple organisms to greater evolutionary heights ensuring their survival in all adverse circumstances. Here also, the basic question is about the deliberate choice of sexual reproduction as a preferred alternative to the simple cell division. How did this exciting idea originally enter into the genes of the biological organism so that organs necessary for sex could be designed to replace the less cumbersome process of cell division? Is it not too much to assume that all intelligent planning involved in this process could be performed by a collection of intelligent molecules and semi-autonomous cells. I am not suggesting inevitability of design, but evolutionary intelligence alone could not have reached such heights to choose sex as the best method for natural selection. All that we can infer now is that some kind of intelligent interaction unknown to us at present is evident at the cellular and molecular levels within the organism and also with the external world.

Born With A Time Bomb?

Ageing is yet another biological wonder that is an integral part of all living organisms. Each cell has a biological clock designed to limit its infinite capacity for division. The DNA seems to contain instructions for terminating the life after a specific period of time. When the cell reaches the preprogrammed terminal stage, growth somehow or other ceases and the cell dies. Only cancer cells with infinite capacity for division continue their uncontrolled growth that ultimately kills the organism. During the cell division, new cells inherit accumulated errors of genetic messages that may also lead to their malfunctioning and eventual death.

Death is an inevitable necessity for preserving the precious resources for the fitter ones capable of successful reproduction. It ensures the survival of the species as a whole by eliminating the spent ones that become the burden of the community. But the cessation of biological life does not destroy the matter constituting the basic bricks of the body. The atoms and molecules are recycled and returned in one form or the other to the environment to take part again in the great cosmic drama of creation and maintenance of life. Ultimately, when the earth eventually vaporizes to become a part of the sun in about five billion years or even less, they will probably begin the return journey to the original galactic warehouses.

Wise Ones From The Ice

Fossil evidences clearly indicate that humans evolved from a species of primates. But the surprising fact is that after the divergence between Hominids and Apes more about 40 million years ago, it took less than 2 million years for the emergence of early human called "Homo erectus". They originated in Africa and spread through Europe and Asia. We can follow their trail from the tools left behind by the adventurous hominids. They represent an important genetic turning point in the evolution of human kind. They had double the brain size of Australopithecus, which probably helped in making of special tools. In fact, Homo erectus almost had the same brain size as the modern man.

Other interesting developments followed the increasing size of the skull. Changes in female pelvis were required to permit the passage of offspring with a bigger head. Another evolutionary requirement was the psychological changes in the female for looking after the infant for a longer period of time. To reach physical maturity, humans need more time and resources to overcome the serious challenges from the bacterial and viral world. The prolonged dependency of the infants had its impact on the life style of the female Hominid. Her role as a gatherer was severely restricted by the highly taxing maternity requirements. We can perhaps surmise that the additional requirement of food and the prolonged dependence of infants must have sharpened the memory and tool making skills of the Hominids. At this point of time, the Hominids would have entered a new evolutionary path leading to drastic changes in learning skill and physical abilities.

The early crude version of the present humankind called "Homo erectus" evolved into the more refined "Homo sapiens" about 250,000 years ago. Their transition into full-fledged humans was completed about 100,000 years ago in Asia and Africa. However, in Europe, Homo erectus continued till about 35,000 years ago in the Neanderthal valley where they eventually became extinct or merged with the more evolved "Homo sapiens." Homo Sapiens completed their evolution in Europe only about 40,000 years ago and they must have even co-existed with the less evolved Neanderthals for sometime. As compared to billions of years involved in the creation and evolution of life on earth, humans seem to have taken an extremely short cut to complete the transition from apes to the "wise ones". Of course, many of our cousins will still be sitting on treetops while we take off to distant planets for building new homes. Our short cut to fame in less than two million years is definitely an enviable feat as compared to the slow evolutionary changes in other varieties of life. They also traveled in the same vehicle of random mutation but could not catch up with the fast moving "wise ones". The full facts of our speedy evolutionary changes will be known when the meaning of all the messages encoded in the genome is understood.

Lucy, The Mother And Father Of Mankind

In the recent past, certain astonishing discoveries about the evolution of sex chromosomes in humans created interesting gender controversies. The genetic family tree conceived by some scientists assumes that the earliest human ancestor was a female who lived in South Africa about 1,50,000 years ago. It is now confirmed that the males evolved out of the females who reigned supreme as the only members of the human race without getting overshadowed by the male chauvinists. Presently, we have no idea how they got offspring but the fact is that the "Y" chromosomes that distinguish males evolved out of the double "X" chromosomes. The female carried them from day number one of the existence of human kind. More over now we find that most of the mutations that carried as to the new evolutionary heights happened on "Y" chromosome. The male who brought out the changes probably moved forward faster by developing the left hemisphere of the brain while the females continued their happy holistic existence.

Another puzzle is the genetic compulsion for evolving the "Y" chromosome when the double X-ed female variety had been successfully achieving large-scale propagation and migration. We have no idea about the forces that could have motivated the "X" chromosomes to get them mutated to make the males. Some environmental factors might have definitely passed on crucial information to the genes about the need for producing a stronger variety of species. Such exchange of information would have created the chemical signals in the genes that mutated to make the male species to combat more effectively the challenges of resource depletion and more aggressive competition. The rapid expansion of the human race would have been the consequence of the emergence of males that left the females free to concentrate on child rearing and house keeping. The hazardous tasks like defending the territories and hunting big games for food were mostly taken over by the stronger male species. The females flourished with less mortality rate and a more comfortable life style. The undeniable impact of the environmental influence is evident in the evolution of "Y" chromosomes that introduced the most significant genetic event of gender differentiation. It boosted the assent of the humans to the highest intellectual pedestal by creating new races having additional capabilities and skills.

Sexless Females

An astonishing physiological change that occurred in the female Hominid during the evolutionary progress was the loss of estrus. We have no idea about exact period of occurrence of this momentous event. But once it happened, the female Hominid was a clearly distinct variety compared to the females of other species. For all females other than the human variety, sexual attractiveness and receptivity are limited to heat periods or estrus. The mechanism of estrus keeps the female ready for sexual act only during certain periods prescribed by the nature. The Hominid female probably could not afford the luxury of estrus, which would have interfered with prolonged periods of child rearing. The Hominid offspring would have been thrown out from the home at a very early age, if the mother got into estrus at fequent intervals. We can clearly see an evolutionary compulsion in the loss of estrus in the female Hominid. It would have taken a few million years to reach complete loss of estrus, but it was an advancement essential for the survival of the species. We can say that the female Hominid made the biggest sacrifice of loosing estrus for ensuring the perpetuation of the species.

Another important offshoot of the loss of estrus was the emergence creation of the family as a core social institution based on sexual love. Monogamous relationship can also be traced to the time of disappearance of estrus. It made females ready for sex at any time when they gave up evolutionary compulsion to perform it at specific periods. We can also find in the loss of estrus the beginning of incest taboos. Prohibited relationships must have been conceived by the society to keep the population growth under control. It would have created chaotic situations if sexually matured adult male were to live in close proximity with females having all time sexual receptivity. Stable family units developed when the rhythm of nature stopped timing of the sexual act. Sex is now the main means for enjoying prolonged companionship based on intimate physical relation and common interests.

The sexual evolution of human female probably began with the Homo erectus. It was Homo erectus who started constructing dwellings with branches of trees and stone slabs.

The highly evolved Homo erectus also created wooden spheres and bowls. Homo erectus whose intellectual capacity far exceeded that of the humble apes probably conceived everything essential for a peaceful family life. No wonder nature decided to gift them with the greatest sources of happiness in the institution of family.

The Fire God

It was probably the Homo erectus who learnt to make and keep fire. The use of fire seemed to have originated in China in B.C. 60,000. It is not clear whether Homo erectus could make fire, but he very well knew how to keep and use it for different purposes. It would have been obtained from the out breaks of petroleum gas or eruption of volcanoes. Whatever be the source, it seems that the Hominid brain perfected the art of taming the fire. The use of fire extended their habitable environment far and wide. It helped them to overcome the challenges of seasons and beasts. The physiological evolution of Hominids was also accelerated by the use of cooked food.

But the most significant contribution of fire was in developing a sense of fearlessness in the human mind. He was no longer afraid of ferocious beasts and debilitating cold seasons. He could make the vast variety of food edible which otherwise could not have been taken uncooked. The beginning of community life can also be seen around the hearth of the Hominid. They might have gathered around the fire in the night to exchange the hunting experiences of the day. Great linguistic skills would have developed during such social interaction which trying to give true description of the events of the day. Fire bearers and Fire makers must have enjoyed the central space in the society for their valuable mastery over the mysterious source of power. Undoubtedly the management of fire and loss of estrus were the two major milestones in the evolutionary progress of human kind.

The Queue Breakers?

Scientists attribute the evolutionary quantum jump of humans to certain peculiar physical features and an intimate social life. The discovery of fire must have definitely accelerated the evolutionary progress of humankind. The development of linguistic abilities helped to preserve and improve the acquired skills from generation to generation. The rigorous living conditions would have brought together small viable groups that developed mutual dependence and specialization in certain skills. The close-knit social life must have created strong emotional bonds that created great civilizations. In the new settlements, women must have learned several housekeeping and child rearing skills that helped in achieving tremendous reduction in infant mortality rate. It must have given great impetus to the growth rate of humans all over the world.

The spirit of adventure to migrate to distant lands, particularly in the last phase of our evolution, was motivated mainly by the steadily diminishing resources and unprecedented climatic changes. Large societies must have split into smaller viable groups to set out in search of a better life in unknown faraway places. It only took very little time for humans to spread out in all major continents for creating new cultural niches. Males hunted and protected the family while females did all the housekeeping and gathering jobs. A sense of reverence developed for elders and ancestors for the skills and information possessed and passed on to new generations. Community life based on mutual dependence enabled humans to survive in serious environmental challenges. Many other species became extinct in the wake of great floods and droughts that frequently visited their habitats.

The greatest human innovation is the cultural evolution that gradually replaced individual ambitions with the goals of community welfare and common interests. While features like free hands and the unusually large brain size are all biological gifts from nature, the cultural evolution that made great civilizations has been the exclusive creation of the collective wisdom of humanity. The linguistic abilities must have cemented social and family relationships and helped in transmitting knowledge and skills from generation to generation. The legacy of skills and knowledge passed on to the new generations took humanity to higher levels of competence. But, more than anything else, it was the emergence of consciousness and intelligence that initiated and sustained cultural evolution. The unique physical features and intense social interactions created a strong identity of self and a sense of belongingness to the clan. From the humble beginnings of small nomadic tribes, great civilizations arose in various parts of the planet. Simply stated, in a short while the wise ones spread far and wide and conquered all forms of matter on earth.

CHAPTER FIVE

MASTERS OF THE UNIVERSE

THE HUMAN SOUL IS A RESTLESS SWAN;
SOARING HIGHER AND HIGHER
IN A PERENNIAL SEARCH
FOR THE TRUTH OF REALITY,
EVENTUALLY WHEN BLESSED BY THE GOD.
IT PERCEIVES THE SUPREME SELF
AND KEEPS FLYING TOWARD ITS ETERNAL BLISS.

[RIG VEDA]

BOTH ACTION AND RENUNCIATION OF ACTION
LEAD TO THE HIGHEST BLISS.
BUT ACTION IS FAR SUPERIOR
AS IT REQUIRES TRUE KNOWLEDGE
TO DO THINGS WITHOUT CARING FOR RESULTS;
INACTION DEFEATES THE VERYPURPOSE OF
EXISTENCE.

[BHAGAWADGEETA]

Coincidence Of Life

We concluded the brief review of the history of life on earth with the emergence of self-conscious humans and the beginning of their cultural evolution. We traced the development of life entirely on the basis of the evolutionary explanation of random mutation and natural selection. The assumptions underlying the Neo-Darwinian model is that chance variations in genetic instructions, which are sometimes beneficial, get passed on to the next generation. Ultimately, they are spread out all over the population. The massive collection of fossil evidences confirms the gradual evolutionary changes in the animal kingdom. We have also incontrovertible proof of slow changes wrought by genetic variations in different species. It is a fact that no other rational explanation has been found for the existence of the wide variety of life on earth. But that simply does not elevate the neo-Darwinian model to a universally acceptable scientific explanation for all the diversity and complexity of life on earth.

Just as some strange coincidences created a stable universe, we come across many inexplicable events in the origin and evolution of life. A live organism functions as a unified entity with several components working harmoniously at different levels. They function in a synchronized manner to achieve a common objective. The possibility of creating life out of inanimate matter through the process of evolution has not yet been established scientifically. Molecular chemistry that conducts all biological functions of life at the cellular level does not indicate the possibility of gradual evolution of different types of proteins. They have to be conceived together to carry out the vast multitude of functions in a living cell. Advanced technology and analytical skills now show us the complete picture of the innumerable interactions of proteins. The wonderful scenario of protein pathways seems to be the outcome of a well-thought-out design to achieve a pre-determined goal.

The complex chemistry of genetic instructions cannot be explained on the basis of the simplistic assumption of random mutation. It is true that evolutionary process can definitely create marginal changes for better adaptation in a fully functional biological organism. But such modifications do not explain adequately the basic question of the origin of a fully functional organism. For about 2 billion years, the bacteria reigned supreme on the planet enjoying infinite self-replication and exchange of genetic information even across the continents. We do not know why random mutation failed to evolve them to higher levels of multi-cellular organisms. The evolutionary ladder can definitely take an organism to higher steps over a long period of time, It cannot create new species with built-in protein pathways and organs and systems working harmoniously for achieving a common goal. We have to seek some other rational solutions to the puzzle of the great human ascent to the top of the biological world.

How Did It All Begin?

To get the true picture of the origin of life, Stanley Miller simulated the primordial atmosphere under laboratory conditions. He discovered the emergence of life-building chemicals like amino acids. It was followed by many more frantic efforts to find more secrets about the processes that created life about 4.5 billion years ago. A large variety of amino acids have been produced in such experiments, in addition to parts of RNA like sugar ribose. It is a fact that in the modern laboratories we can very easily synthesize various amino acids and nucleotides. They are the recognized basic components of life. Further, we can even synthesize DNA strips under controlled conditions from the chemicals freely available in the market.

In a recent study reported in the US journal "Science", Ms Huber and Mr. Waechtershaeuser found that boiling, sulphurous water around active submarine volcanoes contained all basic ingredients to create life. Under similar conditions, they created peptides, which are amino acid chains. But the major problem in conceiving the origin of a primordial cell in this way is the improbability of the assumption that basic chemicals of high purity would have been available in the chaotic biosphere of earth. Nothing could have existed in pure condition nor the parameters for reaction could be controlled as we do in a modern laboratory. Firstly, the chemicals can react only when they are put together in specific quantities. Then we need certain values of temperature and pressure to begin the reaction. The primitive earth was definitely not anywhere near a modern chemistry laboratory equipped with high purity reactants and measuring instruments. Science puts lot of faith on RNA as an ideal candidate for originating life on earth. But RNA also requires several building blocks and processes that are too complicated to occur on the early earth. The evolutionary explanation of RNA acting as a catalyst to create life is too farfetched particularly in view of the chaotic state of the primordial biosphere.

Even for the simple process of joining amino acids to make long protein chain, molecules of water have to be eliminated. It is difficult to understand how they could be removed from amino acids, which are soluble in water. In the early days on earth, we do not know how water molecule was removed without interrupting the process of formation of protein chains. Even in the modern laboratories, we find it extremely difficult to make a protein chain by eliminating water molecules. The explanation that such reactions could have taken place at the rim of an active volcano or in the tidal pools does not sound convincing even to a layman. Unless some rare occurrences happened in the extremely volatile and exposed surface of the earth, life would not have appeared about 4.5 billion years ago.

Why Only Benign Mutations?

Fossils of complex organisms may reveal certain features confirming evolutionary progress of life. But no evidence of a molecular evolution has been found that could have created life out of a soup of chemicals. Complex structures like cells and organs could not have been created without having an initial blueprint of the total functioning of the organism. We should know the specific role of each part up to the lowest level of proteins. No acceptable explanation of the origin of life can be arrived at unless we assume that some supernatural intervention scooped up life from the cauldron of chemicals. We need many more knowledge breakthroughs for getting at the true picture of the genesis of life. A satisfactory solution to the survival of the highly delicate early forms of life without getting disintegrated by puzzle of the cosmic rays is not available in any model. The unprotected surface of the earth could not have offered any niche to nurture the precious bunch of primal molecules. But the saga of their survival to create diverse forms of life is an undeniable fact that is evident in our very existence.

We have seen that Neo-Darwinian ideas falter miserably at the molecular and cellular levels. It is difficult to accept without reservation a purely evolutionary description of the variety of life even at higher levels. The glaring anatomical differences between humans and the great apes like chimpanzees cannot be attributed exclusively to evolutionary adaptations. We know that genetic similarities observed between chimpanzees and humans are about 98 %. How can just 2% of differences explain all the vast variations like brain size, consciousness and linguistic and other capabilities? Evolutionary changes cannot have the sole objective of giving all the preferential treatments to one particular species alone while others are made to suffer genetic stagnation for millions of years. Our genes carry the concise information required for the growth and functioning of all the organs. Most of the random mutations are malignant ones that affect adversely the viability of an organism. But, only beneficial mutations are passed on from generation to generation to give an evolutionary edge to a specie over the competing ones. It looks like a deliberate attempt of nature to transmit only beneficial mutations while suppressing or overlooking the multitude of malignant ones.

The question is how such intelligent choices are made at the cellular level to sort out benign genetic variations from the malignant ones for the purpose of achieving survival of a particular species. It is irrational to conceive that molecules are capable of choosing the best alternatives for creating the fittest organism. After all, evolution is just a neutral natural process incapable of any selective intervention in conveying genetic information. We will need more evidences of causal relationship for correct choices before accepting evolutionary explanation for the variety and complexity even in higher organisms. The available information, indicate that molecules seem to work toward the successful perpetuation of species as if they were guided by some immense intelligence. The inference that they are capable of intelligent exchange of information seems to be an inevitable one when we see the available genetic information.

Who Cares For The Crab?

Another problem with the evolutionary explanation is the enormous time required for visible changes to appear in an organism. The process of evolution admittedly proceeds at an extremely slow pace for spreading the chain of beneficial mutations in the population. In bigger populations of species, genetic improvements through mutations cannot have immediate and universal effects. Of course, the bacteria can instantly upgrade the genes of the entire species through rapid cell division. If we accept evolutionary explanation, it would mean that changes could be created in a large variety of species from a common starting point in a very short period of time. But the fossil evidences tell us that evolutionary changes cannot materialize as quickly as we see in humans. It is estimated that we have at present about 30 million different forms of life on earth out of the more than three billion species that evolved but became extinct. The evolutionary explanation seems to assume that only humans could make large strides in genetic mutations in a few million years using the advantage of the big brain and free hands. There are creatures like the horseshoe crab that remained untouched by the evolutionary efforts of nature for more than 200 million years. It shows that random mutations that worked wonders for humans in a short time, failed to give an evolutionary lift to the poor crab.

No Speed Limits?

It is clear that the extremely slow process of random mutation alone could not have accounted for the sudden increase in the brain size. Even the great civilizations having advanced metallurgical and astronomical knowledge were established in a short span of about 40,000 years. In fact, the estimated time between the genetic split from apes and humans is only about six million years. Fossil studies indicate the possibility that both Neanderthals and Homo sapiens have a common ancestor who emerged about 300,000 years ago. Modern Homo sapiens appeared only about 120,000 years ago and still we have no clear idea about their actual origin. They emerged suddenly with perfect human anatomical features and communication skills. For 60,000 years, they continued with the same skills and intelligence but in 40,000 years they acquired the wisdom to comprehend all profound matters. In just about 10,000 years time, humans created more civilizations and occupied almost all habitable parts of the planet. Fossil evidences show that the average time taken by us for the great evolutionary ascent is much shorter as compared to the progress of other species.

No evidence has so far been found to connect us with the missing ancestor of the earliest hominid, who parted the lineage from the four-legged ones to become distinct sub-species. The fossils found in Ethiopia or Kenya do not give us the correct course of the ascend of humans to the top of the chart. Even four million years ago, there were no species that would distantly resemble the humans. The long periods of evolutionary inaction called "stasis" and the sudden rush of a series of successful mutations cannot be explained in terms of the of changes occurring under the pressure of natural selection. The model of "punctuated equilibrium" that explains stasis and sudden changes really deflates the neo-Darwinian concept of natural selection. Surely, the forces that accelerated the process of evolution would not have worked only for some species. The mechanism of random mutation could not have been accelerated to accomplish vested interests.

But evolutionary explanation assumes that humans are specially chosen for beneficial treatment while other species are ruthlessly neglected. There is no rational explanation for the undue advantages conferred on humans by a purely natural process of gradual changes that should be common to all biological organisms. Can we accept that there is a design in nature to favor just one out of the billions of species? Our ignorance about the actual process that caused the quick ascent of humans has been fully exploited in religious literature to establish the inevitability for divine intervention. We cannot refute such claims unless a scientific explanation of human uniqueness is found that can falsify the mythological stories of genesis.

The Forgotten Cousins!

While the humans were jumping up many steps at a time on the evolutionary ladder, all the great apes remained more or less at the starting point. The evolutionary explanation is that the freedom of hands and the use of tools accelerated mental development. But there is no evidence to establish that the brain mass could develop rapidly with such mental stimulations. In fact, the mind capable of getting stimulated can arise only out of an immensely large brain. The bipeds would not have got much of an environmental advantage over four-legged animals as the latter could move faster with more of leg power. The size of the brain alone cannot automatically confer a higher level of intelligence. It is seen that some animals having much bigger brain are nowhere near us in mental faculties.

The earliest hominids had about 500cc of brain size or cranial capacity, but Homo habilis reached the level of 700cc within two million years of evolution. The Homo erectus that followed had 900-1000cc of brain size. After 1.3 million years of evolution, Homo sapiens got about 1450cc of brain size. The sudden increase in cranial capacity of Homo sapiens in a very short time is extremely surprising and difficult to understand. It is simply unimaginable that within 30 million years, humans could evolve into distinct sub-species with all the great intellectual advantages over others. Nature cannot confer on humans a rapid growth rate of brain size as if to make them the chosen ones to take control of all other forms of life. The poor monkeys never got a chance to reach anywhere near the top seat that seems to have been exclusively reserved for God's own children.

Running Faster With Arts And Maths!

The human brain is a complex mechanism consisting of billions of neurons arranged in a complicated network of systems and sub-systems. From the structural complexity of the brain arises the inexplicable phenomenon of conscious self that is capable of intelligent contemplation. It also enables us to experience emotions of pleasure and pain. The brain works on the basis of a set of algorithms creating holistic images. At the time of birth, it is only about 25% of its adult size, which does not give any evolutionary advantage. The brain is also over engineered with a tremendous amount of about 90% redundancy.

It is estimated that an average adult does not use more than half of the total capacity of the brain. All the algorithms of the brain are not essentially required for the survival of the species. There are specific sub-systems in the brain that deal with mathematics, arts, aesthetics and so on, which cannot contribute effectively towards survival in a competitive environment. The early humans must have faced challenges from fierce predators and unexpected natural calamities. Arts or mathematics would not have been of any practical use for getting away from predators or for fighting the cold. Reading Shakespeare loudly would not have saved our ancestors from an aggressive tiger or lion. All that we can infer is that our intelligent perception and comprehension of the external world is perhaps for purposes other than the mere survival of the species. We cannot overstretch the capabilities of random mutation to account for all the breath-taking sequences of achievements of humans. We cannot forget the fact that even our nearest genetic relations are totally ignored for such exclusive evolutionary favor. The gift of intelligence is something that defies all rational explanations known to us so far. It seems that nature was keen to ensure that the "wise ones" took over some of the divine functions to relive the creator from the monotony of managing the cosmos.

Talking Machines

It is an undeniable fact that linguistic capabilities accelerated our intelligent appreciation of the self and the world. Language not only helped in more effective communication and comprehension of ideas, but also preserved and transmitted acquired skills and new ideas from generation to generation. We are told that even Neanderthal men who lived about 60,000 years ago could communicate effectively. The studies of human mitochondria show that some genetic mutations about 200,000 years ago could have created our speech capability. Noam Chomsky conclusively demonstrated that even newborn babies inherit an in-built language structure. He holds that subconsciously, a child wherever it is born, is capable of creating and comprehending the pattern of speech in the language of its parents. Ardent evolutionists like Stephen J. Gould also find it extremely difficult to explain the universality of linguistic capability as an evolutionary appendage.

The strictly evolutionary needs of sex and survival could have been easily served by a few grunts and gestures that we find in abundance in the animal kingdom. A sophisticated language with logical and grammatical structures and a huge vocabulary of 20,000-30,000 words would not have been essential for ensuring the basic requirement of our species. Speech capability requires specially developed subsystems based on a uniquely designed brain and the correct positioning of the larynx. The shape and structure of the mouth and throat also play an important role in speech. It is difficult to understand how these anatomical features could have developed in the absence of any intrinsic need for an elaborate linguistic capability for survival. Random mutations alone could not have created such wonderful equipments that look irrelevant for survival but are essential for our meaningful existence.

Missing Hair And Massive Penis

Apart from the brain size and speech capabilities, several other prominent human features also defy all known explanations. The outstanding human uniqueness of intense sexuality involves extended foreplay and after play. Such endearing emotional display is not at all necessary for performing a simple reproductive function. In the animal kingdom, females are in sexual readiness only when they are in the cyclical heat period. But females of human kind in reproductive age group are not slaves of such chemical cycles. Freedom from the natural rhythm gives them the choice to perform sex whenever they need it. Apart from its reproductive necessity, sex is also required for creating strong emotional bonds for sustaining the institution of family. Without the physical possibility of monogamy, promiscuous relationships would have created severe social tensions. Consequential conflicts would have destroyed the delicate fabric of community life invented by the Hominids. Another surprising fact is that in spite of the perpetual readiness for sex, the possibility of conception is limited to just a few days in every month. Without such extraordinary and elegant precautions taken by nature, our social life would not have been peaceful. We do not know how genetic instructions could have anticipated the need for monogamy, unless we assume some sort of sentient power in the genes to choose desirable social objectives. Scientific knowledge cannot give us the wisdom to understand the cause underlying the unique changes in human sexuality that began with the loss of estrus.

Moreover, we find that among all the animals, particularly the primates, humans alone enjoy great variety and creativity in performing sex. There are several erotic zones in the human body that are intended to increase the excitement before and during the time of the sexual act. The sexual union in humans is the culmination of a series of physical acts and endearing thoughts involving personal prejudices and preferences. It is difficult to understand the evolutionary need for such elaborate endowments for performing a simple reproductive function. Several minor details like facial mobility, ability to produce copious volume of tears and scent-producing glands are all conceived for the successful culmination of the physical union of the human male and female. The close physical contact and the absence of the thick coat of body hair stimulates the erotic zones. The mystery of the missing hair of humans can be appreciated only in the context of our complex sexual needs and lifestyle.

Yet another baffling puzzle is the absence of the penis bone usually found in other animals. It is probably essential for facilitating the sexual act at short notice and in frequent intervals. Leisurely and relaxed sex is possible only when conception is possible even beyond the limited time of heat cycles. In a competitive environment, humans would have definitely required the penis bone for quick copulation for the survival of the species. Evidently, all our anatomical features point out that they are designed for relaxed mating styles. The hurried and compulsive sexual act of our four-legged brethren seems necessary to beat the competition by all means. In the entire animal kingdom, we are the only anatomically and emotionally designed creatures suitable for living in large communities by establishing intelligent and symbiotic relationships. We have replaced some of the essential tools for survival with the physical and mental equipments necessary for a civilized social life. It is evident that intelligent design operates both at the micro level of molecules and at the macro level of organisms, constantly striving to achieve mutually beneficial co-existence.

Unknown Genetic Agenda

It is assumed that all our anatomical and cerebral advantages emerge from the chemistry of information recorded in the DNA. Using only four bases, DNA can instruct the cell to create 64 different amino acid combinations. The amino acids combine to make proteins, which are the basic bricks of the body. The genes in the 23 pairs of chromosomes give instructions in about three billion chemical letters. If it is converted into a book of normal size, the genetic information will be of about a billion pages. The DNA in a cell when unraveled would stretch out to about six feet. It is difficult to accept that only about 2% differences in the genetic message can be the sole cause for our comparative advantages over the mundane existence of the great apes.

Some people even go to the extreme extent of attributing the creation of the humankind to a process similar to cloning. They feel that the alien visitors from some advanced civilizations in other planets would have left genes to evolve in a hospitable planet. Cloning is now a physical reality successfully attempted in animals. Genetic engineering can cut short the long road of evolution for creating better varieties of plants and animals. New revelations of science in the next one or two centuries will probably give us more accurate information about the basic design that created exclusive human capabilities. But as of now, some hidden agenda seems to control our inheritance, which is definitely not the outcome of the mechanical process of multiplication. The role of an external intelligence shaping our destiny cannot be denied unless we are fully convinced about the feasibility of physical process to bring about the diversity of life.

It is a fact that chance errors that lead to mutation occur at the rare rate of one per several thousand million cell divisions in a generation. Such low frequency of mutation is not fast enough to create great capabilities even in a few million years. Unlike bacteria, we cannot indulge in global trading of genes to recombine genetic information within a short time. The DNA probably prepares the agenda for making an organism using inputs derived from intelligent exchange of information with the environment. The role of DNA has also been reviewed recently when its sequences were finally unraveled. Craig Venter who pioneered the reading of human genome stated that the genes are no likely to be the blue print of humanity. The scientists now feel that the proteins are much more important in understanding the destiny of a biological organism. A million human proteins can keep the scientists fully engaged for the next two decades.

Intelligent Proteins

In addition to unique human anatomical and intellectual features, many more evolutionary improbabilities exist at the micro level. All higher biological organisms are made of trillions of cells that contain the building blocks of life called "proteins". They actually conduct the biochemical functions of the body according to a well-designed program of action. Proteins and nucleic acids are polymers of amino acids and nucleotides specially made for carrying out the multifarious functions of the body.

Amino acids and nucleotides are capable of making a large variety of molecules by attaching to each other in a predetermined pattern. The shape and size of the amino acids required for making a particular molecule is decided much before the intended interaction. For example, we find that, one of the building blocks of nucleotides called "AMP" is synthesized in the cell in a complex and elaborate procedure that involves several enzyme steps. These steps include the use of many intermediates that lead to the end product. It is now known that 13 steps are involved in the synthesis of "AMP" and that it requires 12 different enzymes in addition to the molecules of ATP that provide energy for the chemical reactions at every step.

The surprising fact is that by simply dissolving all the necessary ingredients in a suitable medium we cannot create an "AMP" molecule. The sequential steps required for its production cannot be envisaged by evolutionary urges. Each step could be designed only by understanding the exact need and the mechanism to produce the next one. At the starting point, random mutations cannot conceive all the intelligent steps required for a particular end product having completely unknown properties. The evolutionary theory envisages random mutation as the only vehicle for genetic changes. No role is assigned for any kind of design or forethought in the purely physical processes for making genetic changes in an organism. The protein pathways present the most formidable challenge to our rational worldview based on causal relationships of physical phenomena. We may have to redefine the logical framework of scientific conceptualization that presently preclude the presence of any sentience in atoms and molecules.

Impeccable Defense

Another great mystery is our immune system. It is an intricately conceived foolproof mechanism to defend the body against alien microbes. The system involves several specialized functions performed by a variety of molecules that are networked in a complex pattern. The goal is to prevent any possible attack by intruders. It seems that much before the immune system was devised, the genes had acquired complete information about the kind of alien microbes that would normally enter the body with malafide intentions. The expert defenders in the molecular army protect the vulnerable points that could be easily attacked by the invaders.

The antibodies, which are actually the fingers of the system, can clearly distinguish an alien microbe from the multitude of benign microbes that comfortably co-exists with humans. Trillions of antibodies roam around inside the body in search of aliens. They include specialized agents for carrying out the functions of detection of aliens, production of suitable defense mechanisms and for the communication of messages to certain cells to make antibodies specific for a particular kind of invader. The defense is accomplished in a complex series of steps in which, the invader is first taken as a hostage to the original cell that manufactured the matching antibody. It is then broken up and analyzed for sending the correct profile to other cells for producing effective antibodies in large numbers in the shortest possible time. The immune system is far more effective than the best defense strategy ever conceived by humans.

The real riddle is how the whole system was conceived at the first instance with the clear idea of the role and function of each and every cell and molecule. The immune system is too complex to be created by random mutation or any such mechanical method. It requires complete information about the likely intruders and the entire layout of the body. Intelligent anticipation of a very high order is also essential to conceptualize all possible of sources of attack on the fragile biological organisms. Besides the immune system, there are several other systems like the vascular system that also function according to a predetermined design. It is true that most of the systems are common to many species but the fact that they are specific for the requirements of each one is yet another enigma beyond the evolutionary explanations.

Blood clotting is another interesting phenomenon that proceeds sequentially as if directed by someone in the background. But it is the immune system that is undoubtedly the greatest wonder that helps us to survive from the deadly attack of alien microbes. We have only very recently acquired the correct information about all the intricate processes involved in the production of antibodies. The invention of the electron microscope helped us to resolve many of the mysteries of the dedicated proteins. And the evidences that we now have do not in anyway support the evolutionary explanation of life. They, in fact, indicate possibilities of a deeper design underlying the creation of complex biological organisms. One certainty that emerges from our discussion is that the complexity and variety of life would not have been achieved without the constant exchange of information between the biological organism and its habitat. I will expand this idea in the last chapter to give a cogent explanation of the unique behavior of molecules that give us the marvelous body.

Alternative Explanations: Symbiosis

In addition to the evolutionary explanation, many other scientific ideas indicate interesting causal relationships in the development of complex organisms. Lin Margules attributes complexities in higher organisms to symbiotic relationships instead of competition for survival. It assumes that close cooperation between organisms is essential for accomplishing a common objective. The intelligent organic molecules that perform specific functions inside the cell would have developed in a symbiotic manner by the exchange of information at cellular or molecular level. In the bacterial world, we find examples of such symbiotic relationships of exchanging genetic information across long distances in a short time. The complex cells of plants and animals are the products of several additions and alterations carried out in the simple bacterial cell. But symbiosis like evolution fails to explain the origin of the first live cell with all its intriguing protein pathways and dedicated functions. The higher biochemical systems like humans would not have evolved gradually with the help of a few beneficial mutations unless a fairly functional starting material was available with elaborate genetic instructions.

Co-Evolution

When we put together the Darwinian concept of competitive struggle within the framework of symbiotic relationships, we get the model of co-evolution. The concept of co-evolution focuses on the various instances of cooperation in nature in the interdependence of plants and animals. The negative and positive feedback loops developed by an organism depends up on its competitive and cooperative needs. The mutually beneficial functions of plants and insects give an excellent example of co-evolution. Even genetic messages for the development of an organism sometimes make highly adaptive responses to changing environments. The discovery of jumping genes indicates the possibility of large-scale transportation of DNA messages through some communication medium. Co-evolution can also happen at the molecular level by exchange of feedback through signals between DNAs of cooperative organisms. In real life situations, we find both competitive and cooperative aspects of evolution. The co-evolution model definitely indicates the possibility of intelligent exchange of information between the genes and the environment.

Systems Theory

Some general patterns can be discerned in the functioning of the autonomous and even on interconnected systems. The systems Theory tries to explain the complex systems in terms of the patterns of stimulation or inhibition of components. It assumes that the entire ecology of plants and animals can be understood as the sum total of the dynamics of the various systems and subsystems. The flow of information in various sequences in the system creates effective responses to environmental challenges. We can perhaps restore the dynamics of the organization if missing communication flows are restored and feedback loops are corrected. The systems theory can suggest solutions to improve the efficiency of any functioning organization by rectifying the defects in the components of the system. Even non-linear systems like chaos and self-organization can be explained using the models derived from this theory. But systems approach is more appropriate for computer applications rather than for explaining the functioning of biological organisms. It is difficult to predict the interaction of proteins in terms of systems approach, as the autonomous behavior of molecules does not follow a definite pattern. This theory can only show how a given system functions or becomes more effective, but it doesn't give us the correct answer to the question about the original conception of an organism from the various subsystems working in unison at different levels.

Fractals Everywhere

The fractal phenomenon commonly found in abundance in nature can throw some light on the development of complexities in living organisms. In fractals, when a particular detail is magnified, it shows more and more of the same design. We can see in some fractals infinite repetitions of the same shapes under higher magnifications. The Mandelbrot set is one of the complex shapes that illustrate the fractal phenomenon. The process of iteration using simple algorithms can create fractals.

The human vascular system is an excellent example of fractal branching in which major arteries branch up to even thirty times before the blood supply reaches certain areas of the body. Even in the respiratory system, we find the method of fractal branching. The heartbeat also shows a fractal pattern that produces regular beats. The quantum coherence of the brain is possibly a fractal design unveiled at higher levels of complexities. The brain while at rest shows chaotic electrical activity, but when a familiar stimulus is introduced, it starts firing coherently. Synchronized firing by the neurons clearly shows a pattern emerging out of the chaotic neural networks.

We do not yet know how the iterative feedback from one neuron to the other creates coherent firing. The entire neural network behaves with full awareness of the pattern required for a given stimulus. It seems that some fractal design is ultimately generated in the system out of its coherent activity. But fractals fail to explain how an organism came in to being with all the inbuilt complexities up to the molecular level. The fractal dimension in biological systems indicates that intelligent design with adequate knowledge of algorithms would have existed much before the creation of any form of life. It shows that unless we explain the origin of a complex biological mechanism, the various models that show its functions cannot explain the underlying causal relationships.

Better Patterns From Complexity

The theory of complexity proposed by Stuart Kaufman and improved upon by others gives us yet another explanation of the origin and complexity of life. The concept of complexity suggests that systems with a large number of interacting components can spontaneously organize themselves into orderly patterns. Any perturbation at any where in the system can bring about a total change in the pattern. It has been suggested that the chemicals in the pre-biotic earth would have organized themselves into complex metabolic pathways and systems. More specialized systems developed in course of time by adding further complexities and creating order with the help of perturbations that changed the preceding complexity.

This explanation is the adaptation of a mathematical concept designed to describe computer programs. The problem is that biological systems like humans do not develop from complexities to higher patterns as seen in computer programs. In actual biological situations, perturbations do not create changes in a predictable manner. In biological organisms some kind of a predetermined program is necessary to conceive interconnected parts that function in a coherent manner to achieve a common objective. Even in the controlled environment of the cell, chemicals do not interact spontaneously without the active prodding of catalysts and other contextual factors. Kaufman's model explains certain biological aspects like cell differentiation, stability of cells and even the creation of new cells. But the model breaks down when applied to the cause of the creation of organisms and the confusing behavior of intelligent proteins. We can only conclude here that all the explanations discussed are relevant to a complex organism in some way but they do not reveal the entire story. Our obsessive adherence to reductionist solutions may be the cause for missing out the vital links in the dynamics of creation.

CHAPTER SIX

LIFE: THE UNSOLVED PUZZLE

ONCE UNITED WITH UNIVERSAL CONSCIOUSNESS
WE NEED NO KNOWLEDGE, WEALTH OR
WORLDLY RELATIONS.
EVEN LIBERATION FROM BONDAGE
IS NO MORE A GOAL OF LIFE.
IGNORANCE, FEAR AND DESIRE
THAT SUBSIST IN OUR SENSE ORGANS
DISAPPEAR IN THE KNOWLEDGE OF THE SUPREME
REALITY.

[ASHTAVAKRA GEETA]

FROM TIME UNKNOWN
THE CONSCIOUS SPIRIT AND UNCONSCIOUS MATTER
HELD TOGETHER BY THE BOND OF ILLUSION
CREATED THE PHENOMENAL WORLD.
BUT IN FACT THEY ARE ALL,
THE MANIFESTATIONS OF THE ETERNAL EXISTENCE
OF THE SUPREME SELF.

[SWETASHVETARA UPANISHAD]

Evolution Restated?

In the previous chapter, we discussed various rational explanations of existence. Let us now proceed to evaluate their credibility with reference to the latest scientific information about the origin and development of life on earth. We can also briefly preview the significance of scientific knowledge emerging from the studies of human genome. The objective is to reach some rational conclusions about the real meaning and purpose of existence. If we do not get acceptable explanations, we may have to fall back upon the innumerable speculative explanations about life propagated by the multitude of self-serving sponsors.

The evolutionary explanation of life has a strong case with all the fossil evidences indicating gradual physical changes in various species and subspecies. It is based on the irrefutable premises like common design, random mutation and the migration of changes in the population. The latest analytical tools allow us to study the analogous proteins like hemoglobin which when compared with that of other animals, show several striking differences. The amino acid sequences in hemoglobin are the same in 129 out of 146 positions in humans and horses. Monkeys have only five differences in comparison to ours, whereas the lowly placed chicken shows 26 differences. The striking similarities in sequences clearly point out the possibility of a common origin and the evolution of the diversity of life through similar processes. It could be the one that modified ordinary matter into biological matrix when life originated in the universe.

The lines of descent indicated in DNA sequences and genetic similarities between different species confirm our common inheritance. But there are several genetic factors like the spread of non-selective mutation, incorporation of genes from different populations, linkage of two genes in the same chromosome that cannot be explained by the neo-Darwinian model. We also find possibilities of transfer of genes between separate species even by non-sexual means. All forms of life seemed to have evolved out of the same basic stock but the question is what specific mechanism could have brought about such wonderful complexity and diversity from the original design of life. The mechanism of random mutation is based on the reductionist view that genome as a single unit is solely responsible for all genetic changes. But the genes are only chemical instructions incapable of any independent action to achieve a predetermined objective. It requires a suitable interactive medium and several favorable conditions to create new life. Moreover, now we find that only 1.5% of the entire genome contains real genes and the rest is junk DNA. Since 99.8% of the genetic materials of all humans are admittedly the same, just 0.2% variation cannot possibly account for all the physical and mental differences that we see in the world. It is now clear that more than the genes; the nurture is responsible for the vast range of human diversity.

Again, at the cellular and organ level, evolutionary explanations fail to account for the complex systems and subsystems. They function according to the instructions emanating from the preconceived basic designs of the organisms. Similarly, it is impossible to envisage the creation of an organic molecule outside the biological context of a cell. Without the metabolic mechanism and protection of the cell, no molecule could have survived in primordial environment. At the macro level, evolution may hold good like the theory of relativity, but we can understand the behavior of protein molecules only from a quantum kind of theory. The evolutionary assumption that chance is the only source of all innovations in the genome might have arisen out of the ignorance of the complexities in the world of molecules and atoms. We have seen that the reductionistic dictum that genes are the sole repositories of genetic wisdom no longer holds. The coherent performance of the human genome and the role of the proteins and the environment are the new areas requiring more focussed inquiries. The mystery of life may be resolved with unconventional tools including speculative wisdom, which is consistent with the realities of nature.

Another confounding problem is the long periods of stability called "stasis" during which nothing at all happens to the organism. Mutations might have continued uninterrupted during stasis, but some force seems to put a temporary moratorium on consequential genetic changes. After stasis, mutations suddenly become effective as if the genes were woken up from a long slumber. If random mutations were genuinely random, stasis could not have stopped changes for long intervals. The serious business of natural selection can not afford any intermission or long holiday.

The evolutionary worldview is based on the assumption that organisms adapt to improve fitness for survival and reproduction in a given environment. In every generation, gene mutation happens only once in several hundred million cells. How can we accept that such low frequency of mutations can bring out massive changes in an organism even after undergoing frequent intervals of inexplicable stasis. Only in bacteria rapid self-replication spread gene mutations in the entire population in the shortest possible time. The effect of such mutations is evident in drug-resistant bacteria that develop immunity to new varieties of drugs even in a short time. DNA recombination is common in bacteria that use genetic materials from other strains in addition to their own gene information. In that way, they can achieve genetic changes that would not have happened by the mutation of their own genes. In more complex organisms, genetic information cannot spread at a rapid pace nor can DNA recombine information collected from various other sources.

The evolutionary model supported by fossil evidences points out gradual structural changes in certain species. But we also come across several species totally untouched by any kind of mutation. They either seem to be immune to environmental pressures or fully satisfied with their evolutionary destiny. Evolutionary explanations also fail to account for the intelligent behavior of proteins and the new features in the design of sub-species. The emergence of billions of species from a common ancestor in a short period is also a great mystery. Even if we put all the tools of evolution like random mutation, trading of genes and add more exotic processes like symbiosis and self-organization, we cannot reach an adequate explanation for all the diversity and complexity of life. Some of them point out the causal links between certain features of a dynamic system, but they do not add up to a convincing explanation of the existence of the entire of life.

Designer's Dream

All faiths have the common assumption that an intelligent designer created the universe. Many philosophers and even some leading scientists do believe in the possibility of an intelligent design in the organization of the universe and all forms of life. Of course, evolutionists like Richard Dawkins do not find any room for a designer in the cosmic drama of creation. They firmly stick to the view that in spite of the new revelations of human genome and molecular biology, only evolution or combinations of its variants like co-evolution and complexity can explain the great diversity of life. Some of them accept that we have to incorporate more explanations particularly about the role of environment to understand the latest discoveries from the mapping of the genome The neo-Darwinian model has several analogies to support the possibility of the development of complex biological systems in a gradual manner. But we have seen that the actual functioning of the biological cell does not indicate any step-by-step evolution of proteins to carry out the various pre-conceived tasks like defending the body.

In fact, even some of the analogies relied upon by the evolutionists indirectly confirm the presence of an intelligent design. Their basic assumption that beneficial mutations are generally passed on is an indirect acknowledgment of the possibility of an external intelligence making the correct choice. If malignant mutations were also transmitted to succeeding generations, the entire species would have been wiped out in no time. The exclusive choice of beneficial mutations shows the presence of a design prior to the creation. No rational explanation can be found for such benign natural selection unless we attribute lot of self-organizing capabilities to the molecules. That would be bestowing some sort of sentience to the proteins who perform according to a perfect design.

The long spells of absence of any genetic innovation during stasis also indicate some external intervention for effecting genetic changes. The first hominid species called Australopithecus afarensis remained stable for about one million years. Thereafter, transformations began to appear in rapid succession. But the question is who could have ordered the sudden cessation of all evolutionary activities for several generations? Neo-Darwinians have no answer to the challenges of supporters of design when they seek explanation to the mystery of proteins performing several preconceived functions in a coherent manner. There is also no explanation for the loss of estrus in female Hominids other than simply accepting it as nature's intention to make us monogamous. The genome seems to be acting as a self-organizing intelligent entity in constant interaction with the environment at the molecular level or even somewhere below that. The problem is how the genome itself was conceived at the first instance so that all the proteins created by it could function to achieve the goal of perpetuation of the species. Now that we find only about 30,000 genes instead of the originally expected 80,000, we may have to shift the inquiry into other factors contributing to the diversity of life.

Is Blind Spot A Bad Design?

Evolutionists point out certain imperfect designs in biological organisms as the perfect proof of the improbability of any intelligent design. They argue that a good designer would not have created a product with defective parts. The avoidable errors can be explained only in an evolutionary context of slow changes in an existing structure through random mutations. The human eye is a glaring example of imperfect design as neural connections are awkwardly placed in front of the photoreceptor cells. The neural connections actually block the light from directly reaching the photoreceptor cells. This makes a blind spot in the retina, which could have been avoided, if the predetermined design was to create a flawless visual instrument for achieving optimum visibility.

But the argument that a designed product should always be perfect is also illogical, unless we know the real intentions of the designer. It is not possible to conclude that there is a flaw in the design of the eye without knowing the original intention. Even an imperfect instrument may be necessary for achieving some common objective. An irreducibly complex biological system itself gives adequate proof of an intelligent design. Some faults in the design of certain parts of a system do not mean that the product is an evolved one.

Superfluous Structures

Another argument against design is the presence of superfluous structures in certain organisms. Evolutionists highlight vestigial organs like the rudimentary eye of cave animals, legs of snake-like lizards and pelvis in pythons that can be explained successfully only in the evolutionary context. The very presence of these organs proves their usefulness at some point of time. An intelligent designer would not have retained such useless structures that do not enhance the effective functioning of an organism. The presence of a large number of pseudo genes also indicates the possibility of gradual evolution rather than intelligent design. The trial and error method of evolution can explain the junk DNA that would not have occupied valuable space if the DNA was the product of an intelligent design.

The supporters of design meet such arguments by pointing out the possibility of some unknown use for these organs. They feel that we cannot comprehend their utility at the present level of knowledge. Once the tonsil was considered to be a vestigial organ until its role in the immune function was discovered. Even pseudo genes cannot be considered totally vestigial, unless we have scientific evidence to show them as unrelated to any of the functions of the organism. The junk DNA has now assumed great significance as the mapping of human genome shows only 35,000 genes instead of the expected 80,000. The junk DNA is most probably involved in the sending of some timing signal to carry out the productions of proteins. Our assumption that certain structures are wanted or unwanted only express our limited knowledge of its utility. It is not the proof of any inherent defect in the design of the organ.

Finally Genome To Proteome

Our great expectations of the outcome of human genome mapping project has turned out to be a damp squib. We anticipated confirmation of the number of genes to be about 80,000 to 1,00,000. All that we got out of the mapping exercise is a meager figure of about 30,000 genes. It is all the more humiliating since the lowly placed round worm has 19,099 genes and a simple fruit fly also is endowed with 13,601 genes. We cannot claim any unique evolutionary distinction when the inarticulate mustard plant also shows 24,000 genes to its credit. Another surprise is that only 1.5% of the total genome has genuine genes. Others are junk DNA which are probably involved as a timing device to start and stop the operations of the real one. And yet another mystery is that out of the 3 billion chemical letters in the human genome about 99.95% are identical. The question is how this very small number of genes could achieve such magnificent individual variations in size, color, intelligence and so on. It is also seen that half of the genome has nothing to do with life. They might have migrated from bacteria and continue to multiply like parasites using the cells scarce resources.

For the benefit of scientists, the area of enquiry has now shifted to "proteome", a new branch of study, which will deal exclusively with the proteins. Genes are after all only instructions for making proteins like hemoglobin, dopamine, insulin, estrogens and many others. They are about 5,00,000 to 1 million in number and the data and time required for an in-depth study of all them will be enormous. Each of the 34,000 or so genes is capable of producing several proteins. It also depends on how m-RNA molecules that carry the DNA message to the protein factory of the cell is spliced to produce different proteins. The fact is that the long awaited result of gene mapping does not reveal much information about life. Genes are important but proteins are much more essential and crucial to our survival. Genes are small in number and more manageable but we will find it difficult to handle about a million proteins. They are very smart molecules doing specific functions as if they work under some strict military command. Immense damage can be caused to the organism when they misbehave or fall short in various organs.

As the inquiry goes on and on, we get into deeper waters confronting the elusive and innumerable proteins. Proteins have stolen the limelight from genes and the evolutionary explanation has the additional task of accounting for their variety and complexity. Life is in no way amenable to any easy explanation as we presumed when the genome studies were liberally funded. After the proteins are analyzed we may come back to the genes to find how the instructions are initiated to make them obey a predetermined program. We may also find that the nature is much less responsible for the complexity of life, which is largely the concern of nature. Life may eventually turn out to be the work of the intelligent proteins that exchange information between the organism and the environment. I am not building up a case for proteins but the impression is unavoidable that all are controlled in identical manner by a mechanism that knows all about the necessary ingredients to make life. The same means must have been used for improving life by creating more and more varieties having higher complexities.

New Gods In Old Temples

Religious institutions have genuine reasons for finding fault with all rational explanations that threaten their fragile existence. The believers of all kinds are always on the lookout for any clue or evidence that can support the inference of the intelligent design of God in all creations. Rational explanations can remove ignorance only by properly presenting the undeniable truth of reality available in scientific inquiries. Some evidences surely support the evolutionary model, but several features of life indicate the possibility of a design in the creation of biological organisms. Initially, life could have been the outcome of an intelligent idea but billions of years of evolutionary refinement has created variations in the original plan and product. Even the designer, if at all there is one, might be wondering about the clever handiwork of time that evolved human ingenuities.

With gradual changes over time, life must have reached higher levels of complexity to achieve better chances of survival. From the humble beginning of a single cell, the various evolutionary processes created a wide variety of life. Co-evolution definitely supplements evolution with intelligent inputs from other forms of life. Chaos complexity, self-organization and antipoetic systems are all useful tools in various contexts to reach new heights of evolutionary ascent. Some dynamic systems may even contain features that can be explained by systems theory or fractals. We find merits in all these explanations, which can collectively give us the ultimate answer to the questions of existence. But presently, we need more scientific knowledge about the origin and development of life whether on our planet or in other habitable planets. Our knowledge is not sufficient to reach any rational conclusion about the origin and evolution of life.

Even the idea of alien intelligence experimenting with life cannot be ruled out in view of the possibility of life in advance forms existing in some other planets. With more sophisticated technology, some basic design of life could have been sent to earth for evolving new species fully adapted to the special ecological features of our planet. Presently our space technology is not equipped to reach out to intelligent life on other planets. We have no choice but to wait patiently until science ultimately unravels the real story of the origin and development of life. I will be presenting a comprehensive explanation of the creation and evolution of life in the last chapter by converging the knowledge derived from various sources. In that model, we will examine the possibility of an interactive intelligence emerging as the main cause of existence. But before that, we need to explore the human mind that is the most amazing phenomenon ever created by nature.

PART THREE

WHO ARE WE ?

'INTELLIGENCE TO WISDOM'

The object of your eternal quest
is nowhere but in your own soul .
you grope in the darkness of ignorance
seeking it in heaven & earth .
look inward & see the bright light of truth
burning in your soul & all over the world .
(YAJUR VEDA)

To the pure self, what is knowledge?
Who is the knower? What is the means?
& What is the end?
What is something & what is nothing?
There is no outside or inside
for the self that contains all .
(ASHTAVAKRA GITA)

The knowledge of reality
reached by the wise men
through relentless search
rewarded them with the ultimate bliss
of peace & self-realization .
(RIG VEDA)

CHAPTER SEVEN

IN SEARCH OF THE MIND

BY KNOWING ONE LUMP OF CLAY
WE UNDERSTAND ALL ABOUT OTHER FORMS OF CLAY.
THEY DIFFER ONLY IN SIZE AND SHAPE,
BUT THE INNER SUBSTANCE IS THE SAME.
THE SPIRITUAL WISDOM SHOWS WITHOUT DOUBT,
THAT ALL LIFE IS MADE OF ONE KIND,
AND NONE CAN CLAIM ANY UNIQUENESS.
[CHANDOGYA UPANISHAD]

BOTH ACTION AND INACTION CAN ARISE OUT OF IGNORANCE.
THE PERSON WHO REALIZES THE TRUTH OF REALITY
TRANSCENDS SUCH DISTINCTIONS AND LIVE HAPPILY
WITHOUT DELIBERATELY ABSTAINING FROM WORK
NOR SEEKING WORK FOR ANY MATERIAL GAINS.
[ASTAVAKRA GEETA]

Eventually, We Reach The Mind

After the brief survey of the latest scientific knowledge on universe and life, we are now at the gateway of the mind. It is in fact the central theme of our intellectual explorations. Mind is undoubtedly the ultimate biological wonder that sets us apart from all other organisms on earth. Although its physical location is still unknown, it presumably arises somewhere in the cortical region of the brain. The mind has a variety of non-physical qualities acquired probably during our evolutionary progress. It is true that other animals also possess cerebral cortex, but its size and properties are probably not good enough to create an intelligent mind of our kind. Admittedly, the size of the brain is crucial in creating a complex neural network from which consciousness emerges to create the mind. The mind experiences the perception of the world and creates a distinct identity of self. It categorizes the experiences of objects and events in relation to self on the criteria of perceived preferences. An intelligent mind is capable of making correct choices that enhance pleasure and satisfaction in its interactions with the external world. The ultimate outcome of the correct choices over a long period of time is the acquisition of compassionate wisdom. It extends self beyond the narrow band of personal interests. We tend to devote more time and resources to serve the humanity and preserve the environment for all variety of life to flourish.

A Definition Of Mind

An accurate definition of the mind is necessary for the correct appreciation of its amazing qualities. But mind defies all our attempts to define it in any physical terms so far known to us. It is like an experience rather than a recognizable object or an observable event in time and space. The mind experiences the external world in a private and unique manner. We cannot communicate faithfully the nuances of the feelings within the limited linguistic framework. Moreover, we perceive the world holistically, in spite of the fact that all the sensory inputs that the brain receives are only in the form of vibrations of energy in different frequencies.

The conscious self experiences its own existence as a composite entity despite the fact that the body consists of trillions of semi-autonomous cells. We have several organs that perform independent functions in an integrated framework. The mind can control certain brain processes like attention and memory through conscious efforts. All mental faculties undoubtedly arise from the underlying unconscious physical processes of the brain. The mind is not aware of the great work done by billions of neurons to create it from physical matter. Science has now given us lot of correct information about the nature of brain processes that culminate in the phenomenon of the mind. It is seen that the mind comprises of the integrated images arising out of several processes like perception, emotional feelings, cognition and comprehension. All of them cumulatively contribute to our intelligent choices from the various alternatives in the external world.

The mechanical description of matter is totally inapplicable to the mind. It is beyond the control of the physical laws that govern ordinary matter. The reductionist dictum that the final output of a machine is always determinable from the behavior of its constituent parts breaks down in the case of the mind. From the composition or properties of the brain we cannot even remotely conceive the qualities of the emergent mind. We do not know all its constituents nor can we trace it to any specific location. The functions of the mind cannot be regulated despite the discovery of some molecules capable of altering its qualities and states.

The universally accepted fact about the mind is that it emerges only in a conscious person. The brain actually comprises of a vast network of about 100 billion neurons. What we call mind broadly includes all the conscious and even unconscious experiences arising from the processing of sensory and even extra-sensory inputs. The processed data also require mediation by the memory of past experiences. Another way of understanding mind is to study the effect of its absence in the state of anesthesia, and in less evolved animals. It may not be a very helpful approach but we get some ideas about its qualities when we understand the mindless existence of other forms of life.

Mind Vs. Body

There has been no spectacular change in the physiology of humans for about 10,000 years. It is evident that nature has almost completed an admirable artwork of evolutionary creation that took several hundreds of thousands of years. But the revolutionary changes that took place in the intellectual realm of mankind during the past seven to eight thousand years are far beyond the creativity of any physical forces. Nature has definitely supplied the basic equipments but it is the sustained application of intellectual abilities that took us to the zenith of evolutionary changes.

It is difficult to accept that the intellectual capacity of humans would have undergone such a sea change in a few thousands of years. The genetic blueprint of nature took millions of years for reaching perfection. We have far excelled all evolutionary expectations as each new generation went on improving up on the inherited advantages. Each generation transmitted the cumulative achievements of knowledge to future generations with many more refinements. The mind-boggling maneuverings of nature that we do now is made possible through the sustained application of consciousness. We can be proud of the fact that the mind has conceived much more than what nature has originally designed for our survival. It is no wonder that in a short span of evolutionary time, humans gained considerable insights even into the secrets of the very matter that created them.

Historically, the mind has always been kept at a higher pedestal in relation to the physical body. Plato, Descartes and many other early philosophers held on to the dualistic concept of mind as distinct entity with several celestial qualities. Mind is also known as "spirit" or "soul" to keep it aloof from the baser instincts of the flesh and blood. Even in modern times, the dualistic vision of mind has many supporters including the Nobel laureate John Eccless. The modern dualists do not accept the spiritual attributes of mind but they concede that it is entirely different from ordinary matter that creates the physical world including the brain. The irreversible mental changes in severe cases of brain damage and drug abuse show the close causal links between the functions of the body and the mind.

The brain comprises of many identifiable systems and sub systems. They can be further reduced to components like cells and neurons consisting of molecules and atoms. There are several distinct areas in the brain performing specific functions but the mind is not located in any of them. The monistic view that the mind and body are made up of the same substance is not a scientific conclusion. Of course, it does not rule out the possibility of mind arising out of some uncommon quality of matter like quantum coherence. Scientific studies have identified the parts of the brain that deal with the different attributes of the mind like memory, free will, attention and so on. But, individually, they cannot create the totality of a mental experience. It is an emergent dimension closely related to the collective and coherent function of the innumerable parts of the brain. The brain can, at best, project images like the pictures on a computer monitor or television screen. But just as a TV screen remains a mechanical device, the brain with out the mind is just a collection of neurons.

Even if we locate some neurons or subsystems of the brain actively concerned with awareness, they cannot create the unique experience of the mind. When we converge all the latest findings of science about the brain we may reach some rational conclusions about the real nature of this amazing phenomenon.

Higher Mental Qualities

We have gathered some accurate facts about the sequences of the processing of sensory inputs in the brain. The past experiences stored in the memory help us to identify the nature of innumerable sensory inputs. The output of all the cerebral activities is eventually projected for our perception. The mind evaluates the information to create appropriate responses to the situation. The series of cognitive processes that culminate in intelligent decisions are presumably based on considerations of self-interest. The combined efforts of sensory inputs and memories that carry cultural and social influences sometimes produce rare mental states called "creative intelligence". Scientific discoveries and great works of art and literature emerge from the mind capable of reaching such higher levels of creative wisdom. It is also a proven fact that the genius capable of high level of creativity is seldom distinguished in their physical attributes.

Although intelligence is the ability to think and act in a correct and coherent manner, the ultimate attribute of the mind is the wisdom to be kind and compassionate. It is the ability to forego evolutionary urges of survival and sex to achieve some socially desirable objectives. Such wisdom arises from the perception of the truth of reality that all forms of life in the universe has a common substrata of consciousness. A genuinely enlightened person transcends the immediate individual needs to reach the wisdom to direct all actions for common welfare. The wise ones extend their personal resources to the weaker and less endowed persons in society. There are many intelligent people in the world, but rare are the ones who possess the faculty to find happiness and fulfillment in activities unrelated to personal needs. It is true that these qualities are only inferences drawn from the conscious behavior of a person. They cannot be considered as the qualities present in all human minds. Since individual variations in mental attributes arise from 0.2% of the genetic differences, we have to accept the fact that great minds are also made by nurture and not entirely by nature.

Consciousness To Intelligence

A newborn child possesses very low level of consciousness with out an identity of the self. The infant brain is a fully wired mechanism to make the correct connections for creating a vast neural network. It is adequate to maintain life by regulating the functions of the various vital organs. But the infant cannot recognize objects and events to make a coherent image of the external world. The first stage in the emergence of mind is an enhanced level of awareness. To some extent it is present even in highly evolved primates like chimpanzees. In simple forms of awareness, the external world is not differentiated from the self. The development of the concept of self begins gradually from the early childhood. With the addition of more and more experiences of the external world, a full- fledged mind is formed some time in the early teens. By that time, neural connections are almost complete and the conscious self is firmly established in body awareness. A distinct identity of self entirely different from the external world emerges and gets fully established in memory.

In adolescence, the mind gains more maturity to make intelligent choices in response to different kinds of environmental challenges. All the necessary neural connections are made in the brain by about eighteen years to provide us the emotional and cognitive patterns to create intelligent responses. The quality of responses, however, depends upon the proper appreciation of the external world and the perceived needs and interests of the self. In early childhood, when there is only pure awareness, no rational behavior or intelligent decision can be expected. The conscious self learns from experiences of pain and pleasure and responds to various emotional and physical needs. Care is also taken not to break the barriers set up by a watchful family and alert society. More than inherited characteristics, it is the environmental conditions that sometimes cause early or late emergence of the identity of s unique self.

The Seat Of The Mind

The mind presumably arises out of the innumerable processes in the great network of systems and subsystems in the brain. The brain receives continuous streams of external as well as internal sensory inputs in the form of vibrations of energy. They are processed with the help of memory to project coherent information for the perception of the mind. The mind is totally unaware of the continuous parallel and serial processing of information carried out by the brain. Some scientists claim that such computing processes can be replicated by intelligent machines. They are confident that very soon powerful quantum computers will perform all the conscious functions of the humans. Undoubtedly, the greatest achievement of mankind will be the creation of machines having all human capabilities with the speed of super computing. They can even be made immortal by replacing the defective modules from time to time and updating them with new innovations in technology.

The mind emerges from the activities in the cerebral cortex, which is a huge network of billions of neurons. From the chemical and electrical exchanges in the neural network, the mind experiences the perception of the external world and even its own state of existence. But we cannot locate the mind in any specific cortical area, as it is a consequential effect of the computing processes in several parts of the brain. The mind can even survive minor brain damages, which affects certain faculties like memory and attention.

Cognitive scientists claim that the seat of the mind is in the working memory area that gives us immediate knowledge of the present happenings in the world. Another view is that consciousness is a momentary activation of the working memory area by focused attention. Some scientists believe that consciousness is a limited capacity serial processor that supervises a series of parallel as well as serial computations in the brain. The processes are carried out in a symbolic format and the resultant representations to the conscious self are integrated images of reality. The working memory area generally acts as a controller of various processes in the specialized systems and subsystems of the brain. Definitely, it has all the qualifications to be assigned the honorable seat of the mind. But the assumption that the conscious experiences of the mind are mere projections in the working memory area is to give a simple serial processor of limited capacity, the most important function of life. It is certainly not capable of binding trillions of inputs into a coherent image. The working memory area can, at best, be the location for receiving processed information. But the mind being the ultimate outcome of all perceptions, we cannot locate it in a particular system or area in the brain.

Self-Awareness Neurons

Recently, some claims have been made about the discovery of the system responsible for consciousness in the human brain. It consists of "Self Awareness Neurons" involved in the integration of various processes of the brain into a coherent whole. The actual role of such neurons is ascertained from the study of severe head injuries and the brain scans of patients suffering serious mental disorders. The "Self Awareness Neurons" are found in the frontal lobe of the brain near the corpus callosum that connects the two hemispheres of the brain. These neurons become less active in some mental illnesses but they show hyperactivity in certain other kinds of disorders. Patients suffering from Alzheimer's disease have less active neurons in this area.

The discovery of some neurons having a major role in creating consciousness and self, does not mean that the seat of the mind is revealed. Undoubtedly, a strong link exists between consciousness and the neurons in the frontal lobe of the brain. But it is difficult to accept that this area alone is involved in integrating all activities of the brain to create complete images of self and the world. The seat of the mind is still unidentified in spite of our success in tracing the activities of different systems and sub-systems of the brain.

Hardware Of The Mind

Before we begin our voyage into the complexities of the mind, we should know certain basic structural and functional features of the brain. We have about 100 billion neurons and many other kinds of cells in the brain. Glial cells perform the important function of supporting the vast neural network of the brain. The brain stem situated at the lower end of the brain regulates the basic physical functions like position; balance, control of heart rate and so on. Above the brain stem, the thalamus acts as a relay station of nerve signals between the brain stem and the cortex. Activities like sex drive, feelings of hunger, pleasure and pain are said to be associated with the hypothalamus, which is a collection of neurons below the thalamus. The hypothalamus also sent specialized molecules to the endocrine system for controlling the production of various hormones.

The outer part of the brain consists of two separate lobes, called cerebral hemispheres. A thick cable of nerve fibers establishes close connection and co-ordination between them. The information about the state of the body is processed mainly in the parietal lobes, which acts like a divider. The temporal lobes are concernod with hearing, memory, learning and emotions. The cerebral cortex is the outermost layer of the brain, which looks like a wrinkled blanket. It is associated with all the higher mental activities and is presumably the custodian of the mystery of the mind.

We can trace the organization of the brain to the beginning of life from the single fertilized cell called 'zygote'. Some structures called "neural tubes" develop between the third and fourth week after fertilization. The neural tubes multiply rapidly to form the brain and the central nervous system. After four weeks the cells near the top of the neural tubes form a curved structure that develops into the brain. The general outline of the important features of the brain is fully laid out by the fifth month. The cells begin to migrate to the designated areas according to a predetermined time schedule. The synapses between the neurons that exchange chemical messages develop only after about the seventh month.

The basic functional unit of the brain is the neuron, which is an ordinary cell, with certain additional features. Different varieties of neurons are equipped with special characteristics to perform the vast range of cerebral functions. An average kind of neuron has a nucleus for keeping the DNA and some specific area for carrying out tasks like production of energy. The tree like structure moving out of the central body consists of a main trunk and a lot of branches called "dendrites". Dendrites receive the basic inputs from other neurons. Another long fiber-like branched structure called 'axon' forms the output junction for making connection with neighboring neurons. Nerve signals are sent to other neurons through the axons, in a complicated procedure that involves both chemical and electrical processes.

Every neuron is an input-output system functioning in a vast network of neurons. Signals travel throughout the network by a complex chemical process that consists of the emission and reception of specialized molecules. The membrane of the neuron contains different types of molecules called "receptors". The outer side of the receptor can accept only a molecule with a specific shape. The receptors are channels allowing atoms of sodium, potassium and calcium to flow in and out of the neurons. They can also function as pumps, for removing the atoms from the cell. When a neuron is not sending a signal, the sodium channels remain closed and the potassium channels are kept open. The protein that acts as a molecular pump pushes out sodium ion from the cell to allow the potassium ions to come in. The net effect is an increase in the concentration of potassium ions inside the cell, while the concentration of the sodium ions outside the cell becomes much higher. When the neurons are resting, the axon has a negative charge of a voltage of about 70 millivolts because of the imbalance created by the ions.

With the stimulation of the axon by a signal, a series of processes begin in the neuron with the sodium channels opening up to give entry to the positively charged sodium atoms. They continue to move in by the attraction of the negative charge until the axon becomes positive. The change in the charge opens up potassium channels allowing them to flow out restoring the previous negative charge inside the axon. The flow of charge called "action potential" allows the sodium ions to spread out in the inside of the membrane changing the charge on the upstream. The nerve signal is actually the process in which the sodium ions pour into the axon on the upstream side and the potassium ions move out on the downstream side.

The axons have myelin sheaths impermeable to sodium and potassium ions. The gaps in the sheaths permit the potential to skip from one gap to the next for faster propagation of signals.

When the action potential reaches the end of the neuron, another chemical process begins in little membrane sacs called "vesicles" which contain a collection of special type of molecules. Calcium channels open up for the ions to flow into the neuron causing the neuron membrane to dump the molecules called "neurotransmitters" into the gap between the neurons. The neurotransmitters float across the gap and are received by the receptors in the membranes of the downstream neuron. The neurotransmitters that dock with the receptors begin the complex sequence of chemical process in the message-receiving neurons. Normally, a single neuron receives and processes several kinds simultaneously creating integrated output. The neuron functions autonomously in deciding whether to convey or cancel the message by firing suitable kinds of signals.

A Molecule For Each Mood

The neurotransmitters carrying the signals are special types of molecules that can trigger different chemical processes in the neurons. We have a fairly accurate picture of the role of specialized neurotransmitters that can cause a wide variety of changes in the brain. Different types of neurotransmitters work in various systems of the brain and they can cause several kinds of changes in mental states. Prozac is an anti-depressant drug that blocks a particular receptor to alleviate depression caused by various factors. Noradrenaline stimulates the entire brain while lack of it can create severe depression. Several mental disorders are now being traced to the excess or deficiency of certain neurotransmitters. Actually, it is the chemistry of the brain that decides our perception, emotions and even behavior. In short, we are not what we think or feel; it is just the chemical environment in the brain that decides the destiny. We have already identified the role of specific neurotransmitters like dopamine and acetylcholine in Alzheimer's disease and schizophrenia.

The neuron is made of ordinary matter and it uses both electrical and chemical methods for processing inputs and exchanging messages through molecules. But the basic question is whether all the conscious contents of the mind including its emotional and cognitive experiences can actually be the outcome of some electrical and chemical activities in an advanced variety of ordinary cell in the brain. Our current level of knowledge of the brain and its functions confirms that atoms and molecules are the basic performers of all cerebral processes. So far, we have no evidence of the existence of any ghost-like entity in the brain. It is made of just ordinary matter in a biological matrix.

There are experiences like awareness, emotions and thoughts that cannot be attributed to the known properties of matter. Ordinary matter does not display the quality of "free will" that signifies the intelligence for autonomous planning and decision. The basic inputs that create the free will evidently arise from the computing processes done by ordinary matter in the brain. But the experiences we get out of the cerebral activities are not traceable to any known property of any atom or molecule. Other subtle qualities of the mind such as artistic and spiritual inclinations, caring and compassion for old and needy persons and moral and ethical compulsions also emerge from the brain processes. One simply fails to understand how all such non-physical qualities of the mind can come out of ordinary matter. It is a fact that matter outside the brain is totally devoid of any of the capabilities that make our mind. We cannot understand how the brain alone can create this wonderful phenomenon out of a cluster of ordinary atoms and molecules. To unravel the mystery of the mind we need much more information about the brain processes that initially creates consciousness. And then, we have to see how the unique identity of a self is created to experience the world as well as ones own emotions.

Mind Reading Machines

In the past, dissection and analysis of animal brain or unwanted corpse could be the only way to understand the manifold features of the brain. Fortunately for the animals, advanced technology has now devised gadgets that can study live activities in the live human brain itself. Positron Emission Tomography (PET) and Magnetic Resonance Imaging (MRI) are being used extensively to understand the functioning of the human brain. In PET scans, radioactive isotopes of oxygen are used to detect the level of isotopes that indicate increased blood flow in neural areas. No injection of radioactive substance is required for MRI scan as the electromagnetic pulses that make the atoms align in a particular direction emit radiation when the magnetic field is relaxed. When a particular task is performed MRI can indicate the hot areas that are performing the work. All major chains of activities in the brain such as processing of sensory stimuli can now be tracked in details by scanning. Brain scans are also very useful tools for the accurate diagnosis of mental disorders. The vast collection of clinical data on the effect of brain damages and the new imaging devices reveal a good deal of the causal links between brain processes and mental faculties.

Pre-Installed Software?

The brain is fully equipped to process the heavy flow of inputs received through sensory organs. Since it is purely a physical system with no concealed consciousness lurking in any corner, it should function according to the physiological and anatomical features evolved for specific applications. It is seen that the cerebral cortex is capable of performing several functions that successfully reproduces the image of external reality. But more than 50% of the capacity of the brain remains unused. We find that even when large areas of the cerebral cortex are clinically removed, most of the mental functions are intact thanks to the huge redundancy. The cerebral cortex as a whole seems to act as the main memory storage area of the brain. It is probably some sort of dynamic vibration or oscillation of electrical waves spread out in the cortical area, which is available for instant recall.

The cognitive functions of the brain are carried out mostly in the cerebral cortex containing billions of specialized neurons. For every neuron, about 10 glial cells provide the scaffolding to maintain the huge network. On an average, a neuron in the human brain has between 1,000 to 10,000 synapses or links that connect them to adjacent neurons. The brain, if considered as equivalent to an electronic computer, would consist of about 10 trillion bits of information. The large number of synapses creates a wide variety of configurations that can correspond to the different mental states of an individual. The unpredictable and unique behavior of every individual arises probably from the complexity and variety of these configurations and the chemistry of the brain. It can store about 10 million bits of information per cubic cm, which amounts to 10,000 times more than the capacity of any advanced electronic computer now available to us. But the speed of information processing of a new generation computer is much higher than the pace of cerebral computing.

Two In One Brain

The two spheres of the brain work in tandem to reproduce the closest replica of the external world. The cerebral software is compatible with the separate functioning of the hemispheres that are intimately connected to give us an integrated perception of reality. They process different aspects of the same input but combine them instantaneously to come up with the wholesome image of the world. While the left hemisphere is mainly concerned with analytical functions and sequential thinking, the right one acts like a serial computer. The left hemisphere is like a reductionist trying to break down a system into its various components for better understanding of the composition and properties. The right hemisphere deals with the perception of the spatial relationships of objects to comprehend relative position and properties in a holistic format.

The concept of self seems to emerge from the left brain in the background of the information reproduced by the right brain. The dual processing is perhaps holds the secret of the distinct identity of the self. All rational and scientific pursuits arise from the ability of the left brain to analyze objects and events according to their constituents and qualities. The right brain does not attempt to classify objects and situations but tries to give us the totality of an experience. Both hemispheres carry on their individual functions in total harmony and with full knowledge of each other's capabilities for the true reproduction of different aspects of reality. However, the left brain with its speech center and intellectual acumen dominates cerebral world like a commander controlling various troops without interfering in the performance of individual players.

Since the linguistic capabilities and the decision-making processes are managed by the left hemisphere, it is reasonable to assume that higher mental functions are evolved in that part of the brain. That probably explains the right- handedness of almost 90% of human beings. There are also some evidences of a more active and differentiated left hemisphere in the human male. Moreover, the left-right polarization seems to be less prominent in females than in males. It is the left hemispheres that control the speech faculty and operate the memory of words. The rapid developments in the left-brain are probably related to the more frequent mutations in "Y" chromosomes. Since "Y" chromosomes are absent in females, we can attribute the left-brain's developments to the relentless efforts of the males to meet the innumerable environmental challenges.

In females, the right brain functions are more dominant. It probably explains their highly evolved emotional capabilities. The manner of evolution of the brain clearly shows that it has been developed to convey complimentary qualities of the external world in great detail to recreate the external world. The ascendancy of the left or right brain shows no particular evolutionary preferences for any kind of perception. All that the brain ensures before projecting the external world to the conscious self is that the reality is faithfully represented to respond properly to the environment. In their earnest efforts to control the environment, the males would have brought about more mutations as compared to the docile females who used to follow the leaders.

Reality Reproduced

We have seen that the main function of the brain is the correct comprehension of external reality for eliciting appropriate responses. It is achieved through the processing of various sensory inputs received as vibrations of energy. They are eventually converted to cognizable images of objects by binding the inputs to recreate the external reality. While doing so, the brain attributes several qualities and patterns to the inputs to make the data coherent and meaningful. What we actually perceive is not the real replica of the external world. The perception of the qualities and relationships of objects are simply the inventions of the ingenious brain. The bland and tasteless external world is made palatable to the pleasure centers of the brain only when memories dress it up with all sorts of emotions and imaginations.

It is now well-known that our experience of the universe arises from the vibrations of energy in different frequencies falling continuously on sense organs. The range of vibrations varies from very high frequency to extremely low frequencies. For hearing and touch, low frequency vibrations are good enough, but for vision, we need much higher frequency. The radiations of energy received by the sense organs set off a complex process of neural analysis. The end product of the processing of the energy inputs is a model of the objective reality that is entirely different from the inputs.

The virtual reality projected by the brain is definitely a faithful image of the external world that is tailor-made for our smooth existence. The color or smell that we attribute to various objects may not be its attributes in objective reality. The brain does all the work to convert the tiny packets of energy into identifiable experiences without our knowledge or attention. The subjective reality that we perceive may be just an illusion but the common features of human perception show that the underlying brain processes are identical. The unity of perception undoubtedly gives a touch of authenticity to the subjective reality. It does not mean that we reach full correspondence with all the unknown aspects of objective reality. However, the effectiveness of our physical actions in relation to the external world shows that our perceptions are after all not far from the true state of affairs in the universe.

Creative Intelligence?

The obvious objective of the brain is to give the organism intelligent choices to deal with the environment. With linear or serial processing of information using conventional logic, brain can suggest simple solutions for meeting ordinary challenges. Modern computers do such problem-solving much faster than humans. The neural tracts in the brain can serially process the information and perform repetitive tasks. Even animals do have such neural tracts. They have fully equipped infrastructure to give suitable responses to the problems normally found in their sphere of activity. The fixed programs in the neural tracts regulate the body functions carried out by various organs. Our instincts are also built into the logic of neural tracts, which gives predictable responses to certain situations. In fact, the entire logic of artificial intelligence is based on the premise that serial processing can produce the entire range of reactions necessary to meet the challenges of the world.

The deterministic nature of serial thinking produces the common intelligence that we come across everywhere in the world. It follows the conventional logic in maintaining bodily functions and survival. Devoid of all uncertainties, it tackles all simple problems of life with clear-cut solutions. Children learn the basic lessons in the serial format. If they establish proper neural tracts in the early years of life proficiency is achieved in this type of intelligence.

On the other hand, emotional intelligence arises from associated thinking, which uses another mode of computation. In this mode, inputs are simultaneously processed in them in the backdrop of past experiences. Application of the various skills learned by the body in specific situations requires both serial and parallel processing of the brain. Then we have the rarely found quality of creative intelligence, which is the outcome of more complex processes. It seems that the neural networks are motivated with strong emotional appeals to achieve proficiency in certain attributes of the mind. They learn to associate objects and events with emotions and instincts through the trial and error route instead of the binary logic used in serial computing. There is no fixed program or definite response in this higher level of intelligence. We normally acquire creative intelligence late in life after getting the benefit of various kinds of experiences.

In reality, it is difficult to differentiate between various types of intelligence. We always give a composite and contextual response to the environment on the basis of past experiences. If the responses are not conditioned solely by the instincts and their associated emotions, we are said to possess a higher level of wisdom. Such intelligence transcends the normal horizons of the mind. The metaphysical thoughts require close coordination between serial and parallel processing in the brain and select cultural inputs. They create altruistic intentions ignoring the instinct driven emotional responses. We are not sure whether the evolutionary development of neural network is designed for any ultimate outcome of spiritual intelligence. But in all probability, noble thoughts arise only with some marginal modifications in the cerebral processes in the neural network. If we design new learning programs to improve creative intelligence and develop compassionate wisdom we could reach higher levels of civilized life. The hard ware of the brain is capable of such fine-tuning and adaptations that can take humanity to new evolutionary heights.

Any Spiritual Spot?

Our new tools of diagnosis like MRI and PET scan give plenty of information about the specific brain areas associated with certain mental tasks. In addition, we also have magneto encephalograph, which measures the associated magnetic activity in the brain. Magnetic fields provide detailed information about the brain without interference from any barrier. The electrical activities in the brain are found to be in the range of 35Hz to 45Hz.

According to Dana Zohar and Ian Marshall, synchronized neural oscillations in the 40Hz range occurring in serial and parallel processing of information is probably the neural basis for consciousness and unitive intelligence. They prefer to call the comprehensive intelligence of the mind as Spiritual Intelligence. They also identified separate psychological processes, which roughly represent different kinds of thinking systems or intelligence. To begin with, we have various unconscious processes that go on in the brain with or without sensory inputs. They are performed by serial and parallel processing in neural tracts and networks. Then, we come to emotional intelligence based on the associated memories created through trial and error method. It is created through linear processing and goal oriented-programs. Eventually, we reach the so-called "spiritual intelligence" that presumably includes all ingredients of cerebral processes in addition to the noble thoughts like compassionate wisdom that predominates programs driven by instincts.

It is the typical reductionist approach of western science trying to compartmentalize even intangibles like intelligence on the basis of the computing processes in the brain. From the scientific evidences of the functioning of the brain all that we can infer is that the mind is a composite entity arising out of its computing and even non-computing processes. It is an integrated concept that arises from the sensory inputs processed through the neural tracts and network with the aid of memory. The higher levels of intelligence emerge from the continuous and coherent experiences of the mind in dealing with the external world. An infant can exist with simple serial processing that takes care of the essential maintenance of the body. But in course of time, the parallel processing in the neural network builds up sufficient memory to create the mind including a separate identity. The different kinds of experiences culminate in the acquisition of more intellectual capacities that we can call super intelligence or spiritual intelligence. From our present knowledge of the brain, we cannot conclude that different kinds of intelligence exist to deal separately with spiritual and material needs. Intelligence is a composite capacity to choose wisely between the various alternatives. We act with compassionate wisdom when the mind is broadened by more knowledge and wider experience. It is the true knowledge of reality that can give us the spiritual wisdom to look beyond immediate individual needs and interests. I don't think we can attribute such mental qualities to separate streams or modes of brain processing.

Increased temporal lobe activity is noticed when some people see visions, hear voices, and feel the presence of supernatural powers. It is attributed to the existence of a kind of "God Spot" in the brain. This spot is found to be very active in disorders like schizophrenia and manic depression. The so-called "God Spot" seems to contribute to higher levels of spiritual intelligence as well as creativity in various vocations. While it is true that hyperactive temporal lobe is closely related to mental instability and loss of perception, it is also a fact that the same area is also involved with higher levels of conceptualization and creative thinking. The neural network in the temporal lobe area is definitely very crucial for creating an intelligent mind. But, the idea that different spots in the brain control numerous kinds of intelligence is definitely unacceptable. If consciousness is the creation of 40 Hz oscillations in the neural network, it should also bind the sensory perception for our experience. We have to probe deeper to see how exactly such oscillations are created in the brain. Maybe the quantum properties of matter at the elementary level must have something to do with consciousness as claimed by Charmers. We will address this question separately in our exclusive chapter on quantum mind.

Mindless Animals?

The basic processing of sensory inputs that create images of external reality is probably common to humans and animals. But we seem to possess a highly evolved faculty of perception that serves much more than our survival needs. Of course, we don't have the capacity to perceive certain frequencies of energy like the bat or snake or even the acute vision of the eagle. The higher levels of mental abstraction that create the concept of self and intelligent thoughts are available only to human beings. A closer examination of self-awareness in animals, particularly in higher primates, can perhaps reveal whether the mind is a unique human asset or just a little bit more advanced form of its animal version.

Many scientists examined the possibility of self-awareness in animals. Generally, people believe that self-awareness is an exclusive human faculty evolved out of the large size of the brain. But the latest experimental evidences show that animal brains particularly that of primates; contain certain cells that perform functions identical to that of the "self awareness neurons" in the human brain. Studies indicate that the concentration of "self-awareness neurons" is the largest in humans followed by chimpanzees and gorillas. These neurons are not found in non-primates like bats and dogs but elephants and dolphins do have them.

One way to check the presence of self-awareness in animals is to find whether they can recognize the reflection in a mirror. If an animal marked with a red spot on the forehead touches the same spot on the mirror reflection, it should definitely have a sense of self as against the environment. Chimpanzees and orangutans passed the mirror test, but gorillas failed to recognize their image. In other tests involving practice of various kinds of deceptions by a conscious self, it was found that chimpanzees could cleverly cheat others as if they possessed some form of reflective knowledge of self. It is evident that higher primates are definitely capable of self-recognition but other animals do not seem to reach such levels of self-esteem! The quality of self-recognition in animals is definitely much lower than the kind of our self-awareness intelligent appreciation of the self as well as the external world.

Animal Talk

If some animals like the higher primates are self-conscious, they should also communicate effectively with each other by some means. Animal communications need not be in well-structured, grammatically correct language; a few grunts and screams would suffice to convey the limited range of messages that they want to transmit. Bees communicate the location or source of food by dancing in certain patterns; songbirds give mating calls, while whales and dolphins produce different kinds of sounds for conveying different ideas. Many other animals also use diverse means to pass on the messages relevant to their existence. Humans may have a genetic capability to learn and use language in a grammatical format, but animals are programmed only to convey their messages in certain context-oriented patterns. Some animals may learn the art of communication from their parents and peers. But most of the basic patterns are inherited ones, which are perfected by serial processing in the neural tracts.

Several case studies of effective interspecies communication are reported particularly between humans and animals. Dogs can understand the commands given by humans. They can also follow certain verbal instructions and in response show bodily postures indicating comprehension. Chimpanzees can learn faster and communicate more effectively than all other animals. The case of "Kanzi" is the classic instance of high level of communication skills acquired by a chimpanzee in a short time. Kanzi matched the linguistic abilities of a three-year-old human child, which is definitely a marvelous achievement for an animal. It is pretty certain that other species are not capable of reaching such linguistic abilities.

Theories Of Consciousness

Most of the models and explanations of the mind assume that consciousness and mind are the same phenomenon. Some people treat consciousness as the simple quality of awareness common to the entire animal kingdom. Roger Penrose gives a general definition of consciousness which includes even intelligence. In higher organisms like humans, self-consciousness is the faculty related to the emergence of mind. The mind is generally taken as a composite concept that includes consciousness, self-awareness and intelligence. It also indicates the presence of "free will" to make correct choice between various alternatives. In short, it stands for a comprehensive concept, which is the highest benchmark of evolutionary achievement of humans.

Scientists have proposed interesting theories to explain the phenomenon of consciousness. In the past, philosophers and mystics explained consciousness based on speculative reflections of nature. One extreme view is that we will never unravel the mystery of consciousness in the physical context of the brain. It exists in some unknown realm beyond the reach of our knowledge. But it is irrational to give up the scientific pursuit of consciousness on such arbitrary assumptions. We have already identified most of the functional and structural features of the brain and the computing processes in the neural network. Admittedly, it is difficult to create a coherent model of consciousness and its constituents and qualities. The scientific explanations already available to us definitely hold out the hope of resolving even the apparently inexplicable issues like binding of inputs and location of the mind.

The neurobiologist Antonio Damagio suggests that the constant interaction of the brain's awareness of the state of the body with cognitive functions gives rise to consciousness. The brain through the chemical and electrical interaction with the body constantly updates the state of the body. He explains the phenomenon of consciousness purely on the basis of the complex process of interaction in nural network without the intervention of any extraneous factors.

The Nobel laureate Gerald Edelman concludes that consciousness is a physical function of the neurons. It arises from the reciprocal flow of information between groups of neurons called "maps". His experiments with neurons and synapses indicate that when the brain matures the neurons begin to perform selective functions. The neurons, which are not included in the elite select list, disappear automatically. He assumes that such disappearance of neurons is a kind of cellular suicide or punishment for the failure to make the right sort of connection. Francis Crick and his associates attribute consciousness to high frequency oscillations of signals that permeate all over the brain. According to them, the oscillations of select neurons trigger off the interactions between them producing the state of consciousness.

Daniel Dennet does not find anything more in consciousness to explain or understand beyond the physical functioning of the neurons. He attributes the mystery of the mind to the misconceptions in the speculative thoughts of philosophers. According to him, vested religious interests attribute non-physical qualities to a purely physical entity that can be understood in terms of its composition and functions. Dennet finds that perception is fully explicable in the framework of a "Multiple Draft" theory. The series of perceptions that the brain performs improve upon each other and eventually culminate in the clearest and closest image of reality. The development of the human brain and its functions is explained in terms of evolutionary changes brought about by random mutations for achieving natural selection. Once all the physical aspects of the neurons and their indeterminate but coherent firings are understood, the problem of consciousness will no longer exist. For Dennet, the concept of mind is only an illusion created by the notion that the physical properties of the brain can create a ghost like entity with unknown qualities.

To me, it appears that Dennet oversimplifies the problem of consciousness without making any serious attempt to understand the elusive concept of "I-ness", or mind. The mind obviously acts as a witness or observer but the physical brain has no system or subsystem where such a function can be carried out. After wading through all that science discovered about neurons and their intriguing network, we still find that the mind cannot be understood simply as a product of their oscillations. It supports the view that mind cannot be ignored as a simple illusion. The fact is that Dennet has not succeeded in explaining convincingly the state of consciousness including the binding nature and non-local qualities of the mind.

The theory of complexity considers mind as a purely emergent phenomenon. If there is only one neuron, it cannot perform several functions. With the addition of more and more neurons to form a network, the consequential complex structure becomes capable of performing several additional functions. The structure acquires the capacity to carry out more difficult tasks because of the emergence of new properties and capabilities. The system takes unexpected turns to reach unknown peaks of possibilities with the addition of more units. The emergence of consciousness is attributed to one of such sudden turns that happen with the addition of more neural complexity. The gap between the mental abilities of humans and animals can be explained in terms of the quantum jump that our neural network makes when complexity goes beyond certain limits. It is comparable to a spiral staircase that leads to higher and higher complexities and capabilities through evolutionary changes. The ascent might be motivated by natural selection that suddenly pushes up the rate of random mutation. The complexity model treats the mind as an emergent phenomenon, rooted firmly in the brain processes. However, it gives no convincing explanation of the binding problem and the presence of the mind as if it is disturbed all over the neural tracts and network.

Roger Penrose, the leading consciousness specialist, admits that classical physics cannot explain all mental functions. He attributes consciousness to the mysterious superposition of alternatives that we come across in quantum dynamics. He assumes that chemical forces that underlie the interactions of atoms and molecules being quantum mechanical, the neurotransmitters that convey signals between neurons and the action potentials that control them are likely to have quantum features. But classical physics do not accept this explanation, as neurons are higher level structures that do not exhibit the features like superposition and quantum indeterminacy shown by quarks and electrons. They can be useful to explain the micro-level phenomena of elementary particles, but at macro level, bigger structures demand a different set of rules. Nevertheless, we have to accept the fact that the quantum phenomenon has some striking similarities with the brain functions like the binding of images and non-local existence.

Mind From Memory

Memory is a fertile area to look for a solution to the binding problem of perception. There are several categories of memories like explicit memory, non-conscious memory, short-term memory or working memory and even long-term memory that can be accessed only when the need arises. Then we have what is called procedural memory, that allows us to perform reflexive skills and episode memory that makes us recall the past events. Without referring to memory, the sensory inputs cannot be processed into any meaningful or coherent information. The mind has the capacity to recover even from serious brain damage, but if the memory is totally lost, neural network cannot reconstruct a coherent image for the mind. Memory experts feel that the discovery of the correct mechanisms underlying working memory would perhaps reveal how the mind becomes aware of the reality. Working memory is only a serial processor supervising the innumerable functions of various systems and subsystems of the brain. The question is how the memory of any kind can integrate billions of independent inputs that fall on our sense organs into a coherent image of reality. Since our knowledge of memory itself is vague, it is difficult to attribute the phenomenon of the mind to the unknown process that connects the past with the present.

Altered States Of Mind

Even normal persons reportedly undergo weird experiences of altered states of mind like seeing heavenly visions and having out of body existence. These experiences arise particularly at the time of serious physical stress. Now it is evident that out-of-body experiences can be induced by drugs like atropines, ketamines, belladona, MDA, DMT and LSD. In fact, LSD creates experiences of absolute union with universal consciousness, which was probably achieved by Hindu mystics in their meditative reflections that identified self with the Supreme Being called "Brahman". It seems that LSD can remove body awareness and create an extreme sense of ecstasy in the mind.

Such experiences have no evolutionary or rational explanation. Since many people commonly get such experiences, we cannot simply ignore them as the exclusive delusions of sick minds. Stainislaw Grof, who conducted several experiments with psychedelic drugs, found that LSD could induce experiences relating to the trauma of birth. A large number of people actually felt the perinatal pressures on the fetus. The fetus in its intrauterine phase of life is in a state of blissful existence. But, when uterine contractions begin, its safe haven is mercilessly compressed bring it out to reality. As the head penetrates the cervix, the fetus perceives a brightly lit external world. The first experience of the great light and sound show of the universe must have left some indelible impressions on the nascent mind. The fact that all the psychedelic experiences of the newborn can be reenacted in LSD sessions establishes that the changes in brain chemistry can invoke vast range of dormant emotions and experiences. It is the smart molecule in the brain that ultimately decides what we should experience in the world. More specifically, it is the chemistry of the neurotransmitters that creates hell or heaven for us. There is no way to get away from the fact that we are just the slaves of the brain chemistry controlled by a few select proteins!

Carried By Emotions

More than the cognitive features, emotions of various kinds also influence the state of the mind. We become aware of emotional experiences when they are projected in the working memory area. Emotions represent different closely interlinked states of body and mind, which are difficult to express or communicate to others. The emotional experiences do not create predictable responses in all conscious persons. Emotional disorders sometimes lead to imbalances in perception and also affect the quality of conscious experience. Emotions are experienced when specialized systems in the brain are activated and represented to consciousness. The experience of different feelings arise when the representations with emotional content are projected in the working memory. But much before we become aware of them, the body is fully alerted to face the challenge.

It is a specific area of the brain called "amygdala" that gets activated with emotions. The sustained responses of the body gives the feedback to continue the experience already generated. Emotions and thoughts are probably experienced in the same area of the brain where we perceive the external reality. With our limited knowledge of consciousness, we can only assume that emotions and thoughts are created by different brain systems but get integrated in some manner to give us a unified experience. When we experience one particular emotion, attention is not diverted to other unconnected mental representations. All emotional activities appear goal-oriented to meet given situations. Even our sense of time seems eclipsed at the peak of an emotional experience. The origin and pathways of emotional experience appear intractable in view of the complexities involved in the process.

One thing is certain that in an emergency, emotions and their associated body responses get an upper hand over all cognitive functions of the brain.. Presently emotions control our thoughts more effectively than the thoughts trying to keep them locked up with rational explanations. Ledoux assumes that in the distant future, cortical connections over amygdala may become stronger, giving humans a better grip over emotions. The interface of emotional and cognitive aspects of the mind is an important problem worthy of more in-depth examination.

Intelligent Machines?

When scientists invented expert systems, artificial intelligence was expected to ultimately replace human intelligence. A few robots that performed certain specific tasks gave us great visions of the new era of intelligent machines. But no further significant breakthrough could be achieved to make the intelligent machines self-conscious. The fact is that artificial intelligence experts could not make the software to imitate all cognitive and emotional features of the human mind. Many practical difficulties were encountered even in making a robot capable of performing certain cognitive functions. In fact, even programs for speech recognition have not been successful in spite of some working models invented for limited applications.

The failure of the ambitious plans for achieving artificial intelligence to match human capabilities clearly brings to focus the vast complexities of the mind. So far, we have made a few machines capable of performing certain specific tasks like playing games or recognizing faces or some commands. A computer that can think and act cohesively like a human is not even a remote possibility. The inventers of "Deep Blue" claimed that it could play chess even with grandmasters and beat them comprehensively. But despite all tall claims, it could not consistently perform better than any grandmaster. Even with improved software, the machine is unlikely to the motivate itself to overcome the challenges of a competitive situation. The excellence of the software is only a tribute to the mind that created it in anticipation of the possible moves of the opponent.

In artificial intelligence we try to replicate the individual processes in the brain for accomplishing specific tasks. Finally the outcome of all processes is integrated to perform the intended function. It was assumed that reducing cognitive capabilities to rule-based procedures for serial computing would be possible with the high speed of computing technology. But in practical situations, even with comprehensive programs, computer cannot perform even remotely like humans. In the case of Deep Blue, the knowledge of the rules and the mathematical accuracy of the program were excellent, but it could not draw upon memories and common sense that . the human mind spontaneously gets the reservoir of experience. That could probably explain the basic difference between the man and machine.

We have seen that even a comprehensive set of rules and phenomenal speed of calculation cannot replace the ingenuity and creativity of the mind. Human beings can successfully process large volumes of data simultaneously using several procedures. An intelligent mind possesses many faculties enriched by cultural legacies and past experiences. Even if we create a robot that imitates us well, it will only prove the superiority of the capabilities of the human brain that designed its hardware and software. With the introduction of quantum computing, the scenario may drastically change to give the machine many more capabilities. Finally, we may circumvent the problem of consciousness by implanting capabilities of the machine into the brain. These possibilities could materialize when we understand all about the emergence of the mind from the computing processes of the brain.

"Free Will" Is No Deal ?

The greatest faculty of the mind is undoubtedly the intelligence to choose correctly from the various options that simultaneously exist in the external world. It is called "free will" which has been the subject of several studies using electroencephalograms (EEGs). The results indicate the gradual build up of electric potentials in the brain areas before the occurrence of the actual event of choice. The exercise of free will seems to happen only after the brain has completed all computing processes and decided to act in a particular manner. The free will only gives an official seal to the choice already made by the mechanical processes.

Benjamin Libettes' experiments suggest that free will can some times reverse the decision taken by the brain processes. It is possible that free will can effectively prevent the implementation of the neural choice. It is now known that the neural activity of creating a mental image is completed about half a second before it reaches the mind. The brain arranges the flow of time cleverly to create an impression that we are fully conscious of the actual arrival of the input at the gateway of the sense organ. Similarly, the free will is also aroused to occur simultaneously when the mechanical choice is presented to the conscious self and not earlier. This illusion is to satisfy the egoistic presumption that the decisions are taken by the conscious self and not by the smart molecules. We just want to believe that we are not simple robots run by some cerebral devices solely interested for the perpetuation of the species.

The undeniable fact is that any action that involves external stimulus has a time lag of half a second before it invokes a conscious response. In rapid action like continuous conversation, we may not even get a chance to exercise free will or override the decision already taken by the brain processes. The mind can, at best, act as a conscientious objector of the action replay going on in the brain without being able to intervene effectively or control the predetermined decision. An evolutionary explanation of the passive role of the mind is that natural selection did not require its deliberate intervention. Since all actions essential for survival can be efficiently concluded in the various computing processes in the brain, conscious contemplation is necessary only for higher mental activities. The strange truth is that we are just the slaves of the all powerful neural network and smart molecules that takes decisions without the involvement of consciousness. The highly acclaimed human quality of free will is just another myth created to sustain our incorrigible self-esteem.

If the neural network of considerable complexity can take all the decisions, we cannot claim to possess any exclusive gift of intelligence. Logically, if we create a computer to replicate the entire neural network of a human brain, it should be capable of taking intelligent decisions as we do. But even then, that machine may not attain self-awareness that our conscious mind possesses to experience the entire world including our own state of the body and mind. The mind is a marvelous mystery that makes us proud as well as uncomfortable. But we should not give up our pursuit of mind as more promising explanations are now emerging from the quantum dynamics of the brain that might ultimately solve the puzzle.

CHAPTER EIGHT

QUANTUM BRAIN TO THE PHANTOM MIND

THE SUPREME SELF IS THE BRIGHTEST OF ALL LIGHTS
DISPELLING THE DARKNESS OF IGNORANCE.
IT IS THE KNOWLEDGE AS WELL AS THE OBJECT
OF KNOWLEDGE AND THE ONLY MEANS TO REALIZE
IT.
WHEN FULL FAITH IS REPOSED IN THE SUPREME SELF
ONE REACHES THE STATE OF IMMORTALITY.
[BHAGAWAD GEETA]

I THINK THEREFORE I AM.
[RENE DESCARTES]

FOR THE ONE WHO REALIZED THE SELF
AND DISSOLVED ALL IGNORANCE
THERE IS NO TIME OR SPACE
NOR LIFE OR DEATH.
IN THE ENLIGHTENED MIND
THAT ABIDES IN THE TRUTH OF REALITY
NO EVIL THOUGHT, FEAR OR DESIRE
CAN EVER ENTER OR WILL BE ENTERTAINED.
[ASHTAVAKRA GEETA]

Coherent Firings

Certain characteristics of the brain and our context-oriented behavior suggest a strong possibility of some quantum properties in the brain. We invariably evaluate a situation in terms of several alternatives as if they exist simultaneously in the environment. It is like the concept of quantum superposition offering a multitude of possibilities. In quantum theory, the superposition presumably explores the most stable future energy states. Human beings also indulge in that kind of choice for the selection of a stable future position. We actually seek what is most beneficial to our existence on the basis of the intelligent evaluation of the available choices.

The holistic quality of our thoughts is comparable to the quantum property of omnipresence. Penrose considers it as "oneness" or "globality" like the wholeness of a musical composition. The conscious self experiences an integrated image of all the incoming information comprising of billions of sensory inputs. We can resolve the mystery of binding of input only if some quantum characteristics could be attributed to consciousness. A unified image of reality has to be created out of the various discreet neural activities involving serial and parallel computing. It is actually the binding of inputs that makes all the difference between the mechanistic and the quantum models of the mind. We have not yet found the exact brain mechanism that unifies the energy received by the various sensory organs. But the undeniable fact is that the brain gives us the wholesome experience of an undivided world. Even the latest discovery of "self-awareness neurons" does not reveal any special physical features that can achieve the unity of perception.

Penrose On Quantum Brain

Penrose examined at length the relationship between the state of awareness and the quantum coherence of the brain. Admittedly, non-biological structures cannot create consciousness. Among the biological structures, the human brain is an ideal place to look for the occurrence of the quantum phenomenon. According to Penrose, the microtubules in the cytoskeleton are the probable area where quantum characteristics can be found. Quantum fluctuations in chemical concentration at neuron junctions probably result in indeterminate firings. The growth and contraction of dendrite spines at the synapse junctions can be attributed to some sort of quantum activity.

Since cytoskeleton is a common feature of the cell, it is possible that rudimentary form of consciousness may exist in all forms of life. Penrose uses the quantum approach to explain the interface in the brain between processes working on the basis of Newtonian Physics and the synchronized firing of neurons. The indeterminate firings and the coherent oscillations of neurons indicate the possibility of quantum activity in the brain. The quantum behavior of neurons can also arise from the activities of molecules called "tubulin dimmers". If the quantum explanation were correct, it would rationally resolve the puzzles like the non-local nature of the mind and binding property of brain representations. But since quantum theory itself is in infancy, we may have to await further discoveries to understand the true nature of the brain.

The fact that we cannot replicate conscious experience of self in any mechanical device probably indicates that what we actually miss in our scientific models is the quantum behavior of the brain. The irreducible self and its experiences can emerge only from some sort of quantum coherence. The holistic perception of the external world and our unified responses show that we create reality far beyond the sum of the functions of individual neurons. Our conscious experiences and memories are in the nature of holographic images that contain the whole in every part in miniaturized form.

Mind On A Laser Beam!

In Bose-Einstein Condensates like laser beams, the particles are so highly unified to make their wave fronts overlap and get inside each other. They seem to forgo individual identities to behave as a single unit. In a laser beam, all photons are integrated to act as a single photon. They also display a high degree of freedom of choices between the various alternatives available. In the micro world of particles, we find a rudimentary form of volition similar to the free will found in the humans. The high degree of order in Bose-Einstein Condensates arises from the non-local relationship of the particles and the overlapping nature of the bosons that create a common identity. They fill up all the space at all times as if the whole condensate is a single particle. The coherence and smoothness of the condensate are derived from the inherent quantum properties of the particles in the condensate. Such strange occurrences at micro level have already involved philosophical claims that some sort of pre-consciousness is embedded in all matter at elementary level.

It can be assumed that some evolutionary compulsion might have motivated the brain to assume the unusual quantum coherence to create self- awareness. But it is difficult to extend the concept of Bose-Einstein Condensate to the brain since biological systems cannot normally operate at the low temperatures required for quantum coherence. Some studies of Frohlich, however, indicate the possibility of quantum properties in yeast cells, DNA and certain types of bacteria. It is also reported that quantum effects are seen in some biological processes in the cell walls that contain proteins and fat molecules. They carry a tiny electric charge that is positive at one end and negative at the other. These are called electric 'dipoles' and they are seen out of phase when the cell is at rest. The pumping of energy into the cell makes the dipoles oscillate and broadcast a microwave signal. They seem to oscillate to come into phase for creating a coherent quantum field.

It is true that neurons in the cerebral cortex associated with a particular activity vibrate or oscillate in unison. Wolf Singer found that there are coherent vibrations in a group or bundle of neurons during brain activities like thinking, remembering or feeling. The neurons oscillate in a frequency range of 35 Hz and 45 Hz. The coherent vibrations are probably to synchronize activities of individual neurons to get an integrated image of reality. The area of the brain from where such vibrations emerge can be the lining membrane of the neurons where the ion channels open or close in response to electrical fluctuations. Each neuron has its own cytoskeleton, containing protein like molecules. These molecules are arranged in different structures like microtubules and/or intermediate filaments. Inside the microtubules there are proteins called "tubulines", which are composed of amino acids. Microtubules are responsible for maintaining strengths of synapses and organizing the growth of new nerve ending. If tubulin dimmers in the microtubules do the basic computational work of the brain, it gives tremendous computing capability to the brain to the extent of 10-24 operations per second.

Available evidences do not confirm or reject the possibility of quantum coherence in the activities of the neurons. But the micro size of the ion channels shows possibilities of creating quantum fields in the brain. The oscillations take place when the channels open or close in unison after the neurons get stimulated. We also find pacemaker neurons that induce the whole bundle of neurons to vibrate or oscillate together. The electric field generated by billions of neurons in the brain can create quantum coherence in which all neural vibrations could be in phase. Such fields can also create holistic images to give the experience of wholeness of reality. The quantum field is probably an evolutionary necessity to make the subjective reality correspond closely with the holistic experience of the external world.

Self From The Firing Of Cells

The quantum coherent electric field in the brain is also a must for the high speed of data processing. Visual data processing takes only 1/10 of a second in terms of its color, shape and other characteristics of an object. In a serial or parallel computer, the same processing may require several thousands of years for any comprehensible output. Maybe in a quantum computer, such processing can be done as fast as in the human brain or even faster. It is also seen from experiments using EEG electrodes attached to the brain that the action of switching it on or off interferes with the electrical field in the brain as if interrupting a quantum phenomenon.

Some scientists consider that the quantum field in the brain creates a substrate of consciousness for thoughts and emotions to appear like ripples in a pond. Physicists call these ripples "excitations" or "patterns" on the surface of the Bose-Einstein Condensate. All the molecules in the brain get into a coherent state, to present a meaningful and holistic experience to the conscious self. Only the Bose-Einstein Condensates can give this experience in the shortest possible time without losing the details of the objective reality. As in a laser, the brain uses a large number of particles that participate collectively to form a coherent quantum state.

The quantum coherence is the rare phenomenon that computational devices cannot achieve in the near future. The conventional computing process based on binary logic can be seen in the activity of axons. But the dendrites or the receiving ends of the neurons behave like a quantum computer rather than a parallel or serial computer. Scientists conclude that different types of computational activities occur in the neuron itself, to create coherent oscillations. If quantum fields are not in the brain, it cannot create a mind to experience the undivided self and a holistic image of objective reality. The higher levels of parallel processing in the brain probably builds up recognition skills without the help of language or rules to guide its operations. Even in animals these processes are carried out for creating associated responses. But unless the processed information is bound into a cohesive image, we cannot perceive the reality of the outside world or get a unified experience of our existence.

Is Brain A Hologram?

We find different types of electrical waves in the brain during the waking and sleeping states. In the periods of Rapid Eye Movements (REM) in sleeping state, the electro encephalograph shows one kind of electrical wave. The action potential is an electrical charge in the neuron created by the movement of sodium and potassium ions. Other than neurons, the brain also contains a large number of glial cells that perform certain metabolic functions. Nobili suggests that the electrical activities in the glial cells which are in the form of oscillations can produce a complex wave pattern in which sodium ions affect the movement of potassium ions and vice versa. On the basis of the ionic movements in the glial cells, he created a wave equation that was exactly like Schrodinger's wave equation used in quantum mechanics. Theoretically, this equation shows the possibility of producing holograms in the brain tissues. He concluded that the close proximity of the sources of the signals and the receptors in the cortex are suitable for creating reference waves and information waves.

Another suggestion is that superposition of EEG waves without any distortion can probably create complex images of holographic memory. The linear cortical waves are capable of maintaining their form in conformity with the superposition principle. These waves are found to survive even when anaesthetics suppress other neural activities. The presence of finely tuned resonators distributed throughout the cortex in a random pattern support the view that the brain probably works as a holographic medium. The vast amount of memory that the brain holds could be stored in the form of waves in glial cells. The glial cells can also absorb superpositions of information in the form of waves coming from the past and present. The reference waves can perhaps excite the glial cells to evoke associated memories to bring out the corresponding past experiences.

Whether the brain is operating as a hologram or as a computer capable of serial, parallel and quantum operations, the fact is that a mind emerges out of it with several non-physical qualities. Since self-awareness is not possible without long-term memory, it is probably stored in glial cells as holograms or in some other form in the neural network. Self is recovered when a reference wave is generated in the cortex. In sleeping and dreaming states, self must be in a state of recession as the body awareness and volitional control are at the lowest level. All these possibilities indicate that the body-mind relationship is too complex to understand in terms of classical physics or quantum mechanics. A few facts about the electrical activity in the brain do not give us any clear idea about the emergence of the mind.

Measuring Infinities

If we accept the mind as a quantum phenomenon, which in all probabilities it is, we are simply trying to explain the inexplicable. We first assume that there was a quantum vacuum before the universe came into being with a big bang. In the quantum vacuum, which is the lowest energy state, all vibrations are at zero-point and the field is in absolute rest. It is the substrate that would have given rise to the Higgs field and all phenomenal world of matter and forces. The quantum vacuum contained immense potential energy, as it represented the sum of all possible frequencies of vibration. The information that existed in it created the universe including consciousness, which is a fundamental property of biological matter. If we accept that the quantum vacuum was the source of all consciousness, we need not search for any proto-consciousness in elementary particles or in any other form of matter.

The biological activity of the brain is probably a tool to reach universal consciousness, which is a state of energy permeating the universe. For convenience, we can call it mind or self but the possibility is that the computing process of the brain simply creates a gateway to reality. The mind probably vibrates in unison with certain state of energy in its innumerable manifestations in particles and fields. But these are all only tentative inferences that we can presently draw from the information available on the functioning of the neurons as a quantum field. More solid proof is required to accept the idea that the mind arises from the quantum field in the brain.

Mind From Automaton!

For explaining dreams, Fred Allen Wolf adapted the concept of quantum automaton originally proposed by David Z. Albert. The idea is based on the parallel-worlds interpretation of quantum theory. Automaton is supposed to possess the capacity to store objective information of observed objects including the knowledge about its own experience of such observations. The concept of automaton is derived from the possibility that the image of self can be kept in primary glial cells in quantum super position. It is retrieved from time to time for reaching different levels of self-awareness. An automaton can hold multiple maps consisting of complementary observations including the observer and the observed. The quantum automata, in addition to remembering the observed facts can also understand the state of its own state. All the information about reality is simultaneously available in it for withdrawal if a suitable reference wave is created to retrieve them. According to Wolf, dreams give us an opportunity to measure the difference between self-reflective and unreflective perceptions.

The exact nature of automation and its method of interaction with glial cells for creating the dreaming or waking self are still unknown. There is no physical proof of the existence of automaton in our brain. Fred Allen Wolf assumes that in all probability the conscious self is the outcome of the interaction of automaton with glial cells. Like Dennet's idea of multiple drafts, we have yet another tentative explanation of consciousness in the interactions of automaton. All such explanations do give us some valuable clues about certain features of the mind. But the ultimate unraveling of the nature of the mind still remains a distant dream.

Suspended Consciousness

The large number of case studies of severe brain damage confirms the quantum coherent nature of the brain. It is seen that in spite of serious damage to certain parts of the brain, consciousness remained more or less intact. If the brain functions as a serial or parallel computer, it would not have retained consciousness after such structural damages. The continuation of all normal cerebral activities is possible because of the quantum qualities of the brain. It can be seen that when the brain receives less energy during sleep, consciousness is lost and at higher energy levels, it returns as if nothing happened.

Another important evidence of the quantum nature of the brain is the effect of anesthesia on consciousness. General anesthetics switch off consciousness for a limited period of time depending upon the quantity of the chemical used. Consciousness returns after the drug effects wear off without causing any damage to the mental faculties. Such temporary loss of consciousness can be achieved by using certain chemicals like nitrous oxide, ether, chloroform or even by the chemically inert gas "Xenon". The chemicals probably affect the electric dipole properties of the neurons, which interfere with the switching actions of tubulin. We have no clear idea about the specific action of anesthetics but it is assumed that the "Van Der Val Interaction" of brain proteins cause temporary unconsciousness.

The fact that general anesthetics can also affect animals and birds, suggest the possibility of consciousness arising out of identical processes in all animal brains. Since consciousness can be kept suspended, it shows that molecules of anaesthetic chemicals interfere with some quantum physical action in the cytoskeleton. But we do not know how a small dose of chemical can cause the appearance and disappearance of consciousness and self? We will have to learn more about the role of self in the dreams in which it becomes a witness of the hectic activities in the brain without any external input.

CHAPTER NINE

THE DREAMING SELF

THE SECOND STATE OF SELF IS
THE CONSCIOUSNESS WITNESSING THE DREAM EVENTS.
THE SENSES OF THE DREAMER ARE TURNED INWARD
TO REENACT THE PAST AND ENJOY THE FORBIDDEN PLEASURES.

[MANDUKYA UPANISHAD]

IN SLEEP, THE SELF ASSUMES MANY FORMS.
IT EATS, DRINKS AND EVEN ENJOYS SEX.
TERRIBLE EVENTS ARE SEEN AND MISERIES SUFFERED
BUT BEING DETACHED FROM THE BODY,
THE DREAMING SELF IS UNAFFECTED BY THE EVENTS
THAT DO NOT EMANATE OR END IN IT.

[BRIHADARANYAKA UPANISHAD]

A Brief History Of Dreams

From time immemorial, humans have been reviewing dream events in waking life and pondering over their prophetic and even therapeutic implications. Plenty of assumptions are made in the literature on the physiological and psychological basis for the occurrence of dreams. Since we are in an altered state of awareness during sleep, we should first try to understand the brain mechanisms that create the dreams. When we recall dream events in waking life, we get a weird feeling of being a witness of the dramatic sequence of events without actually performing any physical task. We sometimes experience emotions of pleasure or pain when the dream events are recalled in waking state. In lucid dreams the self is more involved in the events and it experiences strong emotional states that are known as nightmare.

The representations projected in dreams are mostly unrelated images of objects and events. They are not basically different from the images experienced by the mind in the waking state. The dream images seem to emerge from the data already stored in the brain without the initiative of any sensory input. Depending upon the intensity of the experiences in the dream, they are classified as ordinary dreams and lucid dreams. In lucid dreams, the self is more involved and at times it may even try to control the course of the events. There is no scientific explanation about the dominant presence of self in lucid dreams, but the basic mechanism creating the dreams appears to be the same in both cases.

Before consciousness fully dawned upon the human kind to create an image of self, life would have been in a sort of perpetual dream state. After the concept of self got firmly entrenched in body awareness, dreams must have receded to the sleeping state. In the early days of civilization, dreams were taken as the expressions of evil forces that possessed the defenseless sleeping mind. In some primitive societies, dream events are still seriously taken as representing the will of God or the demands of ancestors. The objects and events appearing in dreams are supposed to show the directions to be followed for propitiating some deity or a restless spirit of an ancestor who wants the incomplete tasks to be carried out by the successors.

Aristotle was the first philosopher to give a somewhat rational explanation of dreams. He took dreams out of the spiritual realm of Gods and ancestors and gave it the scientific explanation of "residual impressions". He did not attribute any prophetic value to the objects and events appearing in dreams. Gods, according to him, were too busy to send symbolic signals to the sleeping human mind to communicate their will. He felt the Gods had better ways to discipline the humans.

In the past few centuries, dreams became the gateway to the knowledge of the pathology of the mind. Dreams of abnormal persons were thoroughly analyzed for the hidden symbols that could reveal the root cause of the mental disorder. After detecting the electrical activities in the brain, the focus of attention shifted to the neurons and the various systems and subsystems. Instead of analyzing dreams, reductionism that set the agenda of Western science, focused attention on the various systems of the brain to understand the mind. They tried to find self in the waking and dreaming states through experimental and clinical studies of the processes involved in the emergence of consciousness.

Master Of Dreams

After Aristotle, it was Sigmund Freud who gave a seemingly scientific interpretation of the symbolic significance of dreams. He treated the brain purely as a mechanical device consisting of neurons and the dreams were considered to be the outcome of the discharge of the electrical build-up in the brain. The Freudian concept of the mind has both the conscious and unconscious parts of the brain. According to him, all the unfulfilled and unacceptable desires are presumably dumped in the unconscious part of the brain. Dreams relive the energy accumulated in the brain during the day and the events and objects are represented symbolically to keep the sleeper undisturbed.

Freud felt that in addition to serving the physiological purposes of the brain, the dreams also took care of the psychological needs of the sleeper. He assumed that if the real significance of the dream symbols is understood, the basic cause of mental disorders could be identified and treated successfully. The objects and events appearing in dreams closely resemble the sex organs as most of the repressed desires are related to unfulfilled sexual urges. The socially unacceptable sexual desires dumped in the unconscious parts of the mind get an opportunity to come up in dreams in various disguises to keep both the moralist and the beast contended.

Conceptually, the Freudian approach brought some semblance of order to the chaotic ideas about dreams. People started taking serious note of dreams when Freud pointed out the possibility that dream symbols could reveal certain unknown aspects of human psyche. But more than the interpretation of dreams, Freud's original contribution was in understanding the complexities of the unconscious mind. In the Freudian model of the mind, the ego represents the conscious part of self or "I-ness" and "id" is the unconscious component. He conceived id as a garbage box where all primitive and private sexual desires that are unacceptable to the conscious mind are consigned. The self is the outcome of the holistic projections of images converted from perception, sensation and comprehension. The Freudian interpretation does not give us the actual mechanism underlying the emergence of self or the process of suppression of 'id' by the powerful ego. It is true that the information about the composition and function of the neurons in the brain was rather sketchy and hypothetical at that point of time. But his admirable efforts gave a suitable starting point for the scientific enquiries into the realm of dreams and consciousness.

Jung On Mind

Carl Jung was a great psychologist who gave a detailed description of the mind in the broader framework of relationships. Unlike Freud, he was not obsessed with the concept of mind as a repository of unfulfilled desires. He conceptualized that ego arose from the total psyche and identified itself with the conscious self. Jung extensively examined the broad spectrum of attitudes that characterized human behavior. According to him, the attitude of the introvert relies upon the thoughts and experiences of the self more than anything else in the world. But the extrovert gives more credence to the events in the external world and the thoughts emanating from other persons.

He also conceived "libido" as the flow of total energy without confining it only to sexual urges as conceived by Freud. For him, energy was a universal force containing both intensity and extensity. While the intensity of energy is transferable, extensity can move only with structural changes. Another concept evolved by Jung was "synchronicity" which distorts the existence of an order without establishing any specific underlying cause. In fact, Jung's concept of a non-causal order was probably the forerunner of the idea of quantum coherence that establishes a state of complete order without having any obvious causal relationship. He also indicated the possibility that the mind is the manifestation of a form of universal energy that is non-causal and omnipresent. He did not give much credence to the Freudian concept of mind and significance of dreams.

New Ideas About Dreams

The physiological aspects of dreams were studied extensively in the latter part of the Twentieth Century. It is seen that during the dream period rapid eye movements (REM) occur as if we are actually watching some events in waking state. The studies of Benjamin Libette, a leading neurophysicist, brought out several interesting features of consciousness both in waking state and in dreaming state. Using electrodes inserted in the brain, Libette and his associates found that we become conscious of the outside world half a second after receiving the sensory stimulus. But we always refer to the moment of awareness back in time to the actual time of arrival of sensory input by means of a process called "temperal referral". There is also spatial reference to become aware of the correct spatial point from where the sensory inputs are received. His studies revealed that in spite of our capacity to react to a stimulus within 100 milliseconds, actual awareness of our reaction is delayed by half a second. Libettes' findings indicate the possibility of a time lag between the actual arrival of the stimulus and our awareness. The temporal referral is only for the input that contains a time signal.

Since the brain signals that create dream images have no sensory origin, they cannot be referred back in time. Time studies suggest that unconscious mental functions may represent brain activities of very short duration. If the electrical vibrations or pulses had longer duration, they would have made the sleeper conscious. Similarly, dreams occur during a very short spell of brain activity to keep the dreaming self in blissful slumber. In the absence of external sensory inputs while dreaming, self is aware of only the subjective world created by the memory.

There is uninterrupted activity in the brain in dream state as the inhibitory mechanisms in the cortex become inactive in sleep. Some drugs can also depress the inhibitory mechanisms and create vivid imagery and a different type of awareness. The strange images and inexplicable events that we see in dreams show that the normal mechanisms of the brain in waking state do not function in dreams. The consolidation and interconnection of sensory inputs to project a complete image of the outside world is absent in the dream state. Coherent patterns of dream images arise only when we recall the dreams in the waking state. The binding of dream images in space and time out of the individual firings of billions of neurons seems to happen only in the waking state. It is probably the process of recall that makes the dreams somewhat coherent and meaningful. Without the help of consciousness, we would have made no sense out of the data processed by the brain.

Why Do We Dream?

The "Activation Synthesis Model" of dream proposed by Hobson and McCarley does not find any psychological purpose for dreams. They found that some specific brain mechanisms in the brain stem turned off the waking awareness to create the sleeping state. As a result, only its own sensory and motor impulses activate the brain in sleep. The dreams are made out of memories of past events and future expectations. The electrical wave activity recorded in EEG during REM sleep is known as PGO waves. A specific neurotransmitter molecule generates them in the brain. According to Hobson, sleep is induced when the aminergic system is put off halting the activity of two molecules called "noradrenaline" and "serontonin". The loss of the sequences and absence of any causal link in dreams is attributed to the discontinuities created by the sudden jolts from PGO waves. Hobson finds it futile to search for any meaning or pattern in dreams. They are simply images produced by the mechanical processes of the brain signifying no particular intention. He could not find any evolutionary need for a specific brain mechanism to produce dreams.

Jim Horne, unlike Hobson, found a plausible evolutionary purpose for the dream state. He noticed that the growing human fetus normally sleeps in REM state for about 15 hours in a day. After birth, the REM sleep is reduced to about eight hours whereas in adults it lasts only about 2 hours. The long spell of the REM sleep of the fetus, according to Jim Horne, is an exercise to develop a healthy brain. But, suspended in the amniotic fluid and with no sensory inputs to create memory for making mental images, the fetus is definitely not capable of dreaming like adults. It may be getting some orientation to interpret the future sensory inputs in a meaningful manner. The adult dream in REM sleep may be the hangover of the imageless fetal dreams but it helps our quick recovery from sleep. It may serve some evolutionary need to give us instant alertness to face an unexpected challenge. The suggestion that dreams conceal the remnants of our reptilian instincts looks really far-fetched. It is true that all our modern knowledge of the physiology and psychology of dreams cannot give us the rational basis for the nocturnal drama in the human brain.

Winson, another expert on dreams, suggests that dreams could be acting as a bridge between the brain and the mind. In humans, the same unconscious brain mechanisms are active both in waking and dream states. Winson accepts the existence of an unconscious mind as conceptualized by Freud. But he considers it as a product of the evolution of the brain instead of treating it as a "depository of repressed desires and destructive instincts". It is an active mental structure, which processes external stimuli as well as our responses to the environment. The mind arises in the brain from the unconscious mental structures that are capable of dealing with all challenges of life without the arbitration of the conscious self. Dreams, according to him, are actually the continuation of a mammalian memory processing mechanism in the brain.

He further suggests that the information acquired during the waking awareness is reprocessed probably in the REM state of sleep. Even animals have REM periods during sleep, which indicate the presence of some memory processing program. Winson points out that the beta rhythms seen in REM sleep are indicative of the role of dreams in the refreshing of memory. The evolutionary need to keep a sharp memory is to make the body react quickly to the sudden surprising events of life with confidence and competence. The unusually long period of eight hours or more of REM sleep in infants may be for developing the awareness of self. When the baby reaches the age of two, the REM sleep is reduced to about three hours. The duration of dreams in adults automatically gets reduced for giving more time to perform various functions during the waking life.

Dreaming To Forget

Crick and Mitchson suggest that the actual function of the dream is to remove certain unwanted memories from the neural network. According to them, dreams are a process of reverse learning in the brain, which is diametrically opposite to the findings of Winson. They hold that we dream to forget and not to remember and the net effect is actually to weaken memory. Dreams are necessary to reduce fantasies and obsessions rather than for cementing the memories created in waking state. In computers, overloading of data sometimes creates patterns without any logic or sequence similar to the fantasies of the human mind. Similarly, when the brain is overactive with an abundance of avoidable memories, it would show symptoms of hallucinations. For correcting computer programs unlearning inputs are fed into the networks to weed out the unwanted modes and save the wanted memories. The fact that stimulation of the brain stem during sleep creates dreams supports the unlearning hypothesis. Unnecessary memories are presumably eliminated during the reverse learning process in which neurons give self-feedback without any external stimuli. They are negative feedback loops that render the connections of some neurons weak to erase memories having weak causal links. The cleaning operations of the brain make us feel fully refreshed after a sound sleep. But the idea of reverse learning is not supported by any evidence that deprivation of dream sleep affects the mental functions in any significant manner.

Quantum Dreams

We have already seen the strong possibility of the quantum nature of brain activities. In such a state several superposition can exist simultaneously. On observation, a single state emerges by collapsing the wave function. If we accept that dreams are created by superposition of quantum waves generated by the brain, it explains qualities like lucidity and timelessness. During the walking state, the sensory stimuli interfere with the superposition to create reality, but it is probably the occasional electrical jolts that interrupt our sleep to make way to dreams.

Fred Allen Wolf suggests that lucid dreams can be time resolved holograms or a series of unfolding holograms created by the brain. Ordinary dreams are like images in a hologram made out of converging light rays. In lucid dreams, the presence of self is more focused to give better clarity to the images emerging in the brain. The vividness of lucid dreams is probably on account of the unity of images in relation to the self. According to Wolf, the difference between lucidity and ordinariness in dreams is a question of where the "I" exists and how it is distributed throughout the brain and body and even in the entire universe. When we correctly focus at the center of the hologram, the observer is aligned with the observed and the distinction of separate entities disappears. The reference wave can elicit associated memories from glial cells by exciting them to identify the reality. The combined action of the input wave, reference wave and the associated memory in glial cells collectively create the external world. But all such assumptions still fail to give us any scientific explanation of mind except pointing out a few possibilities to be explored in the realm of quantum phenomenon.

It is now scientifically accepted that the temporal lobe is extremely sensitive to electrical disturbances. Certain areas in the temporal lobe are not dedicated to any sensory or motor function. They are identified as "The Interpretative Cortex" involved in the creation of the present from the past experiences. Penfield and his colleagues discovered that electrical stimulation of the interpretative areas of the cortex creates "dreamy states or psychical seizures". They are definitely not identical to dreams, but recreations of some past experiences. Electrical stimulation of this area brings back past experiences like in a "flashback" consisting of a wide range of sensory experiences like sight, sounds, finger tingling and so on. Persinger suggests that major components of "near death experiences", and several other out-of-body experiences like seeing visions of great luminosity or hearing of soulful music can be duplicated in a laboratory setting by electrically stimulating the temporal lobe. So, ultimately we get some real insight into the brain processes that take us to the realm of God.

Dreaming God Spot

The psychic experiences created by stimulating some particular spot in the temporal lobe cannot be conclusive proof of the existence of a spiritual spot in the brain. It is all the more interesting to note that visions arising from the same process and spot are also associated with epileptic seizures and different kinds of madness. We cannot assume any evolutionary purposes for the development of such a spot in the human brain. The common man attributes Godliness to the kind of visions that some people get from meditation or rituals. We can only say that such visions may also have the same evolutionary purpose of dreaming. The neural network in the temporal lobes associated with such experiences is found to be isolated ones. Even if the visions generated in such neural networks are related to spiritual thoughts, they have to be properly integrated with the totality of the brain processes to make them coherent and meaningful. Just because some neurons in the temporal lobe are associated with psychic experiences, we cannot say that there is a different kind of intelligence exclusively devoted to spirituality. The great visions emanating from them are perhaps a little more lucid than the dreams as the self is more actively involved in such experiences.

Missing Self In Dreams

Scientific studies now suggest that dreams arise in a purely physical process originating in the brain stem. Since the sensory and motor pathways are blocked in sleep, the forebrain is stimulated by random electrical impulses that create the dream imagery. The random nature of the stimuli explains the irrationality and weirdness of the dream events. With the decline of body awareness caused by the chemicals released from the brain stem, the self probably recedes in sleep. In the experiments with small doses of the anaesthetic chemical "ketamine", it was found that the self emerges through sensory inputs. The self is weak in dreams because of the absence of sensory inputs and the lack of volition to make physical responses. In lucid dreams, the self has some more presence and control over the dream events probably because of increased volition. After the drug effect wears off, the volition returns and the self reappears as if nothing spectacular happened in its absence.

In ordinary dreams, image processing is done at the lowest level without the presence of self anywhere in the dream space. There is only pure awareness and no experience of perception of the self in the dream. As the dream gets more and more lucid, the self slowly appears with its emotional and cognitive attributes. At higher levels of awareness, the self is capable of fully participating in dream events and it may even attempt to alter its uncomfortable sequences.

Fred Allen Wolf suggests that we dream for developing a concept of self, capable of experiencing the external world. The different levels of self-awareness during the dream state are cited in support of this idea. The status of self in lucid dreams is that of just a witness not bound to the body or to a sense of space and time. This is the ultimate state of mind that the mystics strived to achieve in ancient times. They might have also experimented with mind-altering drugs like "ketamin" to get into enlightened states of awareness in pursuit of the true knowledge of reality. Applying the quantum model of mind to the dreaming self, Wolf proposes that self-awareness arises from the ability of a simple memory device called automaton to record and retrieve holographic images in glial cells.

In lucid dreams, the self is very much aware of witnessing the dream events. But the self also knows that it is locked up within the dream boundary. It does not experience the intensity of emotions that the dream events would have normally evoked in waking state. Sustained meditation and religious rituals that presumably liberate the self from the physical bonds can probably create similar experiences. The self in all such situations becomes just a witness devoid of any of emotional involvement in any events and situations in which the body is placed.

CHAPTER TEN

RECYCLED MIND IN A RENTED BODY

TURIA, THE FOURTH, IS THE STATE OF SUPER CONSCIOUSNESS.
IT IS NEITHER TURNED INWARD NOR OUTWARD,
AND IS BEYOND ALL SENSES AND INTELLECT,
IT IS INFINITE PEACE AND LOVE,
AND PURE CONSCIOUSNESS THAT CAN BE ACCESSED, ONLY BY
MASTERING DESIRES AND MALIGNANT THOUGHTS.
[THE MANDUKYA UPANISHAD]

IN THE BEGINNING WAS THE WORD
[JOHN 1.1,14]

LET GOD RESIDE IN OUR MIND.
LET US MAKE OUR BODY HIS TEMPLE.
LET HIM PARTAKE THE FRUITS OF OUR ACTION.
LET US PLACE THE ENTIRE HARVEST OF OUR LIFE AT HIS FEET.
LET US ALWAYS REMAIN AS HIS FAITHFUL SERVANTS.
[RIG VEDA 1.91.13]

End Of The Road

We have almost reached a dead end in our search for a reductionist solution of the mind. The emergence of the mind from the purely physical processes in the brain is still an amazing mystery of nature. It is true that the mind can arise only from the material realm of matter and forces but how it acquires the non-physical qualities is the intriguing issue. Some people assume that there are several properties of matter still unknown to science. They hold that the mind arises out of the proto-consciousness embedded in all kinds of matter. Many scientists and philosophers support the idea of such unknown quality of awareness in matter. It definitely gives the requisite causal link between the brain and the phenomenon of mind. This assumption can also explain the binding abilities of the mind that integrate fragmented external realities into coherent images. The mind is not located in any specific area or in the coherent firings of self-awareness neurons. It seems to prevail all over the cerebral cortex as an intelligent state of energy.

The mind-body dichotomy is unacceptable to the supporters of reductionism and artificial intelligence. For them the brain is structurally and functionally comparable to a computer and the mind is only the algorithm or software that operates it. Some proponents of artificial intelligence even claim that a computer-controlled robot will very soon understand the nature of the given instructions and act according to its free will. However, so far no one has created a computer with the software that can enable it to experience its own identity or sensations of pleasure and pain. The new thoughts like proto-consciousness of matter and the evidence that consciousness arises in the realm of 40 Hz oscillations in the brain are welcome developments to further our attempts to understand more about the mind.

Admittedly, the basic differences between the computer and the human brain cannot be bridged so easily. While mechanical operations like memorizing data and performing calculations and mathematical functions are much faster in a computer, it has not so far performed any creative task outside the rigid boundary of a software created by an intelligent mind. Actually, the comparison of a computer with the brain is a serious category error. A computer can work only within the space of the logic invented by a brain. All structural and functional aspects of the brain are the evolutionary achievements of millions of years of struggle to overcome the environmental challenges. But a computer, whether super or ordinary, is only a device created by the intelligent humans. Whatever the computer achieves is only yet another tribute to human ingenuity. It can never be compared to the mind, which is the mother of all man-made tools.

A Mind For Lucy

The electronic logic that runs the computer is only a recent creation of our collective wisdom. It represents the totality of evolutionary efforts of all forms of life. The path breaking designs and perfect functions of a computer are irrefutable evidences of the excellent capabilities of the human brain. Basically, the computer works on the movement of an electric charge in a semiconductor. But the human brain functions on an entirely different matrix by exchanging chemical signals in a huge network of neurons. Computer technology can undoubtedly imitate several functions of the brain and assist us effectively by extending sensory capacities. It can also improve the data storage in the human memory and do more accurate processing of inputs to reach correct solutions. Such complementary functions of machine intelligence can definitely enhance human capabilities by removing the natural barriers to perception and comprehension.

But at the present level of technology, computer cannot completely replace a self-conscious human. Even if we unlock the so-called innate quality of proto-consciousness in matter and create 40 Hz oscillations in computer chips, we are not likely to make them conscious like a human. Assuming that we manage to induct some sort of consciousness in computing machines in future, it will still be an uphill task to develop a mind capable of experiencing emotions and thoughts. We will very soon see the results of the great experiment to build a conscious robot called "Lucy". She is supposed to learn the use of various parts of the body using her neural circuits without getting any program to make appropriate responses to environmental challenges. Lucy will learn to respond to the world only from the pre-installed software of basic instincts for survival and the capacity to process inputs. She is expected to achieve a fairly high degree of consciousness by creating and sustaining the memory of experiences to guide sensory inputs. We will very soon see what kind of mind Lucy will acquire from her silicon circuits.

The Lucas-Penrose argument based on Godel's theorem clearly brings out the ultimate difference between a computer and human. They hold that the "Turing machine" operating on algorithms cannot prove the truth or falsity of a statement. The human brain can state whether something can be proved or not. Even if the computer can state correctly the truth or falsity of a statement, a human brain is required to finally approve its correctness. The proponents of strong artificial intelligence do not have any answer to such arguments. Just because computers can imitate some of the functions of the brain, they cannot assume the role of life capable of creating such machines. If Deep Blue defeated a grandmaster, the credit should go to the marvelous brain that competently programmed all possible combinations of intelligent moves anticipated from the grandmaster. When Lucy's mind becomes a reality, it will only be the fitting finale to the relentless quest of the creative intelligence of its inventor.

Ghost Who Talks!

Historically, the mind has been conceived as an independent entity distinctly different from the physical body. Eastern mystics assigned it a higher pedestal of soul untainted by the baser instincts that corrupt the body. Traditionally, the mind is endowed with several good qualities like intelligence, wisdom and compassion while the source of all evil deeds is identified in the uncontrolled desires of the body. It is also assumed to exist eternally in various migratory forms in the innumerable rebirths in new bodies. In the life after death, the mind or soul is supposed to receive the rewards or punishments for all its earthly deeds. The universal practice of ancestral worship and ritualistic offerings to departed souls shows our firm faith in the survival of the mind even after the physical body. In Western countries the Cartesian notion of the nonphysical dimensions of the mind survived in philosophy and literature in spite of contrary scientific evidences. Of course, the latest discovery that the mind is only an approver of the deeds of the brain removes many misconceptions about its accountability for conducting human affairs.

The basic question that confronts us now is how to accept the nonphysical dimensions of the mind that arise from a purely material mechanism comprising of atoms and molecules. The closest examination of the brain has not revealed anything more than neurons and other cells. But the fact remains that somewhere in the brain there is a mysterious self that is fully conscious of its own identity in the material world. It acts as an observer, informer and even as a critic of its own actions. Above all, it experiences emotions and entertains thoughts without knowing any of the processes that project them to its awareness. Moreover, the conscious experience of one person of the same event is not comparable to that of another similarly placed one. The emotional and intellectual experiences are unique for each individual in spite of the common mechanisms involved in their perception and comprehension. We find that even in modern times, the mind is an elusive mirage that cannot be easily caught in the net of scientific knowledge of the brain.

Finally Quantum Consciousness?

In his book "Shadows of the Mind", Penrose accepts frankly that the mind cannot be explained exclusively by any contemporary physical theory. He feels that a combination of many theories like quantum mechanics and relativity may ultimately create a convincing model of the mind. We will probably understand the mind when a unified theory of everything is formulated to explain matter at all levels. Penrose expects that quantum non-locality and superposition can solve the puzzle of the binding problem. He hopes to find the course of the quantum coherence of the mind from the microtubules of neurons that act as minute tunnels of proteins. A further proof of the relation between consciousness and microtubules is seen in the interference of chemicals inducing anesthesia. If we assume that the microtubules are powerful computers, about 40 billion tiny computers will be working in the human brain. When they fire in unison, a mind-like entity with capabilities far beyond that of an individual neuron can possibly emerge.

In the recent past, the quantum approach to mind has gained many more advocates and admirers. They find that assuming certain quantum qualities in the brain requires only marginal adjustments in the rational wisdom of science. It is now accepted that matter at the elementary level behaves quantum mechanically. Even human thoughts are likely to be quantum fluctuations in the vacuum energy of the universe. The ion channels in the neural membrane are definitely an ideal location for the occurrence of quantum phenomenon. The ions create electrical fields, which can explain the coherent oscillations in the neural network. It has already been confirmed that such oscillations are in the range of 40 Hz. But the problem is how to attribute quantum qualities to neural oscillations since no known mechanism in the brain can create a state of matter that exists in a laser beam. Even the explanation of Micheal Green about the possibility of quantum tunneling does not appear very convincing. All that we can safely assume now is that the quantum coherence of the brain has something important to do with consciousness and mind. No other scientific explanation can solve the binding problem and the non-local dimension of the mind. The quantum route is in fact more promising than the invocation of pre-consciousness from ordinary matter to create consciousness in a large scale.

Some scientists go far beyond even the acceptable assumptions based on quantum coherence and 40 Hz oscillations. They consider that the Higgs field that presumably emerged from the quantum vacuum has created the universe and that it is comparable to a huge Bose-Einstein condensate. Proto-consciousness, which is said to be embedded in all matter, should have also existed in the Higgs field. They find in the presence of the universal energy of the quantum vacuum all the qualities attributable to a God-like entity. It is immanent in all consciousness, 40 Hz oscillations. The mind that emerges from the brain process is probably nature's gift to humans to access this underlying energy substrate. Well, all these are mere speculations without any rational explanation to the real nature of our quest.

The failure to reach an acceptable scientific explanation of consciousness has again revived the idea of the dichotomy of the mind and body. After explaining how the mind works, Steven Pinker concludes that perhaps it would be difficult to solve conundrums like free will and sentience. The mind-body problem would remain alive until the riddle of consciousness is explained by scientific knowledge. Many scientists disgruntled with the unconvincing scientific models of the mind have already started examining mystical insights to understand existence. Some even use psychedelic drugs or follow religious penance to create mystical experiences of the altered states of mind.

As a last resort, it is suggested that Eastern mysticism can probably give us some valuable insights into the mystery of mind.

If scientific knowledge of the brain is coherently correlated to mystic insights, they hope to get the true picture of the mind. There have always been attempts to relate scientific knowledge with the essence of mystic wisdom that treats the reality holistically with total objectivity. But the fusion of quantum mechanics with mystic vision has not yet created any convincing explanation of the mind. It is evident that correct knowledge of elementary particles or DNA would not be sufficient to make us understand the non-physical nature of the mind. For an accurate explanation of the holistic experiences of the mind, we need much more information about the brain and its unknown processes.

A rational explanation of the mind may not be welcome to the vested interests who want to keep it beyond the reach of science and technology. If the mind is another dimension of nature like space or time, it would become explicable some time in the future. True knowledge of the mind will make it difficult for religious faiths to sell their ideas of God and soul to the more enlightened future generations. Some of the leading scientists also admit that the mind should be left to the spiritual realm as it is beyond the reach of the present capabilities of rational investigation. This attitude is self-defeating, as no boundaries can be set for scientific endeavors to unravel the truth of reality. More patient sustained efforts can definitely reveal some of the mysteries of the mind probably well before we complete the third millennium. The 40 Hz oscillations and quantum coherence are all important milestones in our incredible voyage into the complexities of mind. We can appreciate these efforts much better when we put together all the pieces of the puzzle in part IV.

Darwin Can Rest In Peace

Evolutionary psychologists like Steven Pinker and Daniel Dennet try to give Darwinian explanation for all kinds of human behavior. According to them, all our actions and emotions are evolved in response to the needs of natural selection. They even identify the "Universals" of human culture like promiscuity, male aggressiveness and female sexual coyness as examples of evolutionary traits. In physical terms, human brain consists of several modules of evolutionary solutions to the specific problems like finding a mate or learning language or behaving amicably in social situations.

Even if we accept unequivocally all the evolutionary assumptions of the emergence of humans as a species, it is difficult to accept the view that our behavior is entirely dictated by Darwinian urges. Our physical characteristics are definitely developed in response to environmental challenges but the mind shows several adaptive and cultural features that are unique to our species. We do not have precise knowledge of the social and physical environment of our ancestors that developed such specific behavioral patterns. The origin of the mind can be appreciated when we have scientific knowledge about the compulsions that led to the massive cultural evolution of human kind. We have already seen that cultural evolution is the key factor that shaped the human destiny. All that can be said now is that our behavior emerges from the close interaction between the inherited characteristics, cultural and the knowledge acquired by an individual. Evolutionary assumptions cannot explain how the various cultural traits modify the inherited characteristics. We can only say that both nature and nurture contributed toward development of the mind but the dominant role of the latter is becoming more evident in modern times.

Beyond The Mind Of God

The scope of the intelligent machine has so far been confined to the original program and its possible extensions. The IBM supercomputer called "Deep Blue" defeated Grand Master Gary Kasparov in 1997 purely on the advantage of processing speed. It achieved this rare feat by predicting the correct move out of millions of possibilities but strategies for winning the game was not part of the program. But the new technology called "Evolvable Hardware" (EHW) goes far beyond the program by improving the algorithms by upgrading the algorithms through trail and error and from past experience. Our of the billions of possibilities, EHW not only selects the most suitable one on its own but also tunes itself further for creating better algorithms. The creators of EHW claim that the end product can excel the capabilities envisaged in the original design. They point out that some solutions derived from the applications of the EHW are not even conceivable by the human mind that created it. It probably heralds the advent of a super human mind in the machine combing consciousness and the terrific speed pf processing and perfect accuracy of computing.

EHW works on the basis of adaptable hardware called "genetic algorithms". It is basically a learning system, which follows the pattern of natural evolution. with this algorithm, the intelligent machine can evaluate the random blueprint created by its genetic algorithms for performing a given task. A rating system assesses each product and the high performing ones chosen for effecting changing the configurations in the original blueprint. It is also claimed that a single microchip can run thousand of such programs within seconds. Successful application of EHW has already been made in designing analogue circuits. Very soon, we are likely to have telephones using evolutionary hardware technology. Dr. Koza of Stanford has already made circuit design that can surpass the competence of man made designs.

Similar evolutionary shortcuts are also used in designing catalytic enzymes. Stephen Mayo and Daniel Bolon invented a computer program for bypassing evolution. Catalytic enzymes are required to conclude expeditiously the transient states in chemical reactions. Such enzymes are evolved by nature through complex processes of creating amino acid sequences that can accelerate a particular kind of chemical reaction. Dr. Mayo designed a program to evolve the enzyme that can fold into a shape suitable for the desired catalytic function. The number of amino acid combinations being enormous, normal computer calculation cannot conclude such tasks in short time. The researchers used a method that rejects many of the wrong answer right at the beginning. Dr. Mayo claims that they tested the catalytic power of the synthetically made enzyme, which was less than the naturally evolved one. However the performance is highly promising as it ends down billons of years of evolutionary changes to a few seconds on the computers. Chemical application of the new technique can convert proteins to enzymes capable of curing deadly diseases like AIDS.

Now we have machines capable of initiating human capabilities and synthetic enzymes that can bypass billions of years of evolutionary process. In this scenario, the mind that conceives the program also gets bypassed and marvelous new products emerge, which are beyond the ambit of original conceptions. It is definitely an exciting future that awaits the "mind watchers" who will find new kinds of mind having tremendous capabilities emerging from the ordinary matter. It seems that the genetic algorithm that created matter, whether we call it the God or cosmic vacuum has already lost the original inventions. Similarly, physical and cultural evolution has created new minds that are no longer identifiable as the natural product of billions of years of genetic changes. It is prudent to avoid any conclusion about the mind as many unpredictable developments await us in the unknown realm of matter.

PART FOUR

THE PUZZLE REASSEMBLED

'WISDOM TO TRANSCENDENCE'

The magician casts the spell
to creat non-existent objects & events.
When the spell is gone
the truth of reality returns to the senses.
We are all illusions
by knowing the reality of eternal existence.

(SHVETASHVATARA UPANISHAD)

One who knows the reality as
the omnipresent universal consciousness
achieves the ultimate peace & happiness,
As part of its infinate awareness.

(ATHARVA VEDA)

Established in my own grandeur,
I am beyond life & death,
Beyond all deeds & relations,
beyond even transcendence & conciousness.

(ASHTAVAKRA)

CHAPTER ELEVEN

THE SCIENTIFIC WORLDVIEW

THERE IS ONLY ONE GOD OF LOVE
WHO RESIDES IN ALL BEINGS.
HE PROJECTS THE COSMOS, MAINTAINS IT
AND FINALLY WITHDRAWS IT INTO HIMSELF
AT THE END OF TIME.

[SHVETASHVATARA UPANISHAD]

EACH ONE OF US
ADDS A LITTLE BIT TO THE
ULTIMATE KNOWLEDGE OF NATURE.
AND FROM ALL THE FACTS ASSEMBLED ARISES
THE GREAT GRANDEUR OF
THE UNIVERSE.

[ARISTOTLE]

"THAT'S ONE SMALL STEP FOR MAN, ONE GIANT LEAP
FOR MANKIND."

[NEIL ARMSTRONG ON HIS
LANDING ON MOON]

Smart Molecules

The essence of all that we have learnt from the scientific enquiries clearly points out that we are nothing but a bundle of neatly packed smart molecules. Intricately interconnected and chemically sensitive, they seem to work in unison to achieve a predetermined objective. Each molecule has a definite function to perform in the overall context of a live organism. The only goal of the organism appears to be successful replication or reproduction of its kind forever. We have even started calling the DNA that controls all activities of an organism "selfish" as its sole interest lies the perpetuation of the species rather than in the well-being of the parent organism. In sexual reproduction, the DNA is even satisfied with a fifty per cent share of the glory of posterity, since it ensures better quality offsprings. For this purpose, the DNA can even undergo the painful process of unzipping itself in the hope of resurrection in the smarter progeny.

But the basic question is what other nobler purpose can we attribute to the existence of DNA except simple reproduction? From the point of view of the DNA, life becomes meaningless once reproduction is successfully concluded. Nature is totally insensitive to the aesthetics of human existence that we assume to justify our short duration of stay on an insignificant planet. Science has already reached the limits of its explanations about the material world but it could not find any spiritual purpose for life. Since we are not satisfied with the picture that science has drawn for us, more explanations will have to be sought in the realm of speculative wisdom. Having explored all models and theories of science, let us now look elsewhere for the ultimate meaning of life.

Master Of All Matters

It is universally accepted that philosophy is the mother of all scientific inquiries into natural phenomena. From time immemorial, philosophers have been speculating on various kinds of natural phenomena and their causal relationships. Their description of the universe was based on sustained contemplations combined with observation of nature with a detached mind. We find two distinctly different approaches in the realm of speculative wisdom particularly on matters relating to the mind.

Eastern mystics explained the universe in a holistic perspective without probing deep into the minute details of the composition and relationships of any kind of matter. They tried to grasp the totality of the being by relating the individual perceptions to reach out to the ultimate reality underlying the visible manifestations of matter. In fact, they were in constant search of perpetual peace and happiness that material gains could not achieve. They wanted to understand the deepest mysteries of life to get at some lasting solutions for the miseries of existence.

But Western scientific thought, particularly in the last few centuries, took the road of reductionism to understand the truth of reality. They sought the description and causal relationships of all the components and building blocks of matter and life. According to reductionists, once the parts are analyzed and understood, the totality could be re-created by the simple mechanical process of synthesis.

The great discoveries of science in the recent past presented us an admirable description of matter and life. We have successfully understood most of the causal relationships of natural phenomena at different levels. It was reductionism that achieved all these astonishing breakthroughs that enabled us to reach the elementary particles and their dual modes of existence. Everything in the universe can now be explained in terms of electrons and quarks and the basic components of the four forces that hold matter together in a firm grip. Of course, we do not know what lies beyond the elementary particles, or what existed before the big bang, but for the time being, we can safely assume that whatever is worth knowing about the building blocks of matter has already been understood.

Similarly, our scientific inquiries of life gave us valuable insights on almost all the structural and functional aspects of complex life forms. Just as we reached the elementary particles of matter, we have succeeded in mapping the sequences in the DNA that carries the chemical instructions of life. We have some fairly accurate idea of the origin and evolution of life and shortly our genetic engineering skills may even rectify the inadvertent errors of nature. We may also create artificial intelligence and new species of plants and animals that can ensure us perennial supply of food and transplantable organs.

In addition to the unraveling of the DNA, two other major scientific breakthroughs that played key roles in giving us the much sought after mastery over matter are the general theory of relativity and quantum mechanics. The former explains almost all the visible phenomena in the universe giving us an accurate picture of galaxies, black holes and the expanding universe. It describes gravity on the basis of smooth, curved surfaces and forces are said to be created by the distortion of space and time. Although it presents the macrocosm with great clarity, general relativity fails completely when it reaches the micro world of particles or the center of a black hole where conditions similar to those before the big bang are said to exist.

Quantum Schizophrenia

The quantum theory has revealed successfully the mysterious subatomic world and all the known forces other than gravity. However, it falters in the realm of the macrocosm that contains bigger structures. It assumes that the entire stable material world can be explained in terms of the two fundamental particles called electrons and quarks. But the difficulty arises when our inadequate perception and linguistic skills fail to explain the quantum phenomena of superposition and dual states of existence. In the bizarre world of quarks and electrons, nothing happens in the orderly way of the organization of the external world. The uncertain behavior of elementary particles and their simultaneous existence in schizophrenic modes make us feel uneasy as if we are in a phantom world.

The standard model is the most successful application of quantum theory that can reproduce nature elegantly and enable us to make empirical predictions. It leads us to the undeniable conclusion that the wave function is the only reality in the world continually evolving in time. This evolution in time gives rise to new possibilities that are orderly and deterministic until an attempt is made to measure them. Then the wave function undergoes a transformation to create a particle. Until the observer measures an entity like the electron, it can exist anywhere in the waveform. It means that there are no electrons or protons in reality unless we go out to observe them. It means that no independent reality exists anywhere. We are always in a dilemma to describe the nature at that level with any certainty. But at macro level, the uncertainties disappear, giving us a stable reality of objective world accessible to our senses.

It is true that our conventional ideas about nature have undergone a sea change when the quantum world opened up new explanations about the unknown microcosm. Now, we know that without an observer, no phenomena can even occur at the subatomic level. With the observer and his measuring instrument, the wave function gives up its probabilistic existence in dual states to choose a reality. Extrapolating quantum theory to other phenomena, we can argue that all activities and events occur in the world only with the collapse of the wave function. It amounts to admitting the inevitable conclusion that only a conscious mind can create reality, which can exist without an observer. Our sensory inputs are discreet quanta of energy of the objective world. It is the conscious observation that collapses them into the perceptible realities of the physical world. In that sense, the universe is actually created within our consciousness as a sort of virtual reality and no objective reality can ever exist elsewhere. At the time of observation, the universe arises in the observer who is otherwise a mute witness of the eternal evolution of the waves of probabilistic existence.

Symphony Of Superstrings

Science has been eagerly looking for a unified theory incorporating gravity in quantum mechanics. In the quantum mode gravity is conceived as packets of energy called "gravitons". But when gravitons come together the theory fails to explain the resultant infinities. The only model that has somewhat succeeded in removing such infinities is the ten-dimensional superstring theory that includes all elementary particles and their interactions. It is assumed that a subatomic particle is one vibration of the superstring and possibilities are infinite for such particles and vibrations. The vibrations of an electron in different modes give rise to different particles. The laws of physics are the harmonies of the superstrings and the universe is described as a symphony of vibrating strings. The superstrings can also accommodate gravity and explain all the predictions of general relativity like black holes and expanding universe.

But the major problem with the superstring theory is that it is formulated in ten-dimensions. No doubt, it is easier to reproduce all forces by the addition of more dimensions. Even an eleventh dimension has recently been proposed to make this model more cohesive. The main objection to this theory is that all the solutions found so far do not match the known spectrum of subatomic particles. Attempts are being made to reduce the dimensions to a manageable level of eight or even six. Physicists hope to find even four-dimensional universes like ours in a "multiverse". That will once and forever solve the contentious issue of cosmic coincidences.

The reductionist worldview that elementary particles are eternal has now given way to the timelessness of the laws of physics embodied in these theories. It is difficult to explain the hierarchical structure of the universe in terms of a theory applicable exclusively to elementary particles. If a theory holds good for the macrocosm, it fails at the micro level. The elementary particles are the basic units out of which atoms are made. They further get organized into an enormous number of molecules that finally give rise to matter in different forms such as solids, crystals, liquids and gases. The variations in the structural organization of molecules create the diverse physical and chemical properties of matter. Subtle structural organizations are evident even at the highest level of galaxies that contain large number of clusters. We find innumerable complex processes and large variations in different structures everywhere in the universe. The most amazing structure is undoubtedly the massive neural network in the human brain.

Our present state of scientific knowledge of matter at different levels can reveal a somewhat accurate picture of physical reality. Science has made tremendous progress in describing elementary particles and their behavior in the strange logic of quantum mechanics. It has also succeeded in describing the interactions of large structures in terms of general relativity. The variety of complex natural phenomena and their causal relations have also been explained satisfactorily at different levels and states of matter. But the ultimate answers cannot be obtained from simple descriptions of matter or of forces and their causal relations unless the inquiry goes deeper into the philosophical realm of processes. We need to know many more things about the truth of reality including the purpose of its very existence.

No Rational Conclusions

From the uncertainties of the quantum world, let us go to the enigma of our biological existence. The great scientific discoveries of the origin and evolution of life show that the current models are inadequate to explain the complexities of biological systems. Several genetic and non-genetic features of life defy evolutionary explanations. But science cannot accept the idea of a predetermined design without getting some irrefutable proof. It is true that at the microscopic level, the complex biological system looks meticulously planned to the lowest level of molecular interactions. Evolutionary urges do not seem to work at molecular level but higher structures show plenty of evidences of gradual changes creating new species besides improving the old ones.

Molecular biology has now created a situation parallel to the quantum uncertainty that exists in the subatomic world. While quantum mechanics can describe the behavior of subatomic particles correctly, at higher levels of complex structures, it gives way to the general theory of relativity. Some basic changes are required for quantum theory to work at higher levels of matter. Similarly, molecular interactions might indicate some kind of intelligent design for achieving a predetermined goal. At higher levels, evolution can take over giving convincing explanations through random mutation and natural selection.

We reached the current level of knowledge through scientific enquiries to seek the truth of natural phenomena. Our knowledge may be incomplete on several basic issues but that does not mean that irrational ideas can substitute the great achievements of our rational wisdom. We have accumulated it through the relentless pursuit of the truth of reality. Our quest for more accurate and complete knowledge particularly about the mind should continue with the help of the tools created by modern technology. We have some vague ideas about the quantum coherence of the brain that might be the unknown process underlying the emergence of the mind. The binding of inputs and the non-local nature of the mind are closer to the duality and uncertainty of quantum mechanics. Quantum uncertainties can perhaps explain the inexplicable pathways of proteins that seem to move according to the invisible directions of an intelligent designer.

New Tools For Better Clues

It is a fact that the ultimate answer lies everywhere in nature tempting us to discover it with more dedicated efforts. Scientific pursuit of reality is a hide and seek game probably designed by nature to keep the intelligent observers occupied and amused. Without such interesting intellectual preoccupations, it would have been difficult to spend all the time in mundane affairs of life. The discoveries of a few secrets of nature make us sink deeper into the quicksand of more intriguing uncertainties. Nature seems to have set all the rules of the game and keenly watch the unfolding of the drama of our relentless chase of virtual realities.

While we reach some tentative conclusions that appear to be the ultimate answers, some new riddles arise falsifying all our previous knowledge. When we find that at quantum level the elementary particles exist in probabilities or potentialities and that the act of observation alone can materialize them, it is only the beginning of yet another fascinating new game. Just like quantum indeterminacy, all our questions seeking the ultimate answer of the meaning and purpose of the universe and life might also beget some probabilistic answers. This is the inherent defect in our persistence with the tools of reductionism. The true description of matter is only the starting point of the inquiry. For getting at the ultimate meaning of existence we may have to wait till the end of the voyage. In the next part of our exploration, let us use a different set of tools and rules. If we were genuinely interested in finding the truth of natural phenomena, we should not hesitate to go for even unconventional methods and means. All that we want is to get reliable knowledge about the reality of existence.

CHAPTER TWELVE

METAPHYSICAL SPECULATIONS

THE ENTIRE UNIVERSE ABIDES IN INFINITE TIME
PERVADING THE ENDLESS SPACE.
IT MAKES VISIBLE THE WORLD OF MATTER.
BUT
IGNORANT MORTALS SEE IT IN MANY FORMS
AND CALL IT DIFFERENT NAMES.
[ATHARVA VEDA]

THE IMMORTAL ENERGY OF THE UNIVERSE
LIES IN THE SOUL OF ALL MORTALS,
BLESSING THEIR ENDEAVORS
WITH SPIRITUAL RADIANCE
AND INTENSE LOVE.
IT IS THE SUPREME WISDOM
OF ALL EXISTENCE.
[RIG VEDA]

Origin Of Metaphysical Speculations

An important attribute of civilized human existence is its legacy of philosophical speculations on life and death. In fact, of cultural heritage embodied in various features of civilization like literature, art, architecture and great cities eventually give rise to a system of consistent and complex metaphysical thoughts. We have evidence of the early emergence of systematic speculations from the Mesopotamian, Egyptian, Minoan and Indus valley civilizations. The Chinese and Meso-American civilizations that appeared a little later developed their own home-brewed worldviews. The Sumerian Epic called "Gilgamesh" gives us some ideas about the earliest contemplations on life and death. It is probably written in about BC 2000 but rewritten in complete form again in BC 700 .

Gilgamesh, the hero of the epic, represents the first serious human challenge to the laws of the Gods. The epic contains many references to the obsessive reflections of Sumerians about the constant threat of floods. Sacrifices were offered in the magnificent temples for getting better crops. Gods represented the natural forces in human form.

The Mesopotamian metaphysical thoughts emerged from the quest to understand the cause of natural calamities like floods and droughts. The main purpose of their speculative reflections was to find effective ways and means to control natural forces. In Mesopotamian civilization we find deep concern about the life after death. They considered that all land belonged to God's and the King was only a mortal custodian of wealth. The Egyptian theology that followed the Sumerian traditions pondered more on the problems that humans encountered after death. They made great pyramids and mummified the dead in anticipation of an unbroken continuity of existence. They also offered sacrifices to propitiate the Gods for granting bounties of good crops and health. Most of these metaphysical thoughts centered around natural forces or life after death. They did not enter the realm of the origin of the universe or life. It was probably assumed that the Gods took proper care of all such complex matters.

Ancient Chinese civilization focused on ancestor-worship and performed elaborate rituals to propitiate nature Gods. Spirits were exhorted to act as intermediates for achieving the well being of the clan. Mountains and rivers were given the status of Gods and sacrifices were offered for their blessings. Confucian thoughts later on suggested many practical ideas for the proper functioning of social institutions. Greek religion was a complex amalgam of myths and mysticism encompassing the thoughts from other early civilizations. The Gods and Goddesses represented the good and bad qualities of humans in addition to having immense supernatural powers. Omens and oracles gave suitable spiritual advices to conduct the affairs of the mankind. They tried to understand the mysteries of nature through metaphysics, logic and mathematics. The era of intellectual activities of a rational kind actually began with Socrates. Around the 6th century BC, the Greek scholars started systematic enquiries in to the nature of the universe. Platonian thoughts consisted of speculative wisdom into the true cause of natural phenomena. Eventually the Western sciences emerged from the amalgam of Greek civilization ignoring the traditional concern for mythology and superstitious faiths.

Heritage Of Mystic Wisdom

In the previous chapter, we have seen that scientific explanations of matter do not give us a convincing purpose for existence. The biological form of matter is undoubtedly the most complex natural phenomena and humans are the magnificent culmination of the evolution of matter that began with the big bang. We have achieved the unique intelligence to penetrate into the deepest level of fundamental particles and forces. But all these advancements still give us only a fragmented picture of reality. We have no definite idea about the basic cause of the cosmic drama of creation.

Unlike the worldviews of science, the theological insights are not the outcome of unbiased inquiries into the various natural phenomena. They are based on social needs and aspirations of the people at a given period of time. But, scientific methodology transcends all cultural barriers and has universal appeal and application. It does not serve any particular cause as it only intends reveal the truth of reality. Some of the popular and widely practiced religions have successfully got out of the constraints of their initial cultural milieu and motives. But they still retain the flavor of the initial tribal settings. The leading world religions that reached faraway shores in their zeal to proselytize have adapted to the native customs and cultures. Buddhism, Islam, Christianity and Hinduism are the major religions that spread far and wide despite their humble origins in obscure places.

Creator Identified

The common assumption in all religions is a supernatural entity who created life and universe. The believers accept without doubt whatever purpose is indicated in the Holy Scriptures for the creation of the universe. The super natural qualities of a creator are described differently depending upon the requirements of the faith and other spiritual compulsions. The earliest monistic conception of a Supreme Being is in the

"Upanishad"s, which are the philosophical essence underlying the four great Hindu Vedas. Vedic scholars consider that they belong to the period of about BC 2000.

The innumerable sages of ancient India in their meditative reflections envisioned the unique concept of the Supreme Self. They concluded consciousness as the integral part of the Supreme Reality existing in every individual self and even in every form of matter in the universe. The omnipresent entity that they envisaged is entirely different from the plethora of Gods and Goddesses now adoring the Hindu pantheon. They called the Supreme Reality 'Brahman' and the individual self was the 'Atman' or Soul. The individual soul was taken as a localized reflection of the Supreme Reality or the universal consciousness.

According to the Vedic mystics, the realization of the reality of supreme self that unites the entire universe is the ultimate goal of humans who desire to achieve lasting peace and happiness. This supreme reality that creates all forms of existence is not accessible through rituals or other religious practices. The self is the essence of reality existing in all beings that can be realized only with sustained meditation and abstinence from sense-related activities. In the ultimate state of awareness, the distinction between the inner self and Supreme Reality completely disappears and we get a glimpse of the truth of reality embedded in our own physical body. The final experience of enlightenment is the awareness that the supreme self unites everything in the universe as the essence of consciousness in all forms of matter.

By reaching the state of supreme awareness through meditation, we come to the end of our quest for the true knowledge of existence. Pure joy arises from the realization that we are essentially an integral part of the eternal existence of consciousness. In this vision, all separateness dissolves and we see our own selves as the substratum in every being. Self-realization is a spiritual experience that can be reached only in deep meditation with total detachment. Once it is achieved, all desires, distinctions and dichotomies disappear from our thoughts and actions. There is neither love nor hate; past or present; good or bad as all feelings merge into the inseparable totality of universal consciousness. Even knowledge becomes redundant, as the knower can no longer be differentiated from the awareness of the object of knowledge.

Aftermath Of Self-Realization

What we get after self-realization is the exquisite experience of undifferentiated unity with all beings. It gives us the compassionate wisdom to be kind and truthful and to act with self-restraint. The selfish motives that create the urge for more material possessions and power become less compelling than before. The individual self transcends into the radiant splendor of the Supreme Reality gaining the feelings of love and kindness toward all creatures. Separate identity is no more relevant as one merges spontaneously and irretrievably in the unified awareness of the Supreme Self.

Vedic Sages envisioned the total dissolution of the individual self when one reaches the fourth and final stage of consciousness. It is called "Turiya" or the "fourth" that lies beyond the consciousness in waking, dreaming and sleeping states. By reaching the fourth state, we get "ultimate liberation" or "release from all earthly bonds". It brings to an end all searches for the meaning and purpose of life. The true knowledge that "I am the universe" (Aham Brahmasmi) and "you are that" ("Tat Twam Asi") became the abiding faith of the enlightened ones. The great mystics who reached the fourth state of consciousness through meditative reflections found that it is the one and only spiritual achievement worthy of all intellectual pursuits.

Supreme Reality

Apart from the philosophical reflections of self in the Upanishads, the most ancient concept of creation is described in the Hindu scripture called "Rig Veda". It is assumed that the universe was created from a state of potential that arose from some kind of completeness like infinity. The whole reality, matter, forces and energy were embedded in the original energy, which the Upanishads call "sat". It is comparable to DNA or a seed that contains all potential for creation. Everything in the universe arose as manifestations of this single, formless and all encompassing entity. It is the Supreme Reality that preceded all existence and beyond time, space and all other conceivable dimensions. The universe is just one of its manifestations and it pervades in everything, everywhere with infinite powers and properties far above our capacity for comprehension.

Another specific description of creation is given in the "Chandogya Upanishad" which is the philosophical essence of "Sama Veda". It is in the form of a dialogue between a father and his 24-year-old son who wanted to know more about the Supreme Self. The dialogue reproduced below reveals the profound vision of the mystics who traced the creation of the universe to the Supreme Reality.

"There was only the Supreme Being in the beginning,
With no second or third.
He brought out the entire cosmos from himself, and entered into all beings.
As the innermost self
He is the truth, and the Supreme Reality,
And my son you are that and nothing else,"

The son then insists upon further clarification about the concept of self, which is given in the following verses:

"When we enter dreamless sleep,
We are one with the Supreme Self.
When death takes the self out of the body,
The body dies but the self survives.
The Supreme Self is the hidden essence of the seed,
From which the whole tree grows,
And spreads itself everywhere.
He is omnipotent, omnipresent and omniscient,
All living and non-living matter
Reflect his eternal glory of existence."

In a later Upanishad called "Svetashavatara" belonging to "Yajur Veda" the mystics try to give the comprehensive meaning and purpose of human life. They examine several tentative answers but finally prescribe a pathfinder to reach the ultimate goal of self-realization.

"The body and mind should together concentrate
To see the Lord of Life dwelling in all beings,
We should try with devotion to reach,
The Lord through blissful meditation.
He is the cause of all cosmos and he alone
Can relieve you of all miseries and
The endless cycles of Karma for ever."

The modern followers of Vedic philosophy try to draw parallels between such explanations of genesis and scientific descriptions of the initial conditions. For our purposes such analogies are not relevant, as we are not seeking to establish the superiority of science or religion. We are not interested in the merits and demerits of different schools of thoughts as all that matters to us here is to find of the truth of reality irrespective of the means to reach it.

The mystics of Vedic tradition did possess the uncanny wisdom to visualize the act of creation. The dark primordial world visualized in the "Rig Veda" is equivalent to the concept of singularity. The idea of a Supreme Being that existed before the creation but became manifest thereafter, shows that spiritual contemplation based on observation can grasp the truth of reality. It was achieved without the aid of scientific knowledge and tools that now enhance our perception. Only an intelligent observer can appreciate the fact that the universe is one of the manifestations of the non-existent. If we accept the quantum theory, it is the collapse of the wave function of the non-existent that would have created the reality of the phenomenal world.

Cosmic Vacuum

Buddha emerged as a great spiritual teacher at the end of the Vedic period (BC 563-483). He challenged the traditional Hindu belief in the multitude of Gods and the expensive rituals required to propitiate them. He traced the problems of mankind to the wrong practices of society and our greed and ambition to amass wealth and power. Buddhism envisaged some sort of cosmic vaccum as the initial conditions and denied the role or existence of any supernatural entity. Initially, it began as a scientific search for truth discarding irrational faiths and practices. Buddha rationally analyzed social and individual problems and identified their causal relationships. He pointed out an eightfold path to overcome the perennial human miseries arising out of desires and passions.

Buddhism conceived the beginning of the universe in a void called Shunyata. It is said to be a combined state of non-existence and existence. We can assume it as the totality of everything without any differentiation into animate or inanimate matter. The Buddhist concept of "nirvana" indicates awareness with complete detachment, permanence, stability and incomprehensibility. The blissful state of "Nirvana" can be attained by the realization of the true nature of self and causal knowledge of existence. In the original Buddhist philosophy, the supreme reality that transcends all changes is not any entity but a process of achieving detachment from all desires. It is not the being but the cessation of all changes, forms and properties. We can only compare it with the infinite singularity or quantum vacuum of the initial conditions that evolved into matter and forces after the Big Bang. Buddhism considers that the ultimate goal of humanity is to reach the void, which is nothing other than pure consciousness.

An important feature of Buddhism is the firm faith in the virtue of the rejection of all passions, desires and attachments. Eternal wisdom arises in the human mind when it breaks all such bondages. The supreme state of "Nirvana" is no God or creator and it can only be reached by following the noble paths to liberate the mind from the tyranny of senses. "Tathagata" that means "suchness" is the only reality, which is also called "dharma" or "wisdom". Strangely, Buddhism also reaches the same vedic conclusion that consciousness is the ultimate truth of reality.

Yin And Yang

The "Tao Te Ching", presumably written by Lao Tzu, is the basic book of Chinese spiritual wisdom. It is the "way" or the rhythm of the universe. Tao does not indicate the presence of any ultimate reality unlike in the deep metaphysical concepts of Hinduism or Buddhism. It is assumed to be the womb from which all life arises and to return after death. Tao also show the correct path for leading a righteous life. The basic premise of

Tao as an inactive power is equivalent to the Buddhist concept of Nirvana and the Vedic idea of Supreme Reality. Tao assumes that something that is the mother of many things mysteriously formed in the silence and void before the creation of heaven and earth.

Another basic assumption in the Chinese metaphysical thought is the interplay of two opposite forces called the "Yin" and the "Yang". The "Yin" is the feminine quality in nature and the "Yang" is the symbol of masculinity. The right proportion of the opposite but complementary forces is required to make a well-balanced human being. The harmonious and mutually dependent relationship of the opposites preserves the universe and all forms of life. In Chinese thoughts, we find the interplay of opposite forces and the Tao instead of the concept of any Supreme Being, Formulation of such practical ideas maintained peace and harmony in China in spite of the massive political upheavals.

The great practical wisdom of Confucianism is the main pillar Chinese way of life. While retaining the ancient practices of ancestral worship, Confucius emphasized the principle of Ken, which is a special kind of force binding the heaven, earth and all structures in the cosmos. Humanity is an integral part of the cosmos and all our activities relate to some deeper reality. Confucian wisdom was intended to create close family ties and more meaningful social life based on mutual respect and humility. Unlike the Vedic and Buddhist thoughts, Chinese philosophy does not ask people to shun attachment and desire for material gains. They are more concerned about improving the quality of the earthly existence rather than seeking the truth of ultimate reality.

Islam

Several common metaphysical thoughts link the conceptual framework of Judaism, Islam and Christianity. All of them believe in a supreme entity who created the universe and in whom all the values converged. The Book of Genesis says that in the beginning the earth was some sort of void a definite without form. Utter darkness prevailed over the abyss and then God light from darkness. After the creation of the heavens and the earth, God reviewed everything and saw that it was pretty good. Although Judaism and Islam arose from tribal societies, both had the same idea of one God. They repose faith in the God's will revealed in the holy books.

Islam emerged as a distinct faith after the battle of Mecca. In Islam, God demands complete submission from the followers. He is perceived as merciful and compassionate to the faithful but angry and ruthless toward all non-believers. The infidels are invariably condemned to the misery of eternal torture in hell. Islam does not tolerate any form of polytheism and believers are all united in their faith in one God and his commands as reveled in the sacred book. The enemies of God are those who refuse to follow the holy path of Islam, which is elaborated in great details in the Holy Scriptures. According to Islam, Allah, the Great, created the world which is perfect in all respects. We cannot find any fault with God's creations so long as they live according to the divine will.

Judaism And Christianity

Judaism began as a violent, tribal religion with Yahweh as the God at whose behest the armies of Israel destroyed the people of Palestine. Moses created a new religion with the concept of a creator who is also the author of the moral law for humanity. Satan is the opposite of God and an independent power center of all the evil in the universe. The concept of the evil force creates the moral dualism that leads the righteous to God's way and the wicked into the trap of the devil. The vision of eternal misery of the non-believers keep people on the right track and the institutionalized religion ensured that the faithful are not led astray. In Jewish mysticism, through the concept of Kabala, moral dualism is transcended to perceive the supreme reality. There are several forms and beings that emerge from the ten spheres of divine manifestations. Our universe is the derivation from a kind of spiritual universe and it is the manifestation of the infinite wisdom of God.

In course of time, Christianity became a totally independent religion cutting away from the patronage of Judaism. Jesus of Nazareth, a Jew who was crucified by the Roman rulers, is the central figure on whom all variants of this major religion converge. Christianity is now the leading world religion with maximum number of followers. It holds that the divine reality or the absolute truth is made accessible to human consciousness through concrete symbols or signs. These symbols are not comprehensible to non-believers. The supreme reality is revealed in the flesh and blood of a human being who, in spite of the attempts of evil forces, rose to eternal life in the flesh. God expresses his infinite wisdom in the structure of the universe through the Holy Spirit or divine energy. The father is the source of all being and the Holy Spirit is the eternal energy of love. The wisdom of God is fully revealed in the human life of Jesus Christ.

The Gospels of the life of Jesus were initially written in the second half of the first century AD. They were in Greek and then got translated into Aramaic, a dialect, which Jesus and disciples spoke. The first ten chapters are taken from Mark and the teachings of Jesus are given by Luke. It is the fourth Gospel that gives the universal wisdom of love conceptualized in Jesus. Every event in the life of Jesus has a symbolic meaning that expresses the wisdom of the God. The life of Jesus is the ultimate divine wisdom that God presented to humanity. The fourth Gospel reveals the unique relationship between Jesus and the God.

Christianity did not conceive the act of creation of the universe as an isolated or unintended incident. It is created in accordance with the will of God and the existence of all forms of life is an expression of God's grace. Like Jesus, those who follow the path of righteousness enter into a unique relationship with God. The Holy Spirit is the source of all wisdom and goodness. It is also considered as the love that sustains the world with compassion, mercy and forgiveness. The God is the ultimate custodian who controls the universe with order and care. Christianity lays more emphasis on a good and compassionate worldly life that follows the path of love in devotion to God. It does not go deep into the casuses of genesis as the entire world is conceived to be the outcome of the infinite compassion of the God.

Common Spiritual Legacy

The common feature of all major religions is a supreme being who created the universe and life. The concept of the

"Brahman" of Hinduism, the "Shunyata" of Buddhism and the "Tao" of the Chinese, and the "Allah" of Islam are all examples of identical approaches in the contemplation of conscious humans irrespective of different cultural and temporal contexts. The idea of a creator with infinite powers probably serves our social need to keep people on the path of righteousness. While the big bang gives us a rational version of creation, it has not yet succeeded in replacing the concept of a Supreme Being. Science has clearly failed to unlock the mystery of cosmic coincidences and evolution of life. In spite of all the accurate knowledge we have so far accumulated no convincing scientific explanation available to the common man to put his faith in its rational wisdom.

The great discoveries of science that enhance of our perception have not yet given acceptable answers to the intriguing ultimate question of the purpose of existence. While theological explanations can safely attribute all coincidences to a Supreme Being, science cannot afford such simplifying assumptions. It has not yet developed the technology to replicate the act of creation to test the hypothesis that a quantum vacuum can give birth to an inflating universe. The validity of scientific knowledge is evident in the vast multitude of technological achievements. Undoubtedly, we are now much more comfortable with all new appliances than in the past. But for the common man, in the absence of a spiritually fulfilling alternative rational knowledge cannot replace his sustaining faith in a Supreme Being. Such a rational model will be presented after we examine the unique concept of universal consciousness propounded by an ancient Indian mystic called "Ashtavakra".

CHAPTER THIRTEEN

GRANDEUR OF CONSCIOUSNESS

KNOWLEDGE, SCRIPTURES AND DISCOURSES,
CANNOT DISCLOSE THE SOURCE OF SELF.
SEARCH FOR IT IN EARNEST DEVOTION,
BY FOLLOWING THE RIGHT DISCIPLINE.
IT IS THE LORD OF LOVE THAT UNITES
ALL BEINGS IN HIS ETERNAL WISDOM,
SEEKER OF TRUE KNOWLEDGE LOSES THE SELF
BUT GAINS THE KNOWLEDGE OF EXISTENCE.

[MUNDAKA UPANISHAD]

WITH THE REALIZATION OF SELF
WE TRANSCEND EXISTENCE AND NON-EXISTENCE.
ALL DUALITY DISAPPEARS,
IN THE PUREST OF VISION OF UNIVERSAL
CONSCIOUSNESS.

[ASHTAVAKRA GITA]

Discovery Of Self

Our forays into the realm of the latest scientific knowledge provided no rational explanation to the irreducible nature of the mind. It is evidently beyond the control of the laws of physics that governs the material world. When we come to the speculative explanation of the mind. The earliest reference is found in the Upanishads composed by Indo-Aryan mystics in about BC 2000. Their search for God and the meaning and purpose of life concluded in the great discovery that self is an integral part of "Brahman" or pure universal consciousness. They identified the self in all beings as the essence of reality and found the ultimate truth of life in pure consciousness. The mystics reached the rational knowledge of self through meditation, which minimizes body awareness. It would have given them the vision of unity of existence of all beings in the Supreme Reality of consciousness. In this ultimate awareness, all individual identities are dissolved forever along with the causes of human miseries.

In spite of these astounding rational revelations, blind faith in a multitude of Gods continued to control life in the early Indo-Aryan settlements. "Ashtavakra", a great scholar of consciousness, devoted his entire life to explain this concept in a secular and logical manner. "Ashtavakra Geetha" or "the song of the supreme self" contains the dialogues between the sage and his royal disciple called Janaka. Although, we find several references to self in the "Upanishads", a complete analysis of consciousness is seen only in "Ashtavakra Geetha". The sage conceives consciousness as the embodiment of all mental activities like thoughts, emotional experiences, ego and the unconscious tendencies of the mind.

He propounded that the self is the essence of consciousness embedded in the core of the human mind. It would become evident to us only when the illusion or "maya" that binds ordinary matter with biological matter is finally dispelled by true knowledge. Self-realization is the ultimate achievement that can remove the fear of death and all other miseries of life from the mind forever. To reach this state of awareness the, Vedic scholars suggested the path of meditation. But Ashtavakra found that self can be realized only by internalization of the true knowledge of reality by the seeker. The fact that the self is only the reflection of universal consciousness and that it is present in all beings has to be accepted beyond doubt for reaching self-realization. Religious practices and meditation can give us only an occasional glimpse of the real self. Our own existence should become an inseparable part of the eternal splendor of consciousness to remove all inherited ignorances of identity, faith and other illusions. In short, it is true knowledge alone that can show us the path to the immortal existence of universal consciousness.

The greatest contribution of Ashtavakra is his single-minded pursuit of pure consciousness as the sole cause and effect of all existence. He conceived self as something for beyond all physical attributes and qualities of the phenomenal world. The self is the individualized form of universal consciousness that materializes the phenomenal world in our perception. Universal consciousness that embodies all reality in its ambit is the only eternal truth of existence. It brings to light the physical reality including our biological life and also the capacity to conceptualize the self. The self is actually an extension of cosmic consciousness, which temporarily abides in the body made of biological matter. The realization of the unity of all kinds of matter in consciousness removes the wrong notions of dualities and individual differences.

We experience the objective world when it is projected to the conscious self. Consciousness is actually the interface between the physical and non-physical dimensions. It creates the illusion that what we perceive through our senses is the actual reality. The conscious self that experiences everything for and on behalf of the body is beyond all definitions and descriptions applicable to biological or other forms of matter. Its comprehensive, non-physical nature can be understood only by visualizing the broad and all-inclusive entity of "Brahman" or Universal Consciousness. The phenomenal world of matter and forces has no relevance to self, which is inseparable from the eternal reality of consciousness. The realization that the self is only the extension of universal consciousness gives us a totally different perspective of life.

Dichotomies Disappear

After establishing the self in universal consciousness, Ashtavakra proceeds in a systematic manner to explain the application of this new knowledge in life. At the very outset of the dialogues, he advises the disciple to avoid sense related objects and be straightforward, compassionate and truthful. It is pertinent to note here that identification of individual self as a part of universal consciousness does not mean that we are free from all the moral and social responsibilities and constraints. Knowledge of self is not a license to do whatever the body desires. A truly enlightened person would automatically detach himself from all pleasure-seeking activities. When the self is envisioned as the embodiment of pure consciousness capable of only witnessing the events and objects in the world, the greed for material wealth spontaneously vanish from the mind. The physical body becomes a transient medium with the self as a window to experience the external world. The body is seen as a simple manifestation of ordinary matter, with a false identity and pleasure-seeking tendencies created by the illusions of the mind.

Once the true nature of the body identity is understood, all individual differences would disappear from our thoughts. Nationality, race, caste or creed are creations of the mind to put artificial barriers between the same kinds of biological matter. All such feelings arise from the misconceived perception that attributes non-existent qualities to the physical body and environment. Emotions like pleasure, pain, hatred and love are all derived from the unreal physical experiences of the body and not the true expressions of the self. The self is the neutral witness in all beings to enable us to perceive the existence of matter in different forms.

Mind Is A Magician

Ashtavakra asserts that the mind is a magician creating innumerable illusions to make us feel a part of the physical body. Several qualities like intelligence and free will are normally attributed to a person as his mental faculties. But the fact is that the conscious self is just a witness and not the performer of any physical deed. In fact, it is the physical body that acts and enjoys the fruits of action. The self is just a concept emerging from a conscious human brain to perceive the world. The egoistic feelings attributed to the mind by the ignorance of reality are actually the pleasure-seeking tendencies of the physical body. The self is only the reflection of the consciousness that permeates everywhere in the universe. It is the essence of some sort of unknown intelligence. By the illusion created by ignorance, we connect the self to the body and crave for sense-related objects of pleasure. Similarly the body avoids situations perceived as potentially dangerous and capable of giving pain. In his exposition of the concept of consciousness, Ashtavakra summarizes the great saga of all kinds of existence.

It follows that the self is not affected by the changes in the phenomenal world of matter, as its pure intelligence is immutable. The universe arises and subsides in the self as waves appear and disappear in the ocean. But the fact remains that the ocean is always unperturbed. The ego is a body related concept to differentiate it from the external world so that the ignorant ones can feel that the actions actually emanate from an identified physical source. The self only illuminates the world to a physical body and does nothing more than to sustain the illusion of an egocentric existence. Existence is, in fact, an assumption of the mind emerging from its perception of some material differences between the physical body and its immediate surroundings. It enables the body to correlate the experiences of the external world as if they actually happened to it.

The mind is also capable creating the illusions of having unique thoughts and emotions. The self has no qualities other than pure consciousness and it is not a part of the physical world of biological or non-biological matter. The delusion of self emerges from body attachment with out any external causal relationships. It may probably arise when the complex computing processes in the brain reach a high degree of coherence. The self gives the body a glimpse of the universe through consciousness like the lens imprints the physical world on a film in the camera. The physical world is neither the lens nor the film on which a picture is recorded. All that a mechanical device or medium can do is to make things visible to the senses. The self catches the reflection of reality in a physical body and retains it in memory for a finite period of time. Since it does not belong to the body, the mind that embodies the self survives the death of biological matter. The self cannot make any differentiation between classes or categories like knower, knowledge and the object of knowledge. It exists beyond the illusions of bondage and goal of salvation in the integrated domain of universal consciousness.

Self In All And All In Self

Once the truth of reality removes all misconceptions about self, the mind spontaneously becomes a part of the eternal wisdom of universal consciousness. This realization extends ordinary awareness to reach the unbroken unity with the external world. The objects that give sensory gratification no longer hold any attraction for an enlightened person. His needs for material possessions vanishes and body-related actions gradually subside to the barest minimum. The self realizes that all beings are embodied in it and it is also present in everything in the universe. It cannot be tied down to any particular physical object like the body, which is only seen as a temporary abode of the mind. The desire for sensory inputs of a particular kind or close physical proximity of other persons becomes less persistent. The vision of eternal wisdom of the unity of existence gives us freedom from all attachments and removes the mind-body distinction. Other polarities like happiness and unhappiness, pleasure and pain are also slowly removed with the knowledge that all such experiences are transient states of body. The true-knowledge of self creates the ultimate awareness that self is in all and all is in self.

Life After Self-Realization

After self-realization existence becomes a spontaneous dream without any desire for worldly possessions or pleasing experiences. The true knowledge releases the mind from all disturbances created by thoughts and emotions. It makes one fearless and full of love and kindness toward all forms of matter. The wise man who knows this truth treats his own body as if it belongs to another person. He is fully convinced that death can destroy only the physical body and not the self that belongs to the eternal wisdom of cosmic consciousness.

On the other hand, the ignorance of the truth of reality engenders endless miseries arising out of the intense greed for worldly possessions. The mind attached firmly to body awareness considers the self as his own exclusive identity. Everything that happens to the body becomes the nagging burden of the mind. Meditation or religious practices may prepare the body to reach a state of readiness to realize the self. But awareness of the true nature of the self happens only when knowledge removes the ignorance of reality. Once the dualities of emotions and thoughts are united in the perception of the self, the only feelings that can remain in the mind are compassion, contentment, truthfulness, forgiveness and straightforwardness. These are the qualities that emanate from the mind that can see its own reflection in every being. Ordinary persons succumb to the endless demands of pleasure-seeking physical body. But the enlightened one is free from all attachments and enjoys eternal existence in pure consciousness.

Supreme Reality Of Consciousness

When we accept universal consciousness as the Supreme Reality and the self as its integral part, the feeling of all separateness vanishes from the mind. In "Brihandaranyaka Upanishad", the consequence of such deep realization is clearly brought out in a dialogue between sage Yajnavalkya and his wife Maitreyi:

> "When the self is realized in the indivisible unity of life, there can be no separate sight, sound, smell or speech. No separate thought or knowledge can exist when separateness itself disappears and the knower and knowledge becomes one in the unity of perception."

The Supreme Reality is the pure intelligence that brings the phenomenal world into our perception. As we are normally driven by the needs of the physical body, the important first step is to, understand that the mind-body duality is just an illusion. The intelligent appreciation of the Supreme Reality of consciousness removes the misconceptions of all dualities and polarities including the separate identity of the body.

The dissolution of the self ushers in a sense of benign detachment from the objective world. The relevance of the physical body diminishes when the mind is united with the Supreme Reality. The visible universe becomes an integral part the self, which loses the individual identity. Ashtavakra describes the process of dissolution of self in several illustrative metaphors. The Supreme Reality is compared to the infinite space and the physical body to an earthen pot contains the space. Eternal space exists both inside and outside the pot in spite of the existence of the pot. The individual self is only the space enclosed temporarily in the earthen pot and it neither belongs to the pot nor does it become inseparable from the infinite space. Similarly, the Supreme Reality of consciousness is compared to the ocean in which innumerable individual selves arise like waves. What happens to the waves is of no concern to the ocean as all kinds of waves are only the extensions of the ocean in different shapes and sizes. They all ultimately return to the ocean after the physical disturbances that cause them to rise subside. The individual wave or self has no separate existence outside the ocean of consciousness.

Once the true nature of self is understood, there is no need for renunciation or acceptance of anything in life. Nothing matters to the self after it casts away the separate body-based identity, which is the source of all miseries. The concept of a God or creator also becomes redundant once the entire universe is accepted as the manifestation of the pure intelligence of consciousness. The same consciousness is the God that gives rise to all the metaphysical thoughts. In fact, with the acceptance of this ultimate truth, the individual self reaches the serene state where actions like worship, renunciation, acceptance, love and hate become expressions of ignorance. Life becomes meaningful only when it perceives unity with the eternal existence of the Supreme Reality. This true knowledge settles all disturbances created by egocentric thoughts and emotions. Even the physical body attains perfect serenity, as it is not perturbed by self-related thoughts. Nothing further can be gained in life even if we acquire more knowledge or wealth, as the realization of the ultimate truth of Reality puts an end to further intellectual and material pursuits.

We can get the full impact of the liberated self, only when the mind is unbound from the physical body. Bondage is created when the mind gets a feeling of separate identity through the sense organs that perceive the phenomenal world. Experience of happiness, anger, pain, hatred and all other feelings arise when sense organs in the brain convey them to the conscious self. Liberation of the self from this bondage is possible only when the mind gets detached from these experiences and the assumptions like "I-ness" are completely extinguished with knowledge. The truly liberated self becomes totally indifferent to the changes in the phenomenal world, which are illusions created by the mind that sustains as body-awareness.

Indifference But Not Insensitivity

But indifference to the phenomenal world does not mean total insensitivity to life around us. It only means the correct perspective of equal mindedness to all objects or lack of attachment to anything in particular. A truly indifferent person has no passion for enjoyment of life or for its rejection. He does not differentiate between objects of enjoyment and those that are pain inducing. Everything in the world holds the same appeal, as awareness is undifferentiated between the qualities of objects. When all thoughts converge on consciousness, the cause of mental conflicts related to the gain or loss simply disappear leaving the self at total peace with the phenomenal world.

The enlightened self is not at all affected by the passage of time or ageing. He is fully content with the awareness that self transcends all temporal and spatial dimensions. Perfect tranquility is established in the mind and body when dichotomies and differences of opinion cease to affect the indifferent self. He does not get into any argument or debate with anyone, as he abides in the totality of pure intelligence. No spiritual training or initiation is required for him or practices like meditation to reach any goal of life. The self is its own pathfinder to the Supreme reality of consciousness and no Guru or god man can show him the wisdom of existence. In fact, once we know all about consciousness secrets of nature will no more be worth any further probe.

In the phenomenal world, we find changes constantly occurring in various objects. These changes are only fluctuations in matter in their primary or secondary forms like atoms and molecules. Such changes cannot affect the basic character of the self that is pure consciousness and no physical matter. The self is not made of biological or inanimate matter to crave for the objects of the phenomenal world. All the wealth in the world cannot create the lasting peace that comes with the ultimate realization that the eternal truth of existence is consciousness.

When the liberated mind is firmly united with the Supreme Self, the body becomes less amenable to the fluctuations in the material world. The self is now no more concerned with the fate of a particular configuration of biological or inanimate matter at any point of time. Any kind of purposeful activity distracts the self from its peaceful existence in the wisdom of consciousness. More than the minimum routine activities of life can cause disturbances to the serene self. The enlightened one avoids spontaneously all activities, which are not essentially required for the maintenance of body functions. He performs normal functions necessary to discharge the moral responsibilities to the family and society while abstaining from self related activities.

Meditation Is No Pathfinder

To take the mind out of mundane worldly affairs so as to reach the goal of universal consciousness, one has to first transcend the illusory perception of body awareness. Two types of meditations are generally suggested to reach the realm of super consciousness. In concentrated meditation, attention is focused on a particular thought or object that could presumably bring about transcendence by excluding all other sensory inputs and thoughts. But the concentration required in focusing the mind demands tremendous efforts that distract the self from the objective of self-realization. In fact, detachment cannot come through any taxing mental activity like concentration.

In the second type of meditation, we try to withdraw the mind from all sense objects and thoughts. But such intentional inaction creates more fleeting thoughts and negative feelings. The mind automatically leaves all attractions and distractions of the phenomenal world only when it internalizes the rational wisdom that consciousness is the only truth of reality. We cannot acquire it through any physical efforts or mental labor. Sustained speculative reflections on the truth of reality alone can lead us to the desirable state of self-realization. Only true knowledge can be the pathfinder to the eventual enlightenment of self.

Bliss Of True Knowledge

While our physical body and the material world are created out of matter, the Supreme Self existed before the beginning of the universe. The unborn Supreme Self is the intelligent energy that pervades the entire universe and is inherent in all objects. Whatever happens in the world are changes in the forms of matter brought out by the interaction of the physical laws of nature. They do not affect the qualities of the immutable Supreme Self embedded in all forms of matter. All rules and patterns are qualities emerging from the properties of the original complexity. We are capable of understanding only a limited range of the rules of nature through the consciousness that reveals to us some features of reality.

The final outcome of self-realization is a spontaneous and simple attitude to life. The consequential changes in the lifestyle would reduce physical activities to the barest minimum. The enlightened self becomes neutral to the results of his own action and resists all unreasonable demands of the body. The fluctuations in fortunes or pleasure and pain in different circumstances do not affect the self. But neutrality does not mean total neglect of the physical needs of the body. If the essential functions are ignored, the body will become sick and unfit. Consequently, the rhythm of life will be upset, causing serious distractions to the self, abiding in the bliss of universal consciousness. So long as the mind resides in the physical body, it has to ensure perfect health to avoid any cause for disturbance. Similarly, one should discharge all essential social and family obligations without making strenuous efforts to amass wealth by unfair means.

With the realization that consciousness is the eternal reality, all egocentric thoughts slowly leave the mind. Empowered with the new vision, one likes to live only within his means and through fair methods. Even in his waking state, his existence is only an enjoyable dream. His unwanted memories get obliterated and perception becomes an act of effortless physical process rather than focused attention. The burden of life slowly melts away as he gets detached from wealth, friends and even family. He is left with no desire for bondage or liberation, nor does he care for any salvation from material life. All misconceived notions about the physical body and its fortunes in the phenomenal world will vanish from the mind forever.

Once true knowledge of reality enters the mind, an eloquent person becomes silent and stops all unnecessary activities. Those who are keen to enjoy the pleasures of the phenomenal world should avoid such knowledge that creates feeling of detachment. The sudden realization that the self is neither the doer nor the enjoyer, could bring about drastic changes in an active person. Only matured and balanced persons who can get the benefit of true awareness without causing damage to the worldly life and society should access such knowledge. In fact, it is more desirable to reach this ultimate truth after discharging essential social and family obligations and all moral responsibilities. Otherwise, it can affect the very survival of the human species, which solely depends upon the illusion that it is the self that performs all physical functions. If all individuals lose the sense of separate identity, life will become more chaotic and uncontrollable.

We have a rich legacy of ideas, explanations and opinions about the meaning and purpose of life in the overall context of its evolution in the universe. But the undeniable fact is that the entire world of existence becomes perceptible only when we become aware of it through consciousness. The genuinely enlightened man realizes this ultimate truth that consciousness encompasses all ideas and opinions, divisions and differences experienced by the mind. The fact is that nothing can exist independent of consciousness, which transcends all manifestations of matter including us. It permeates the universe and all forms of matter emanate from it without any initial differentiation. The intelligent energy that must have existed eternally in the universe is nothing but pure consciousness. We realize that the self, which, is a kind of proto consciousness abides in every individual as the reflection of cosmic consciousness. Its wisdom is beyond our comprehension, as our intelligence is derived from it. The life long pursuit of knowledge therefore ends in the realization of the supreme wisdom of universal consciousness.

The joy of realizing the true knowledge of existence is the unique experience of enlightenment. Buddha and many other mystics probably reached it through meditative reflections. The self is the silent and inactive witness of everything that arises in the mind from the physical processes in the brain. The wise ones recognize it as a reflection of the Supreme Self of universal consciousness. In short, one begins to live in total peace and harmony with nature and fellow beings when it is know that the entire phenomenal world is a manifestation of consciousness. We can call it more rationally as intelligent energy or the believers can even take it as the God or whatever suitable terminology they might find for identifying this concept. The qualities that we attribute to it only show our ignorance of the inexplicable nature of consciousness. The truth of reality should enable us to perceive the objective world correctly without getting confused by the innumerable illusions created by the transient images projected from the brain.

It seems that what Ashtavakra wants us to learn from his vision is the practical wisdom of compassion, straightforwardness and simplemindedness. The true knowledge should make us enjoy every moment of existence without indulging in competitive activities that create avoidable mental stress. There is no meaning in seeking deliverance from life, as the self can only return after death to the original energy of consciousness or its manifestation in some form. A spontaneous life is all that is required for achieving peace and happiness with the knowledge that the mind is inseparable from the wisdom of universal consciousness. And that is the essence of the wisdom of universal consciousness envisioned by Vedic mystics and elaborated Ashtavakra. It is prescribed as a way of life for the common man who readily understands that all realities arise from consciousness. Let us now examine how much of this mystic vision is consistent with the latest scientific discoveries about the brain and mind.

CHAPTER FOURTEEN

MISTICS' FIND THE MODERN MIND

LIKE THE AWARENESS OF WHAT IS WITHIN AND WITHOUT
DISAPPEARS WHEN ONE IS UNITED WITH THE BELOVED.
WITH REALIZATION OF THE TRUE SELF,
SEPARATENESS MERGES IN THE HARMONY OF EXISTENCE.

[BRIHADARANYAKA UPANISHAD]

WE KNOW ONLY A FEW NAMES AND QUALITIES
OF FINITE NATURAL PHENOMENA.
BUT THE INFINITE IS THE SOURCE
OF ALL ENDURING QUALITIES OF EXISTENCE.
THE KNOWLEDGE OF THE UNITY OF ALL LIFE
IS THE ULTIMATE GOAL OF ENLIGHTENMENT.

[CHANDOGYA UPANISHAD]

Fully Wired Survival Machine

The recent scientific discoveries reveal most of the structural and functional features of the brain that creates the magnificent mind. The modern gadgets can trace the sequences of the functions of the brain in the minutest details to get the correct picture ideas of what we are. We now know how the brain creates an experiencing self. Let us now converge our knowledge from various sources to explore the possibility of demystifying the mind to reach the ultimate truth of existence.

We perceive the external world mainly through the visual inputs. The retina is constantly bombarded by billions of photons from various objects. They interact with molecules in the retina to modify the shapes suitably to unravel the inputs. These molecular changes further affect the shape of a protein called "Rhodopsine". This information is conveyed by molecular interactions and consequential changes down the line to the visual cortex. The sensory inputs are then processed and projected with the help of long-term and short-term memory data stored in the brain. The working memory area is supposed to receive the projections, which are presumably experienced by the conscious self. Actually, what is projected by the brain and experienced by the mind is only a replica of reality. It is the final outcome of the innumerable molecular transformations in the brain. The references made to the memory data make our perception contextual and meaningful.

It is now confirmed that the neurological processes that create the image of the external world in the brain are carried out continuously without our conscious participation. Only in the last stage of all the neural processes, somewhere in the left hemisphere of the brain we experience the perception of reality. The so called "interpreter" in the left hemisphere is probably the conscious self that evaluates the sensory data conveyed in the concrete form of a coherent image. The recognition of the image is facilitated by the memory of similar experiences in the past. The important fact discovery is that the conscious self actually receives the experiences half a second after the brain completes all processes in the neural tracts and networks. The inference is unavoidable that the image of the external world that we get is in a fully cooked form. It is made edible with all spices and sauce and the mind simply enjoys the dinner as if it created the hearty meal.

Every newborn child is equipped with all the essential wirings in the neural tracts and network to lead a normal life. The brain is fully programmed to learn many things about the world without any conscious efforts. Individual differences particularly in the matter of intelligence are based on only 0.2% genetic variations in the neural wiring. Our accomplishments are largely due to the environmental influences during the early childhood. The brain contains specialized systems and subsystems created serially through various evolutionary processes to ensure reproductive fitness and survival. Scientists claim that every important addition to the brain systems is built up on the original neural equipment inherited from the ancestral species. We have the remanants of the bacteria in the cells in the body that carry out independent functions. Prefrontal lobes represent the latest evolutionary achievements consisting of intellectual faculties like compassionate wisdom. Our primitive instincts are still carefully preserved in the neural tracts and networks that respond automatically to the known challenges of the external world.

Miracle Of Molecules

The latest breakthrough in biochemistry gives us a totally different picture of the cellular and molecular activities that appear to be predetermined. The new revelations cast a shadow of doubt over the purely evolutionary explanations of the development of a complex organ like the brain. Various specialized systems of the body like the neural network in the brain, the circulatory system, the immune system and the metabolic pathways involve several interconnected interactions of protein molecules. It looks like a perfectly designed flow chart that works on the basis of certain chosen parameters for achieving a preset objective. The immunological system reveals a fool-proof design for detecting the presence of disease-causing alien microbes. The choice of the appropriate molecular response to the invading microbes and consequential instructions to produce massive numbers of accurate antibodies show a highly imaginative system to ensure a trouble free existence for the organism.

The brain contains several complex systems designed to perform functions that presumably contribute to the effective functioning of the organism. But certain areas of the brain deal with functions, which are not even remotely concerned with any sort of survival strategy. We cannot hold that mathematics and music are essential for the reproductive success of any organism. No evidence of improved reproductive fitness has been found in great musicians or scientists. We have also no explanation for the brain getting saddled with all these additional responsibilities if it was not meant for achieving some goal unconnected with evolutionary purposes.

Superb Self-Deception

But the astonishing discovery is that all the processing of information at the neural level are concluded much before the conscious self becomes aware of the outcome. Thereafter nothing is added or subtracted by the mind that assumes everything as its own achievement. Our motor system is designed to function independently without availing the intervention of any conscious perception. The fact that conscious perception can be erroneous is now fully established by blind sight experiments. It is claimed that about 98% of what the brain actually does is outside our conscious experience. Our sensory and motor activities are planned and executed without any knowledge or involvement of the self. The mind is simply made to believe that the multitude of simultaneous tasks performed continuously in different parts of the brain is its own creation. The fact is that it simply receives the end product of the processes without having much of an option to reject it. More often than not, the self confirms the decisions taken by the brain may be after adding some justifications if they are unacceptable. The mind creates an impression that all the work done by the brain is according to its own conscious direction. It also gives causal explanations to impart meaning to the perceptions. The masterly self-deception of the mind conceals the secret that it is the ordinary matter in the brain that does all the basic work.

The view that the brain is just a dynamic, rule-driven, computing device has gained widespread acceptance in the scientific community. It develops in a guided manner according to the instructions from the genes and certain environmental influences. The axons of neurons can pass through even uncharted areas to reach their destinations. They are probably guided by some molecular sensory device or signals coming from the area to be linked. The retinal connections are already established even before birth and neural signals go through the designated pathways safely to their ultimate cortical targets. We have no idea about the causal links that determine the goal or design the necessary mechanisms at the micro level to achieve all this connectivity within the limited intelligence of an organism. The mind is totally unaware of the programs laid down in the genetic instructions much before the systems are made fully functional.

Slave Of Matter!

The cortical surface of our brain is many times larger than that of monkeys. The expansion of the surface area represents the addition of several new brain processes for performing additional tasks. After the eighth week of conception, the fetus has all the nerve cells ready for dispatch to the designated zones. By the fifteenth week, billions of neurons leave the cortical plate and from the twenty-fourth week to birth the cortex develops so fast that all the known adult type of cells are already present. They are raring to perform the exciting job of cerebral computing. About eighteen months after birth, the gray matter dramatically expands in the language region.

In the initial stages of our evolution some vague form of mind must have emerged to motivate further modifications in the brain. The cortical areas would have enlarged to accommodate all the new systems and sub systems. The brain contains several maps that roughly correspond to the layout of the external world. Specific areas are designed to handle special visual tasks such as motion, color and shape detection. When attention is stressed and divided between different tasks, the phenomenon called illusory conjunction comes into play. Many sensory inputs recombine in the brain to create an object that did not exist in reality. The limited capacity serial processor that controls our attention does not fortunately affect the faculty of imagination, which is surprisingly boundless.

Our scientific knowledge of the brain shows that it can carry out a series of computing activities in a network of neurons. It seems that memory imparts coherence to the perception of the objective world. We make sense of what is going on around us by reconstructing from the memory the identity of the current inputs. The interpreting self appears to be more active when misleading memories baffle its comprehension. Most importantly, the illusion that the mind controls all activities is also rooted deep in the memory. This particular mechanism is probably not available to animals, because of the inadequate size of the cerebral cortex. They have very little concern for any separate identity probably because of the inadequacy of the memory to create self-awareness.

In humans, the mind must been have developed out of extended awareness for achieving a competitive edge over powerful predators. It seeks order and patterns in all the natural phenomena to find causal explanations of the objective world. However, it breaks down when confronted with meaningless or voluminous data having no causal correlations. The conscious self creates an exclusive identity for the physical body as distinct from the external world. Our notions about existence have to be modified to accept the fact that it is the brain that does all the hard work much before the mind gets it into awareness. The only contribution of the mind is in the experiencing the events coherently with certain causal links to justify our choice among available alternatives. The mystic vision that self is an integral part of universal consciousness unrelated to the body processes is fully consistent with all the latest scientific findings about mind. It shows the mind as an emergent non-physical entity without any independent existence. The mind that comprises of consciousness, an experiencing self and body identity is nothing more than just an illusion created by the computing processes in the brain.

Self From Nowhere!

Unlike the neural network, mind is not the inherited property of the body. An infant has only pure awareness without experiencing any separateness from the external reality. In the early days of humankind, there must have been a similar state of simple consciousness. The innocence of the childhood is actually corrupted when we acquire the separate identity of an experiencing self. Some primates also possess consciousness without developing a clear and continuous identity of self. Experiments with the anesthetic drug "ketamine" clearly bring out the distinction between self-awareness and pure consciousness.

Saul-Paul Sirag, a renowned physicist recorded his personal experiences of altered states of mind after consuming small doses of ketamine. He found that the disappearance of self depended upon the drug-induced processes in the brain. The feeling of pure awareness followed the loss of identity of self. In that state, the visual field became multidimensional and dynamic. When music was played, it perfectly synchronized with the visual field. A sense of elation mixed with awe created an inexplicable experience of pure and undifferentiated awareness. The perception of the external world was unfocussed with no orientation towards any particular object. Everything appeared to be a part of some vibrant reality of great brilliance. The experience of total unity with the perceptual field alone prevailed.

When the effect of the drug started wearing off, the self slowly returned with the three-dimensional vision and a clear perspective. The focus of the perspective brought the concept of the self and sense of volition back into the being. It also created a sense of clear identity in the world of perception. Volitional activity in relation to the external world is found to be essential for creating self-awareness. Simple subjective awareness does not give us an identity unless the ability to manipulate the external world fixes an idea of self in consciousness. If it is ensured that the self is not in the external world, the consciousness assumes it as the identity of the body. It is actually body-awareness and the ability to control reality that makes us conscious of our own existence in the world.

Highest Awareness Is Perfect Vacuum

In the absence of the self, our perception becomes pure awareness, which is the simple reflection of external reality. In undifferentiated awareness, with out any self-related thought or action, our perception is fully integrated with objective reality. It is a rare experience, which the mystics must have reached through meditation, yoga or some herbal medication to alter the normal state of mind. We see colorful displays of sight and sound in a synchronized field of perception. Pure awareness is like a dream, but unlike in dreams, even a weak self not available to relate the events coherently. The self becomes united with external reality as no barriers are present to indicate separateness. The perception seems to become a continuous flow of information uncontaminated by the memories of past or expectations of future. While dreaming, the self is weak as the motor system is inactive. In dreams, there is no volition to direct events, which creates the idea of separateness.

In ordinary dreams, the self is a disinterested witness of the unfolding drama but in lucid dreams, the dreamer is vaguely aware of the act of dreaming. We can even move some muscles but the concept of self is not strong enough to alter the dream events. The self needs many ingredients like body awareness, volition and memories to create the illusion of an identity to own up the commissions and omissions of the body. It seems that without the concept of self, we can still exist in pure bliss of universal consciousness. If we really know who we are, it may not ensure the survival of the species or improve reproductive fitness. But our knowledge is much more precious as it can transform mere survival an enduring experience of existence.

Finally, Mind Demystified!

The phenomenon of consciousness has not so far been found in any inanimate matter. Many scientists and philosophers hope to discover even in ordinary matter proto-consciousness or some sort of innate capability of becoming conscious. Russel, Huxley and many other philosophers welcomed the idea that some volition is dormant at the elementary level. In quantum world, we find volitional activity of elementary particles before the act of observation creates an event. But all these ideas are still in the realm of speculation and we have no confirmation of the capability of ordinary matter to become conscious in any context. The essential condition for consciousness to emerge is the network of specialized cells called neurons. They are highly evolved building blocks of intelligence capable of simultaneously receiving and processing billions of inputs. They seem to possess even free will to respond or not to respond to an input. The concept of self appears in a conscious organism when it develops devices to store its own image probably in glial cells or in some other devices of the brain.

Before developing the concept of the self, the brain simply receives inputs from the external world. Without focused perception, the inputs remain inseparable from the external world. In other words, it is possible that through consciousness the neural network reconstructs reality from the inputs received by sensory organs. The inputs are basically vibrations of energy that get integrated probably by the process of coherent firing of the neurons or through some other mechanism unknown to our scientific wisdom. The electrical activity of the brain in the 40 Hz range and the increased activity of self-awareness neurons and certain select spots in the prefrontal lobe indicate that neurons conceal some missing link to the mind. The conclusion that emerges from the convergence of all our scientific knowledge is that universal consciousness is most likely a kind of vibration of energy that we are unable to understand but the neurons are capable of resonating with its frequency. No wonder the mystics concluded that we are nothing but the mere reflection of universal consciousness. The coherent firing in the neural network may be the means to reach the reality of supreme consciousness.

The more intriguing question is how the self-image gets embedded permanently either in glial cells or in some other area of the brain. We can assume that some quantum mechanical superposition of images or some sort of synchronized oscillations of neural firings create the concept of self. It is also possible to store memory of the images of self as holograms. We now know that certain drugs can temporarily obliterate the memory of self. All our rational knowledge put together do suggest the idea that self is an acquired capability, which was not a part of the brain at the time of birth. It emerges from the highly complex and delicately interconnected neural processing in the brain. We cannot find it as a physical entity inside or outside the body. At best, we can consider it as a variable concept or assumption arising out of the persistent interaction between the body and the external world.

The secret of reality lies in the mechanism that creates pure consciousness to give us the access to the material world even before we acquire the concept of self. The mind actually distorts the objective reality for its own vested interests by adding the legacy of past experiences. The consciousness that makes the objective reality seems to be something imperishable whereas the material world is truly transient. The self just reflects the objective reality through the brain processes to give us a comprehensible image of the world including our own identity.

End Of All Search For Meaning!

When we finally reach the end of the road, we find that Ashtavakra correctly surmised the mind as an illusion created by the body. We now find that consciousness is the eternal truth that makes reality of the phenomenal world accessible to us. The world is comprised of energy vibrations in different frequencies some of which are not intelligible to our range of perception. The composite images of the experiences of reflected reality gradually build up body awareness and the idea of the mind. It gets irretrievably erased in serious brain damage but can be held in abeyance by chemical action as in the case of anaesthesia. It is capable of acting only in the context of consciousness arising from the coherent activity of the neurons.

But without an experiencing self, our perception integrates fully with the objective reality. Then we simply have a dream or trance-like existence. Extremely prominent self gets into avoidable conflicts and competition with the external world. We experience acute pain and discomfort when self-related objectives are not achieved. Without the self we reach total unity with universal consciousness as thoughts and actions become synchronized with the rhythm of nature. The entire being merges with the eternal existence of objective reality, which would be a rare experience beyond description. The essence of knowledge that gives us total peace and happiness is the acceptance of the unity underlying all creations in the universe. Mystics like Ashtavakra might have reached the extended state of awareness with the realization that the truth of reality in the universe is consciousness.

Ultimate Answer

We have concluded that the self is just a reflection of pure consciousness that fills up the entire universe. The next step is to internalize this truth and adapt it for guiding the self through the turbulence of ordinary life. Forms, properties, polarities and all other attributes of matter are applicable to perishable physical objects but consciousness being an emergent quality is clearly outside the scope of such constraints. If we assume that proto-consciousness is an inherent quality of matter, it would definitely survive when the matter changes its present form. In that view, both matter and energy should possess the property of pre-consciousness. It means that before the appearance of matter in the big bang, pre-consciousness must have been present in the quantum vacuum or singularity of the initial conditions. The fact that universe is perceived only in our consciousness, which is beyond all changes, unborn and infinite, shows that we are only an advanced molecular manifestation of matter. Our greatest asset is the capacity to perceive the universe through consciousness. We can create the illusion of self and sustain it through various mental and physical activities.

We have seen that the concept of universal consciousness is consistent with all the latest scientific knowledge about the mind and reality. The dualistic nature of the mind and body is now revealed to be just an illusion. The mind actually belongs to the realm of universal consciousness, as it is only some state of the energy embedded in biological matter. The body does all the processing of the information about the external world but it is the mind that makes it an intelligible experience. The mind is actually a window to the external and even internal reality and only our assumption makes it an integral part of the body. When we understand this true nature of the mind, all puzzles of existence are resolved forever. The mind and universal consciousness survives the changes in the form of matter whether it is animate or inanimate. Our awareness continues even after the physical body perishes with the passage of time.

The mind and universal consciousness must be the same unknown state of energy that exists everywhere. Even before the big bang, the universe existed in that unknown state of energy with all the potential for creating the cosmos. It is this self-organizing intelligence of the pure, original energy that unfolded the universe with all the correct physical constants and created various structures including biological matter. No other explanation can give a rational solution to the puzzle of cosmic coincidences and the evolution of life on earth. The same state of energy continues to condition and control the universe in the form of interactive intelligence shaping the destiny of all forms of life. It contains all the information about the past, present and future and self-organizes eternally for purposes not known to us.

The elementary particles of matter like quarks and electrons or some other entities with wave particle duality must be instrumental in exchanging intelligence at primary level. The context for the exchange of intelligence must be some sort of unique quantum coherence. In course of time, our scientific knowledge will reveal the exact mechanism for exchange of such intelligence. The ultimate answer from our present level of knowledge appears to be that it is the unique state of energy containing the original intelligence that drives the self-organizing cyclic processes of creation and destruction of its own manifestations. We have no idea why it indulges in such cyclic experiments on existence. Our intelligence fails to fathom the intentions of the original intelligence that created the universe.

What It All Means?

It means that our existence is a unique experience of acquiring and enjoying knowledge, which other forms of life cannot achieve. In addition, with conscious efforts, if we reduce our body-related thoughts and emotions and contemplate on the truth of reality, we can reach the greatest experience of undifferentiated awareness. Our perception then gets totally integrated with the intelligent energy that pervades the universe. By becoming one with the universal phenomenon of consciousness, we reach the blissful state of existence, which is beyond all descriptions. The problems created by divergent thoughts disappear with the correct perspective of the unity of all beings in the self. In that state of mind we experience only love and compassion towards all forms of matter including our own body. We find that all beings co-exist for a finite time in a limited space and nothing can perish as they are integrated in the existence of universal consciousness. The realization of this truth releases us from all fears including the greatest fear of death. We understand that death can only make a change in material form and that such a transformation neither increases nor decreases the amount of energy in any manner.

To attain this highest level of understanding, one has to first seek the true knowledge of reality and then let it become the guiding principle of life. In meditation we try to switch off sensory inputs and concentrate attention on a particular object or thought. Such exercises cannot take us to the experience of undifferentiated awareness. It can become a part of the mind only by internalizing the rational worldview of scientific knowledge. It will help us to contemplate on existence in a dispassionate manner with minimum body awareness. True knowledge alone can remove the inherited ignorance of reality and take us to the ultimate awareness of self. The sheer splendor of existence lies in the realization of self and not in any material position or possession. In brief, the only valuable acquisition of life is the compassionate wisdom to love equally all forms of matter. We should feel fully contented with the available means of life spontaneously given by nature according to our abilities. Devotion to whatever works comes in the course of life and avoidance of ill-will towards anyone are the other attributes that can make life worth living even for a short span of few decades.

CHAPTER FIFTEEN

A RATIONAL MODEL OF UNIVERSE AND LIFE

I AM THE BOUNDLESS OCEAN;
IN ME THE WAVES OF PHENOMENAL WORLDS
SPONTANEOUSLY RISE AND DISAPPEAR.
I DO NOT EXPERIENCE ANY GAIN OR LOSS
BEING ENSHRINED IN THE PERFECT VACUUM OF
ETERNAL CONSCIOUSNESS.
[ASHTAVAKRA GEETHA]

THE SELF MEDITATED UPON ITSELF
AND PROJECTED THE UNIVERSE AS EVOLUTIONARY
ENERGY.
THE ELEMENTS, LIFE, MIND AND THE CYCLE OF
KARMA
THAT ARE ENCHAINED IN CAUSE AND EFFECT,
AROSE FROM ITS INFINITE INTELLIGENCE.
[THE MUNDAKA UPANISHAD]

ONLY THOSE WHO KNOW
THE SECRET OF THE VISIBLE WORLD
CAN GET A GLIMPSE OF THE INVISIBLE,
THAT CREATED ALL PHENOMENAL WORLDS
[ATHARVA VEDA 10.8.37]

Ultimate Model For All Reasons

A rational model of the universe and life should give us the correct and complete description of all the known physical and even non-physical phenomena. It should also provide us all the ultimate answers with the causal and non-causal relationships of objects and events at various levels. Theoretically, it should be capable of giving predictions and propositions that are verifiable by means of scientific methods. The model should also be consistent with all the commonly perceived features of nature that we generally accept as reality. Presently, we have a fairly correct scientific explanation of various natural phenomena both at the microscopic as well as the macroscopic levels. But they fail to give us satisfactory answers to the amazing array of coincidences that culminated in the creation of the universe. We also need an explanation of the origin and evolution of life and the mysterious non-physical qualities of the mind. To create a correct worldview, we have to consolidate our rational wisdom into a sustainable substratum that can explain all kinds of phenomena. We may have to supplement certain missing links and extrapolate some accepted facts to make complete picture of reality.

We know that the truth of reality, in all its splendor and complexity lies everywhere in nature including within our own body. In our vast treasure of knowledge, we find many models and explanations containing some facts relevant to the ultimate answers. Unfortunately, our fragmented vision does not give us the complete idea of the reality and its causal relations. The inability of our sensory organs to comprehend the complexities of nature beyond or below certain frequencies of energy may be an important reason for our incomplete perception of the truth of reality. We have also seen that mystic insights of universal consciousness give valuable insights relevant to the understanding of the mysteries of the mind.

We began our search for a rational worldview to set right the inherited misconceptions about existence. To achieve this end, we brought together several capsules of information from scientific knowledge about the universe, matter, life and consciousness. In the scientific explanations we noticed several inexplicable coincidences and improbabilities particularly about the origin and organization of the universe, the evolution of life and consciousness. We concluded tentatively that more accurate knowledge and new approaches are required to understand the causal links of non-physical phenomenon like consciousness.

The model outlined here convincingly describes the initial conditions that prevailed before the big bang and created the universe. It also tells us the probable cause of cosmic coincidences and correct choice of various physical constants that organized the universe and evolved matter and life. The basic assumption of the model is that before the big bang, an unknown form of intelligent energy subsisted with absolute qualities. It could have been something like a neutron star or a point of infinite singularity or a quantum vacuum. This primordial energy is the original substratum of all kinds of known and unknown matter and forces in the universe. It is the highest and purest state of energy in which everything was united in a state beyond quantum theory or classical physics.

First Premise

At the outset, let us examine the concept of energy, which is the central theme of our model of the universe. We know a lot about energy from the theories of classical physics and quantum mechanics. Energy is scientifically described as the capacity to do work. It gives the broadest measure of the state of a physical system. In an isolated system the total energy remains constant in spite of any change in the form. Energy is the basic measure of all changes in a system like the money flows that keep an account of various transactions in an economy. The greatest attribute of energy is that it can neither be created nor destroyed. Not only that, it can take many forms, some of which are quite familiar manifestations like kinetic, thermal, electrical, chemical and nuclear energy. Heat and work signify energy in the process of transferring from one system to another. Kinetic and potential energy refer to the source in terms of the position or motion.

Einstein's theory of relativity explains that mass and energy are equivalent. But in spite of all our knowledge of energy, it is only a useful concept to understand the physical world and not a concrete reality. It is not entity like matter that can be physically described or defined. The presence of energy is normally felt when a physical system undergoes transformation. In terms of the principle of conservation of energy, its totality is not subject to changes in manifestations of various states. When a system undergoes change of state by losing or gaining energy, a consequential balancing effect is always felt in another state. This abstract concept is also beyond causality and the constraints of time and space.

The primordial energy that existed in infinite state is beyond our comprehension. In that form it would have contained all possible vibrations and frequencies of energy. We can take it as the potential energy that to created matter, forces and all kinds of structure in the universe. It should have had all the intelligence required for choosing the physical constants in some manner unknown to us. Some basic design must have been present in the original states of energy to creat the universe, matter and life.

Our scientific knowledge of the universe begins only with the big bang. We have unquestionable proof of a cosmic explosion in the red shift and the background microwave radiation. This cosmic explosion must have taken place about 15 billion years ago. The timing of the explosion is also somewhat accurate from the astronomical observations of the farthest galaxies.

In the primordial state of energy before the big bang, all the matter and forces in the universe should have been existent in potential state as intelligent energy. The explosion has only brought about a transformation in the state of energy. The law of conservation of energy tells us that the total energy in the system would have been the same as the energy presently in the universe or universes if it created more than one universe. It could have been infinitely dense and totally opaque. No photon could have existed independently outside the system. Of course, no observer could have described the system, which had nothing external to its ambit.

It is from this infinite state of energy that our universe came into being in a sequential manner. Theologians may call it the creation of God and the rationalists may simply assume it as a change in the state of Energy. We have no means to understand the true nature of the transition of energy from one state to another at the highest level. We cannot even imagine the amount of heat energy produced for creating the context for the separation of forces and making of matter in its elementary forms. No conjectures are possible as all the attributes of the initial state of energy are far beyond our comprehension. But the fact is that such an energy transition of tremendous magnitude gave rise to our universe in a series of processes involving variations in temperature and other parameters.

Second Premise

The second premise is that the initial state of energy had all the basic intelligence necessary for unfolding a viable universe. It would have known the correct values of all constants, which became operative only in the interactive context created by the transformation of energy. In fact, ingredients for a stable universe were inherent in the original energy in some unknown form. The basic design needed an appropriate thermal condition separating forces and creating matter. It is like a seed containing all genetic information gradually growing up to a full-blown plant with all the inherited features and qualities embedded in the embryonic cell.

The origin of life is analogous to the origin of universe. Life must have begun on earth in as a single-cell organism. Firstly, it became capable of differentiating itself from the external world. The DNA gave all the information for creating energy and replicating itself to perpetuate existence. In course of time, the variety of life that emerged out of the original cell would have undergone several evolutionary transformations. The cosmic intelligence must have created the first live cell using the information stored in its eternal memory bank. At certain higher levels of complexity, the interactive intelligence must have given rise to the phenomenon of consciousness that enables us to differentiate the self from the external world.

Extrapolating the conservation of energy principle, we find that the end of the universe will only be a change of the present state of energy. Assuming that a big crunch or fiery collapse will be the probable end, all matter and forces will again return to the original state of energy. While regaining the primal state, it will probably carry the memory of the earlier states of existence. The physical constants and their combinations required for creating universe would not have emerged from any design other than the intelligent energy. It may take hundreds of billions of years for yet another explosion to initiate the cycle of creation. But the information would probably remain dormant in the purest state of energy to be utilized for the self-organization of another universe in due course. The concept of time is not applicable to this phenomenon as it includes both the forward and backward flow of time in its self-sustaining loops of intelligence. Only the appropriate context can unfold the information that contains both the knowledge as well as the object of knowledge. So, this possibility settles the basic issue of the creation of the universe and origin of life.

Third Premise

The third premise of our model is that it is the interactive intelligence that gives rise to structures, forces and the diversity of life. The intelligence encoded in the original energy becomes interactive under suitable conditions and in a manner presently unknown to us. Atoms and molecules must have been the outcome of such intelligent interaction. We have sufficient evidence to prove that everywhere in the universe, matter interacts intelligently at quantum level. The structures emerged through such network of relationships at the fundamental level of particles. On our planet also we find that every form of life interacts with the environment to decide upon the desirable course of action for maximizing chances of survival and improving reproductive fitness. We have seen that even at molecular level, exchanging of information is absolutely necessary for the existence of a biological organism.

In classical physics such intelligent exchange of information at elementary level is an impossibility. Only quantum theory can provide the necessary conceptual framework for creating instant correlation between distant particles. Quantum non-locality does not require mediation by a local force or even some kind of a signal between the particles. Two particles can be related instantaneously without any intermediary, if we assume that they follow quantum dynamics. The spins of two photons are spontaneously correlated, when the spin of one of them is known. Aspect's experiments confirmed Bells theorem that the intelligence exchanged between the particles has indeterminate potentialities. It is something like telepathic communication of an elementary kind.

Since interactive intelligence is a clear possibility at quantum level, our assumption that the original state of energy contained universal intelligence is an acceptable proposition for a rational model. It is not only possible to encode all the intelligence in a state of energy, but also to transmit it instantaneously beyond space and time. Just like the potentiality collapses when it is measured or observed, the intelligence also creates matter and forces, when the appropriate context arises to interpret the information in the primordial energy pool. Even after the formation of matter and forces, the interactive intelligence can continue to create new forms of matter like life and evolve them to more complex varieties. This was probably the cause of all evolutionary processes on our planet.

Our perception of reality gives an undeniable proof of interactive intelligence at the biological level. Neurophysiologists, led by Wolf Singer of the United States, found that when we see a familiar object, all the neurons receptive to the qualities of that object fire together. The coherent firings of neurons while recognizing a known quality in the visual object clearly show the exchange of intelligence between the object and the molecules in the neurons. Classical science has no rational explanation for such coherent firing of neurons. It shows that neurons are sensitive to some features in the outside world. The brain can differentiate unfamiliar objects and features in the world only after they are broken down to the basic level and then put together to create an identifiable image.

The brain takes about 1/10th of a second to synchronize the processing of information at different areas dealing with various features of the visual field. During this period, it integrates the data on color, motion, shape, past experience and so many other features before identifying an object. It is evident that the brain is in constant communication with the interactive intelligence that permeates the world. Classical physics cannot accept this idea, as it requires local forces and causal relationships for explaining all natural phenomena. The unified perception of an object by the conscious self is possible only if we accept the quantum indeterminacy of the Bells theorem.

Creation Of The Universe

From the premises so far discussed, we can finally unfold a rational model of the universe. The main assumption of the model is that there is interactive intelligence everywhere in the universe at the level of elementary particles. Our knowledge of matter now clearly indicates that at the elementary level, up quark and down quark are held together by gluons to create protons and neutrons. Electrons held by photons to the nucleus make a complete atom. Molecules are combinations of atoms that ultimately create matter. The elementary particles such as quarks, gluons, electrons and photons do not have any size or structure. They are the building blocks of matter that possess the quality of non-locality for interacting universally with the intelligence in the memory inherited from the primordial state of existence.

Our model is essentially based on the process of self-organization. In self-organization there is a complex and indeterminate substrate that creates patterns at different sizes and scales. We find examples of self-organization in Bose-Einstein condensates, living organisms and crystals. It is an open system without entropy. All biological organisms develop according to self-organizing patterns initially embedded in a fertilized egg. Similarly, it is definitely possible that the universe also developed as a self-organizing pattern in accordance with the intelligence inherent in the original state of energy before the big bang. It could have been in the form of quantum chaos with non-linear properties.

The basic intelligence must have been derived from the memories of the events in a collapsed universe. In cellular chemistry, we find that the gene components are turned off or on by each other depending upon the requirements of the cell. In the computerized model of the behavior of genes developed by Kaufman, components remained constant with sparse connections. With more connections, interesting patterns began to develop from the self-organizing network in the program. After the self-organizing network of the primal energy created an original pattern, evolution must have taken over the task of further refinement to ensure the survival of the product and creation of better varieties by exchanging relevant information between the genes and environment. This also explains the exclusive choice of benign mutations in evolutionary changes of life.

In a similar manner, the information embedded in the self-organizing pattern before the beginning of the universe must have given rise to the structures like stars and galaxies. The context was the lowering levels of temperature that created conditions necessary for exchange of information for arriving at the correct values of physical constants. The information exchanged must have been on the basis of the memory of past structures that would have returned to the original form of energy in a big crunch after the completion of inflation. Even the critical rate of inflation would have been chosen on the basis of the information available in the initial conditions. The ripples in the microwave background radiations could be indicative of self-organizing patterns of original intelligence to form bigger structures.

The self-organizing model is also evident in the growth of a fertilized egg. The embryonic cell contains the information coded in chemical language. The egg while growing in a suitable medium unfolds its own genetic instructions. The very fact that random mutations of a beneficial kind alone are passed on to future generations clearly indicates the possibility of intelligent exchange of information with the environment to ascertain the future consequences of present choices. But the exact processes involved in self-organization and exchange of information is beyond our current level of knowledge.

Unconscious Perception

Our perceptive abilities can decipher only what ultimately reaches the conscious self. Humans possess about twelve perceptual senses but much of the information gathered by the sense organs does not reach our awareness. Some of the information that flows along the optic and auditory nerves never enters our consciousness at any time. Blind sight is an example of brain-damaged persons spontaneously responding to objects within the visual field without being aware of seeing any object. Similarly, people suffering from hysterical deafness show EEG brain response to sounds, when they are not at all conscious of hearing them. The fact is that the information resulting from the processing of all the inputs received by sense organs does not reach our perception.

The fact that such unconscious perception exists in reality confirmed the clear possibility of exchange of information at elementary level. Some people possess a magnetic sense of direction without their being aware of it. We try to explain such unconscious perception as intuition or insight. We sometimes arrive at correct conclusions without being aware of receiving and processing any information related to that topic. Such intuitive perceptions cannot be explained rationally at the present level of knowledge of the brain. In the same analogy, the process of exchange of information at elementary level is unknown to us, but it does exist at the level of electrons and quarks. We can correctly conclude that all processes in the universe are conducted by the constant exchange of information at some elementary level.

Wisdom Of Existence

We can now sum up our model of the universe, life and mind by explaining the whole sequence of creation in terms of the basic intelligence in the primordial energy. We have seen that this energy would have been in an unknown and intense state before the big bang. It would have had all the intelligence to create everything in the universe including elementary particles, forces and structures at various levels. It would have spontaneously arrived at the correct value of physical constants necessary to create matter, forces and even the critical rate of expansion of the universe. The intelligent energy would have been interacting continuously with all forms of matter and forces at the level of elementary particles or even below for further evolution into more complex structures.

When we look closer at the quantum world, we find that the interchange of photons by electrons is essential to create a negative or positive charge. The photons interchanged are known as "virtual particles" which emanate from a quantum field. We have seen all existence as excitations of quantum fields. The possibilities of finding such excitation in respective fields gives rise to the wave function. The fields can also interact and the field theory gives us the basic scaffolding to construct our ideas about transformation of entities. What we understood from all this high-energy physics is the simple truth that there is constant communication at elementary level of particle waves in a quantum field. Now we have to accept that the exchange of information is done intelligently in accordance with some pattern or design inherent in the original intelligence.

It is the same original interactive intelligence that created biological matter out of ordinary matter. The possibility of exchange of information at elementary level would explain the development of life in the primordial cell. It would also explain the vast complexity and diversity of life created through the process of evolution of the first primordial cell. The selection of beneficial mutation that got propagated in the entire population of species can also be explained only in terms of such interaction that can choose the ones, which are useful for the survival and reproductive fitness of an organism. The chemical instructions on the genes create intelligent proteins that carry out dedicated functions as if they had some blueprint or agenda for action. It is the constant exchange of information that actually conducts the cellular and molecular level activities in biological organisms. Evolution becomes a meaningful process only when it is capable of exchanging information between the organism and the environment.

In our new knowledge of the mind, the question of being, non-being and becoming has no relevance. Traditionally, science and philosophy keep their enquiries confined to systems at or very close to equilibrium like man or machine. But in modern times attention has shifted to self-organizing systems where transformations take place constantly. The new tools for understanding of becoming are non-linearity, chaos and self-organization, complexity, feedback loops, bifurcation points and so on. The philosophical basis for the new line of enquiry is Hegel's Dialectical process with the focus on becoming. The being is to be understood from becoming that represents the complex and inexplicable processes consisting of several coincidences.

This model does not make any distinction between being or non-being or becoming in view of the basic assumption that the entire existence was originally contained in the undifferentiated non-being. Our current preoccupation with becoming arises from inadequate knowledge of the evolutionary process. In our model, becoming is an automatic process containing several steps in different contexts in which the information in the original energy interacts with various manifestations of its own creativity. Each manifestation tries to arrive at an optimum level of existence by exchanging relevant information with the environment. Consciousness is one form of this interaction where the neurons in the brain receive inputs from the external world for our experience on the basis of the unknown exchange of information.

Even in the lowest possible energy state of absolute zero, the quantum vacuum is active in terms of the uncertainty principle. When we add up frequencies of vibration in that state we reach a kind of inexplicable infinity. The infinite energy of the vacuum in just 1 cubic centimeter is said to be more than the energy of the entire universe. I think the quantum vacuum that existed before the big bang must have contained supreme intelligence beyond our comprehension. Even some great scientists accept the possibility that quantum vacuum is the ultimate transcendent really in which our existence appears like waves in the ocean. So far, we have no experimental proof or evidence of the existence of such phenomena. But the undeniable fact is that the original state of energy whether in the form of quantum vacuum or some other state had the intelligence to create all entities in our universe.

In short, the universe is the outcome of the activity of a self-organizing intelligent form of energy and human life is a manifestation of its ingenuity to create the highest order of complexity. The synchronized oscillations of neural network raise the level of our perception to comprehend holistically the consciousness pervading the universe. Our capacity to experience the world including the various states of the body should be the extension of the interactive intelligence of the universal energy that exists everywhere. We can call it God or universal consciousness or any other name. Simple truth is that it gives us the mind to perceive the reality. Universal consciousness may exist in the form of quantum waves continuously evolving super positions without any past or present. Our quantum coherent perception may be collapsing the wave to gain access to external reality.

From the model described here, one would get a deep and abiding understanding of the unity of existence of all forms of matter. We are all evolved from the same original state of energy. The realization of this truth makes us free and fearless in a state of super awareness. It also establishes the fact that nothing can perish in the universe including life, as all events are only transformation of energy from one state to another. The intelligent energy exists eternally while the forms of matter or forces may change depending upon the variations in the context. The Supreme Reality envisioned by the mystics in their deep contemplation is probably the primordial state of energy revealed as undifferentiated awareness. Death is like a lump of salt fallen in the sea, where it is neither lost nor perished but simply changes form by dissolving its individual identity. It becomes one with the supreme state of existence of intelligent energy in yet another unknown form. This is the sum and substance of all the wisdom that we have learned by converging scientific knowledge and mystic contemplations on existence. In fact, self-realization is both the end and means of our search for the truth of reality that is evident in all the manifestations of energy permeating the universe and even beyond.

Emergence Of Matter And Life

Condensing all the premises we discussed in the model, we can now reach some tentative conclusions about the process of evolution of intelligence in the universe. For this purpose, we can identify a few stages or contexts in which the intense activity of exchange of information suddenly upgraded the level of complexity in the universe. These changes must have come about in certain special circumstances suitable for the exchange of information between various entities. We can sequentially examine these stages, which I have arbitrarily bunched for focusing on the highlights of the period.

STAGE 1: This stage belongs to eternity before the big bang. From our present time, it would have been about 10 -15 billion years ago. There was no matter or forces as everything was united in the unknown form of energy having absolute qualities. Whatever properties we assign to matter, forces and energy would have been at the ultimate level in the original state of energy. It must have contained all the intelligence including information about its earlier forms of existence and the possibilities of future events.

STAGE 2: The universe begins with a big bang. We have no idea about the specific cause of the great explosion. But we can presume that whatever it was, it would have been present in some form in the original state of energy. When the temperature cooled down to about 100 million trillion, trillion degrees, gravity began to exert its presence. The universe would have been in the form of a blur in what is called Planck Era, which was followed by GUT Era that lasted 10 -42 seconds after the big bang. In this era, the temperature cooled down to 1 billion, billion degrees and matter emerged as quarks and electrons along with antimatters. During this stage, the universe must have expanded manifold and the critical rate of expansion would have also been chosen by the intelligence in the original energy.

STAGE 3: In stage 3, which lasted up to three minutes after the big bang, we have the intense interaction of matter and forces by exchanging intelligence and evolving several cosmic coincidences of physical constants for creation of matter and forces. With the temperature at 1 trillion degrees, electromagnetic and weak forces appeared and protons and neutrons were made out of quarks. The photon emerged at this time after the collision of protons and anti-protons. Electrons also appeared about one minute after the big bang, after completing their quota of collisions with positrons. The intense activity of neutrons and protons created elements like helium, lithium and heavy hydrogen.

STAGE 4: Stage 4 began one billion years after the big bang with the formation of bigger structures like galaxies, quasars and stars. About three billion years after the big bang, we find formation of distinct stars and solar systems in the galaxies. The stars started fusion reaction at this time creating heavy elements. Massive stars would have thrown out the products of fusion reaction into the intergalactic space. New stars and planets were made out of the remnants of old stars.

STAGE 5: From now onwards, we can confine our discussion to the formation of our planet, which was about five billion years ago. The planet was created out of condensed intergalactic dust containing elements like carbon. The planet was in the form of a fireball that went on cooling and solidifying. The cooling process created rocks and condensed steam, which became shallow oceans. Plenty of carbon-based compounds were created from the interaction of various chemicals under the primordial conditions. During this period, the intelligent energy must have started exchanging chemical information for creating new structures based on designs and patterns that would have already existed in its pre-big bang memory.

STAGE 6: In stage 6, we have the beginning of biological life on earth. Microorganisms prevailed everywhere inventing different ways to create energy through processes like fermentation, photosynthesis and so on. During this period, DNA also appeared and the bacteria learnt the process of trading of genes and even repairing its own DNA. DNA recombination by bacteria must have created a wide variety of bacterial life fully adapted to the environment. At DNA level, the live organisms must have constantly interacted with the environment to invent changes in the chemical instructions for creating more viable forms of life. The bacteria worked hard to create an atmosphere conducive to life by inventing the optimum oxygen levels and other parameters. About 1.5 billion years ago, a suitable atmosphere was created on the surface of the earth for evolving more varieties of life.

STAGE 7: In this stage, we find the slow evolution of higher forms of life. About 1.2 million years ago, organisms evolved locomotion along with the invention of sexual reproduction. Early animals appeared about 700 million years ago and plants appeared around 500 million years ago. During this period, we can see the most wonderful evolution of intelligence in the form of the Cambrian Explosion, in which several new forms of life appeared with hard body parts. Land-based animals and plants started evolving about 400 million years ago and dinosaurs and mammals got themselves established by about 200 million years ago. This period came to an end about 70 million years ago when dinosaurs and many other species suddenly disappeared, probably in the aftermath of the impact of a meteorite measuring about seven miles across. The dust created by the collision must have blocked out sunlight for a very long period creating impossible conditions for continuation of life of large animals.

STAGE 8: This stage witnessed the great evolutionary ascent of primates, which must have begun about 65 million years ago after the extinction of the dinosaurs. The first humanoids appeared about five million years ago. They began to walk on two legs, started using tools and domesticated fire. They also used language to evolve faster to emerge as homo sapiens about 500,000 years ago. About 40,000 years ago the only humanoid subspecies on earth was homo sapiens as all other subspecies disappeared. At this stage, there was constant interaction between neuron-based intelligence of the humanoids and the information available at different levels in the external world.

STAGE 9: This is the beginning of the era of technology, which began with big agricultural settlements. The great cities in Mesopotamia were made about 6,000 years ago and written language seems to have appeared about 5,500 years ago. During this period, the main inventions were wheels, boats and calculation methods using abacus. In China, Egypt and Assyria several new inventions like the clock and a variety of architecture began to appear. The intellectual revolution began in about BC 2000 by eastern mystics when they compiled holy scriptures based on insights derived from their meditative reflections. In the Western countries, between 400 and BC 200 the rationalistic philosophy of Socrates, Plato and Aristotle laid the foundations of modern science.

STAGE 10: The modern era of science and technology began with the great discoveries of Newton in 1687. In the realm of philosophy also, several new ideas emerged in the West beginning with the rational skepticism of Descartes and the rationalism of Emanuel Kant. The industrial revolution began during this time with the invention of several new technologies. Another great idea that emerged was the concept of Darwinian evolution, which completely falsified the religious interpretation of life. The discoveries of Albert Einstein, Neils Bohr and Verner Heisenberg explained matter at various levels by about 1928. During this period, we saw the development of the Church Touring thesis that reduced problems to some algorithms. With this invention, we have entered the latest technological era of intelligent machines that even surpassed the highest level of human intelligence. The evolution of intelligence continues at a much faster pace now with the help of tools like computers and other electron-based inventions.

CONCLUSIONS

They asked," Are you the God?"
He said, "no."
" Are you an angel?"
He said, "no."
" Are you a saint?"
He said, "no."
Fed up with his denials, they finally asked, "Then what are you?"
Buddha said, "I am awake."
The answer became his title.

[FROM A FOLKLORE]

THE GOD OF LOVE PROJECTS HIMSELF IN THE UNIVERSE IN MYRIAD FORMS
ALL BEINGS ARISE IN HIM AND ALL RETURN TO HIM
WE THE HUMANS ARE THE GRACE OF HIS ETERNAL WISDOM.

[SHVETASHAVATARA UPANISHAD]

WE SHOULD SEEK THAT HIGHEST GOAL OF LIFE
AFTER REACHING WHICH NO ONE
WOULD TURN BACK.
LET US FIND A PERMANENT PLACE IN THE ORIGINAL ENERGY
FROM WHICH ALL ACTIVITIES
HAVE BEEN EMANATING FROM TIME IMMEMORIAL

[BHAGAWAD GITA]

Ultimate Enlightenment

Our intensive search for the ultimate truth of reality in the accumulated wisdom of scientific knowledge has given us some tentative conclusions. We have briefly reviewed our rich cultural inheritance of theological worldviews and mystic insights to reach certain acceptable solutions. We found that the recent discoveries of science on various processes in the brain are fully consistent with mystic insights on self and consciousness. The epilogue that follows this chapter, presents a preview of the great future awaiting us in the third millennium.

It is true that in spite of all our enquiries, we are still unable to discover all the ultimate secrets of nature. But the available information can enlighten us to a large extent if we evaluate it in a detached manner. I will now try to lead you to the truth of reality envisioned in this book in a symbolic dialogue between the self and the Supreme Self. You can assume that the Supreme Self, who answers your question, is actually the collective wisdom of humanity that becomes the pathfinder to the truth of reality. In the dialogues, the self seeks rational answers to all fundamental questions that we discussed in part one to four of this book. The answers presumably present a rational worldview, which is quite intelligible to the common man.

We evaluate here various options and alternatives available to us without any preconceived notions about the outcome. You can substitute in the answers, your own personal views and preferences, wherever you want, to create a suitable worldview that would meet your spiritual requirements. But you will be surprised to find that despite all additions and alterations, the truth of reality remains firmly fixed in the intelligent energy that pervades the entire universe in one form or the other. The concluding part of our voyage of discovery will begin now with unfolding answers to all fundamental questions of existence.

WHERE ARE WE?

A Self-Organizing Pool Of Energy

Self:- **"In part I, the scientific explanations of the process of creation of the universe, its infinite expansion and probable end are given. Can we substitute them for the religious worldviews that give different versions of creation?**

Supreme Self: " Yes, there is no doubt that it all began with the biggest of all cosmic explosions. We cannot falsify the astronomical observations of the red shift and the presence of background microwave radiation. These are the two irrefutable evidences of the explosive beginning of the universe. The huge quantity of hydrogen and helium found in the universe also confirms it beyond any doubt. Explanations of creation in religious scriptures various cannot survive in the absence of observational or experimental evidences. All attempts to resurrect the steady-state hypothesis simply failed in the face of facts. The truth is that the universe is steadily expanding after its creation with the big bang. We may not accept the explanations of the cause of expansion given in various inflation theories, but we cannot deny the fact of the big explosion and subsequent steady inflation.

Self:- **"How did matter and forces evolve in the universe, presumably from the absolute vacuum of the initial conditions? Could a big bang create a context suitable for the emergence of structures like stars and planets?"**

Supreme Self: "It is true that the nature of the initial conditions are still unknown to science. All attempts at giving rational descriptions are inadequate to convey the bizarre state of primordial energy possessing probably all the absolute qualities that are beyond even our imagination. The descriptions like quantum vacuum and infinite singularities do not give a meaningful representation of the true state of energy in its original existence. The proposition that a black hole can give rise to a universe is also not acceptable as there are billions of them even in our present universe. All our knowledge about the creation of matter and forces is based on the standard model of the universe. First, we have no idea about the state of the universe in the Planck era that extends up to 10-43 seconds after the big bang. Something tangible like hydrogen atoms and free photons emerged only 300,000 years after the big bang. Our ideas about creation of matter in the universe are still speculative, particularly the events that are said to have happened in the first few eras. Some of the experimental evidences do confirm the creation of matter as predicted by the standard model. But conclusive proof is yet to come for all the high-energy, high temperature phenomena that are now theoretically explained on the basis of the scientific knowledge of elementary particles and their evolution after the big bang. "

Self:- "What about the present state and future prospects of the universe?"

Supreme Self: "According to the inflation theories, when the universe was 10-34 seconds old, there was a tremendous expansion that inflated the nascent universe like a spotted balloon. The spots did not move on the balloon but there was more space in between them making the balloon flatter by a factor of about 1050 or more. The specific cause of such inflation is still unknown, but some scientists attribute it to the crystallization of color force from the united force of nature. The problem is that the predictions of the Grand Unified Theory about the possibilities of such massive expansion cannot be tested in any particle accelerators in the foreseeable future. Moreover, such theories do not account for gravity for which we may need a new theory of everything. There is also no explanation for the specific value of omega, which is keeping the universe delicately poised between collapse and infinite expansion. If the universe began with a slightly lower value of omega, it would have re-collapsed a long time back. If the omega was greater than 1, the gravitational force would have been very weak and no stars and galaxies would have appeared. So, in spite of all inflation theories and grand unified theories, it is difficult to explain the flatness of the universe. The model suggested in the preceding chapter explains all such phenomena as occurrences arising out of self-organizing properties.

***Self:-* "Can the proposed model explain cosmic coincidences and the mystery of the origin and evolution of life?"**

Supreme Self: "Cosmic coincidences are the correct choices of certain basic values like the density of matter in the universe, mass of the elementary particles and relative strength of various forces. If the numerical values of physical constants were not correctly fixed, the universe would not have emerged with stable structures. Galaxies and stars are essential for life to appear in our planet. The choice of physical constants has no scientific basis or explanation other than the speculations proposed in anthropic reasoning. At best, it assumes that the universe is there just because we are observing it. The different kinds of anthropic reasoning appear more irrational than some of the religious explanations. The creation of a stable universe is possible only if we assume that intelligence was embedded in the initial state of energy before the big bang. The model outlined in the preceding chapter can explain the coincidences more coherently and convincingly.

***Self:-* "What about the mysterious behavior of matter at the quantum level?**

Supreme Self: "Classical physics cannot explain the strange behavior of elementary particles that do not require mediation by any local force. Quantum mechanics assumes that it is possible to establish non-local correlation to transmit information instantaneously across space and time. This phenomenon is explained by quantum indeterminism that has been established in the experiments of the French physicist Alain Aspect. It is not possible to extend quantum indeterminism to bigger structures as it fails to integrate the impact of gravitational force. In the super string theory, an attempt has been made to account for both gravity and quantum mechanics, but this theory requires more than 10 dimensions. But quantum mechanics really works in gadgets like laser machines and holograms. All that we can accept now is that different explanations are necessary for physical phenomena at different levels of matter. Our inadequate knowledge fails to integrate all matter and forces in a singularity, as it existed before the big bang. But the model we discussed takes care of the problem of integration, as the basic assumption is that all the intelligence was embedded in the original state of energy before the big bang.

WHAT ARE WE?

Life Is No Coincidence

***Self:-* "Is it true that biological organisms were created out of the interaction of ordinary matter in the universe?**

Supreme Self: Our scientific knowledge clearly establishes the undeniable continuity between the creation of matter after the big bang and the first appearance of life on earth. All biological organisms contain atoms and molecules that are constituents of ordinary matter. Live organisms are distinguished only by certain properties like reproduction, metabolism, DNA and so on that are probably acquired after inanimate matter got organized in a biological configuration. Alternatively, we can assume that some innate quality of matter like proto-consciousness was involved in the evolution of life on earth or any other suitable planet.

***Self:-* "How did biological life emerge on earth and evolve in to a wide variety of complex organisms?"**

Supreme Self: "For the emergence of biological life in the primordial conditions of earth, several coincidences should have occurred simultaneously. It is difficult to presume that controlled laboratory conditions existed on earth 4.5 billion years ago. One possibility is the evolution of self-organizing matter having interactive intelligence for reaching higher levels of complexity in an appropriate context. It is just like the formation of matter and forces in the universe as it cooled down after the big bang. Biological life could have also reached the earth on some meteors. Since earth did not have an effective cover of the atmosphere at that time, several meteors must have landed safely carrying some startup bacteria to begin life.

The undeniable fact is that for two billion years, bacteria ruled the earth without evolving into nucleated cells or higher forms of biological organisms. It indicates the possibility of meteors playing a crucial role in the sudden appearance of the variety of life on earth. We cannot also rule out the possibility of the symbiotic relationships of bacteria creating nucleated cells, which are the basic building blocks of the higher forms of life.

***Self:-* "Is it true that all forms of life on earth has a common origin?"**

Supreme Self: "The common origin of all forms of life on earth is self-evident from the common features that all plants and animals carry in their cells. In fact, we still have in our cell many properties of the first single celled biological organism. We share about 98% common DNA features with higher primates like chimpanzees. Not only that, we still carry several imprints in our organs that reveal gradual changes in the structural and functional feature of a common ancestor. The latest results of the mapping of human genome show that hardly 0.2% individual variations exist in humans. It is also clear that there is no genetic basis for racial or intellectual differences.

***Self:-* "Evolution seems to be the only rational explanation of the variety and complexity of life on earth. Does it actually account for all the diversity of life we find on earth or some other explanation is needed?**

Supreme Self: "The evolutionary explanation of life assumes that chance variations in genetic instructions pass on to future generations. They ultimately spread out the beneficial changes in the entire population. The only purpose of the transmission of such variations to the progeny seems to be better adaptation to the increasing complexities of the habitat for ensuring the survival. There are incontrovertible fossil evidences that indicate gradual evolutionary changes in various organisms over a long period of time. It supports the role of evolutionary intervention in creating the vast variety of life on earth.

Assuming that the evolutionary explanation of life is true, at the starting point we need an original live organism that can undergo random mutations to alter its own original genetic instructions. The minimum requirement is a single cell organism like bacteria that can further evolve into a more complex form of life. But we find that in spite of two billion years of existence, evolution obviously did not work any wonders in the bacterial kingdom. They did not evolve into advanced multi-cellular organisms during their long period of undisturbed reign on this planet. Moreover, molecular biology now reveals that proteins follow some predetermined course to achieve a specific goal. Evolutionary changes are meant only to achieve the Darwinian goal of reproductive fitness for the survival of species. But we see that at the molecular level, the activities are so intricately organized as if they were to follow some design to accomplish a common objective.

We found it difficult to justify the assumption that evolutionary changes promote only beneficial mutations and the malignant ones are ignored. If we simply add up all specific functional objectives of molecular interactions we will not reach at any evolutionary goal of an organism. The fact is that, we have no acceptable explanation for solving the puzzle of the origin of life and the great evolutionary quantum jumps of humans. The phenomenon of the mind has apparently no evolutionary purpose. We discussed this question at length in Part II, but no rational conclusions emerged in support of a purely evolutionary model or any intelligent design. All that we can say is that evolution was not the only means for achieving the great diversity of life on earth.

***Self:-* "In addition to the evolutionary explanation, what other factors could be responsible for the origin and organization of life?"**

Supreme Self: "We find that the possibility of life originating from self-organizing molecules in the volatile surface of the primordial planet was rather remote. Other speculations about the aliens sending designs of complex life to earth are interesting ideas worthy of serious contemplation. But such exotic explanations do not solve the puzzle of the origin of life as they only shift the focus from indigenous to alien intelligence. We have many more explanations like co-evolution, complexity, chaos, systems theory, self-organization and even fractals that relate to some features of the organization of biological life. But, none of them can truly account for the development of diversity in a complex organism. At cellular level such explanations break down leaving us to admire the inexplicable intelligence of the building blocks of life.

What we have so far collected are only fragments of information that do not add up to a convincing picture of reality. They offer explanations, which are as good as assuming supernatural interventions. The mystery underlying the beneficial coincidences that culminated in life cannot be understood if we totally rule out the possibility of some sort of design. An intelligent design for life can arise probably out of the constant interaction between various elements at the level of electron or quark. All the evidences clearly point out that the basic design of the universe and life should have been present in the state of energy prior to the big bang. It must have evolved various kinds of structures through the exchange of information in suitable contexts. DNA recombination in bacteria, support such an explanation. The creation of meticulously designed systems like the immune system and blood clotting system involve constant exchange of information at molecular level."

WHO ARE WE?

No Mind Anywhere!

***Self:-* "How do we become aware of the difference between the self and the external world?"**

Supreme Self: "The analytical study of the brain indicates that it consists of billions of neurons and other cells. They create a massive network of about 100 quadrillion connections. The neural connections perform serial and parallel processing of information received through various sensory inputs. We find that consciousness arises when the brain reaches some suitable level of coherent electrical activity. Studies of visual and olfactory sense organs show that the neurons begin to fire in a synchronized manner when input is familiar. In the absence of consciousness the electrical waves in the brain are in a chaotic state. It is evident that consciousness emerges when some quantum coherent neural oscillation reaches at some optimum level in the chaotic electric field of the brain.

Experimental studies of altered states of mind and the weak presence of self in dreams and childhood also show that consciousness is the first stage in the emergence of a clear identity of self from the external world. We are not sure whether consciousness is an external or internal reality, but the experiences of the self are always within the boundaries of the brain. The computing processes of the brain undoubtedly create the illusions that the mind experiences as objective reality corresponding to the details of the external world. We have to accept the fact that the brain mechanisms are capable of giving a reliable reproduction of reality in spite of the limited perceptual capacities of sense organs and slow computing speed of the neural network."

***Self:-* "How does the mind emerge from the brain processes?"**

Supreme Self: "In Part III, we examined the emergence of conscious self in an altered state of mind. The concept of the self is absent in infants and lower level animals. The conscious self emerges when body awareness reaches a state capable of differentiating the external world. It is also seen that the self is strongly attached to body awareness and the ability to control the physical world. In sleeping and dreaming states the self disappears as body awareness is at the lowest. All these findings clearly indicate that the conscious self is an emergent quality of the brain.

The conscious self experiences the representations of processed sensory inputs fortified by the memory. Vector coding is the methodology used for creating the impressions through parallel processing networks. The synchronized firing of nerve cells at 40-cycles per second or so enables the mapping of multi-sensory impressions. The reality experienced is the true prototype or replica of the outside world with matching details of all aspects of objective reality. It can also create alternative scenarios, which are not related to reality but can help in making correct choices for future.

If we accept such scientific explanations of mind, no room is left for any conscious self to monitor or experience the activities of the brain. According to Daniel Dennet, the brain has no specific area where scenarios of mental images are played out in a coherent manner. There are only multiple streams of activity and it is assumed that the aggregate of all interrelated patterns of neural activity creates consciousness. The mind is something like a self-organizing mechanism consisting of several scenarios that appear and disappear creating an illusion of reality. Some psychologists assume that short-term memory or working memory is the seat of consciousness or mind as it maintains contact with all the current inputs and stored memory data. It is a limited capacity processor, which can handle only about seven words or symbols at a time.

Another mystery that still baffles us is how memory is created and stored symbolically in neural circuits using several concepts associated with the qualities of a particular scenario. It is difficult to admit that mind is just an emergent product of such manipulation of symbols. Moreover, no scientific explanation gives a satisfactory account of the binding of various stimuli to create a holistic reality in the brain. The mind is also not localized in any part of the brain and it can even be held in abeyance by anesthetics or by brain injuries. What we really get from scientific knowledge is a detailed description of the processes in the brain and not the emergence of the mind from it. Our last resort is just to accept the mind as the totality of all processes in the brain. We become conscious when there are coherent oscillations in the neurons in the 40 Hz range and the mind perhaps emerges after the subjective experiences create the illusion of self. The virtual reality is sometimes fortified or modified by an emotional content. The emotional input overrides the other streams of information and directs the body to higher or lower levels of activity. Strong emotions can always create new thoughts in the mind and thoughts can also affect the intensity of emotions. The subjective reality is a unique one to every experiencing self with several qualities added by the memory to the sensory inputs. Certain standard mental images of common objectives and situations can be transferred to other persons, but the exact effect of the experience of emotions cannot be fully conveyed in any verbal transactions."

***Self:*- "What about "free will"? Can it be explained by the laws of matter that evidently control the brain?"**

Supreme Self: "It is true that the mind is not amenable to any exact description in terms of known physical laws. Free will is an important quality of the mind that is not subject to any state of the body or even to the control of the mind. The concept of free will is that the mind acts as if it is an independent entity beyond the control and constraints of the body. The body cannot exist for a long time without the active mind nor can the mind subsist without body support. Experimental evidences now suggest that it is the brain that does all the computations for arriving at a decision much before the mind becomes even aware of it. The decisions taken by the brain are experienced by the mind as its own because of its close link with the body. Even the concept of free will seems to be an illusion created by the subjective reality to make the mind believe that everything emanates from its holistic wisdom. "

Self:- **"What is the scientific view on the mystic vision of self as an extension or reflection of universal consciousness?"**

Supreme Self: "From the scientific explanation of the mind, we understand that it experiences only a kind of virtual reality created by the processing of information inputs in the brain, which are marginally modified memory and by emotional contents. Consciousness is the universal quality enabling all humans to access the external world when the neutral activity reaches a high degree of coherence. The objective reality is never experienced as a direct reflection like in a camera but only when they are processed and projected for the perception as customized images. These images create the subjective reality that opens the gateway to the outside world. Luckily, they correctly match the objective reality in dimensions and properties. Otherwise, it would have been difficult for us to physically move about in the external world and manipulate the objects with precision to make effective changes in the habitat.

It shows that consciousness is only a medium to experience the external world and is not an inherent quality of the brain. The neurons in the brain start coherent firing when they recognize an object or pattern in the external world brain only creating a conduit to the external world through the medium of consciousness. It is consciousness that makes us aware of our own self and the outside world. The mystic vision of Ashtavakra that consciousness is a universal phenomenon seems to be an accurate description of this strange entity. Probably, the quantum coherence of the brain enables us to access external reality in a holistic manner through the window of consciousness."

Self:- **"What is the ultimate solution to the mind-body conundrum?"**

Supreme Self: "We have seen that the concept of mind is derived from the original intelligent energy that pervades the entire universe. The dualistic nature of mind and body is just an illusion. There is no place for the mind in the brain, which contains only physical matter. It is the brain that does all the processing of sensory inputs received from the external world as well as from its own body for creating experiences of the external world. The conscious self or mind is only a conceptual derivative from an unknown form of energy that exists everywhere.

The constant interaction in the brain at some quantum level of electrons or quarks interchanges intelligence with objective reality that consists of vibrations of energy at various frequencies. The synchronized firing of the neurons when they recognize a familiar pattern in the external world gives a clear indication of exchange of intelligence at some basic level. The mind is an assumption that follows the creation of virtual reality in the brain by its computing processes and it is definitely not an independent entity or biological organ. In fact, the mind is better conceived as a coherent correlation with external reality rather than as a concrete physical phenomenon. It emerges from consciousness that reveals the entire external world for our experience through highly synchronized neural activity. The mind itself is an experience that arises only at a high level of neural activity, which is required to establish proper connectivity with the external world. We can demystify mind by understanding it in the proper perspective of an experience or memory created by the various brain processes."

***Self:-* "Is it true that altruistic behavior is an exclusive human trait?"**

Supreme Self: "Neo-Darwinian explanations of life give no scope for propagation of compassionate wisdom in the population of any particular species. Those who possess this quality are not likely to be adept in surviving higher competitive environments. Altruistic genes, if at all there are any, are likely to fade away in course of time, as selfish genes would ultimately dominate with their aggressiveness and ability to eliminate the docile ones. In the case of social insects, the scope of natural selection has probably been widened to include selection of stable social relationships and specific task assignments. Individual and collective behavior of social animals like ants is intended to promote the common welfare of the community. Compassionate wisdom in human society is the outcome of a parallel process of cultural evolution. Some genetic influences for creating strong protective emotions towards infants, elders and weaker persons would have accelerated such cultural evolution conferring compassionate wisdom to humans. Since the number of genes revealed in the human genome mapping is only about 35,000 or so, we have to concede the possibility that nurture plays a major role in shaping our destiny".

***Self:-* "Is there any rational basis for gender bias?"**

Supreme Self: "In early tribal societies, there was a clear division of labor between the man who hunted for food and woman who attended to domestic chores. In agricultural and industrial societies also, the distinction persisted, but it became less sharp as women got gainfully associated in agricultural operations. Some genetic bias in fitness arises from the anatomical differences, but there is no reason to believe that only the males could take up the dominant predatory role. In fact, in the animal kingdom, we find exceptions in several species. While the female lion stalks the prey, the male comfortably often settles for a passive role but joins the dinner party with all gusto. In communities of bees and ants the division of labor has no gender bias. In modern societies it is based on cultural factors but certain genetic explanations are possible for more active or less active roles in the past.

The structural evolution of the brain indicates dominance of left and right hemispheres in males and females respectively. Women are capable of doing certain tasks like providing service and caring for the young and sick in a much better and dedicated manner than men. The dominance of the left hemisphere in the males indicates that they can do analytical jobs involving logical operations more easily than females. Basically, we still display certain legacies from the hunter-gatherer practices of the early tribal societies. But it is not correct to claim any genetic determinism in favor of any particular gender. The behavior pattern change with new social roles and gender distinctions automatically disappear with improving literacy that removes inherited misconceptions about divine preferences. But it is now well known that most of the mutations in the evolution of humans happened in the "Y" chromosome that distinguishes males. We can probably infer that females are less amenable to changes. It may also be on account of their relatively conventional role and lack of opportunities to meet fresh challenges from the environment.

***Self:-* "In brief, what is the overall meaning of existence?**

Supreme Self: "Existence is essentially a biological process common to all forms of life. It is dictated mainly by the genetic compulsions created in a highly adaptive process of evolution in response to the challenges of nature. For human beings, existence is not only driven by the biologically designed computing system of the brain but also by certain cultural factors. They are inherited from the interactions of several generation with the external world in a social context. The mind is primarily motivated by the basic instincts seeking food, sex, safety, parenthood and so on but this list of essential urges now includes the quest for intangible concepts like knowledge, power and positions in life.

Some parts of the brain receive sensations of pleasure even by attaining increments of fitness arising out of altruistic behavior. Genetically, the mind has the singular tendency to move toward fitness-promoting environments and objects. In reality, our existence is an incessant search for pleasure giving patterns in the environment that now includes cultural values such as social acceptability. Cultural evolution has inducted several new dimensions in our mundane biological existence. Intellectual pursuits have now become a much more absorbing activity for some people than biological urges like reproduction. A lot of re-engineering is probably going on in our neural tracts that result in profound genetic changes in the original instinct-driven pleasure circuits.

Humans are now realizing that compassionate co-existence is ultimately more rewarding than the selfish pursuits of survival and fitness. Such attitudinal changes may not have any evolutionary significance, but life is now undoubtedly less conditioned by genetic compulsions. As Ashtavakra correctly puts it, our existence becomes meaningful when we accept whatever comes to us in life spontaneously without craving for any undesirable or undue advantages from society. Life is to be enjoyed fully with simple, straightforward and honest activities that would maximize happiness for both the individual and the society. The purpose of life is harmonious existence with nature; one's own self and with all forms of life. It is self-evident to anyone who acquires true knowledge of reality."

***Self:-* "Is there any ultimate purpose for biological existence?"**

Supreme Self: "In evolutionary terms, the purpose of life is to improve reproductive fitness that ensures perpetuation of the species. The genetic goals are fixed with reference to the basic requirements of the organism like food, sex and security. But the evolutionary purposes relevant to tribal and nomadic societies are not strictly applicable to the present agricultural and industrial contexts. Many of the essential needs of life are normally taken care of in modern societies leaving the individuals with plenty of leisure to pursue other pleasure-enhancing activities. It seems that the purpose of life has switched over to new modes of intellectual pursuits including creation of new knowledge, aesthetics, and altruistic and adventurous activities. In fact, human behavior is now determined mainly by social compulsions rather than genetic instructions. The keen desire for reproductive fitness has very little relevance in modern times, as the purpose of existence has become the pursuit of culturally determined social goals. They give us more lasting sense of fulfillment and achievement in life. The purpose of existence in modern societies is to maximize individual and social welfare by choosing wisely from the various alternatives.

***Self:-* "What is the role of nature or God in the scheme of existence?"**

Supreme Self: "It is evident from our knowledge explorations that intelligent energy is the substrata of everything in the universe. It is highly interactive maybe at micro level, without the mediation of any local force or medium. Such quantum non-locality can exist between two or more particles without any kind of signals exchanged by them. They can also relate instantaneously across all barriers of space and time.

The intelligent energy that created the universe and its structures at different levels including human life can be named as Nature, God, Destiny or any kind of Supreme Being. The undeniable fact is that it had all the intelligence for the creation and maintenance of the universe even before the big bang. It is selectively interactive in certain contexts and also possesses indeterminate potentialities. Nature or God, or whatever we call it, has created the universe out of its interactive intelligence. We have to accept the fact that all of us are the manifestations of the same energy in different shapes and sizes. The unity of all existence is the fundamental principle that should guide our thoughts and actions."

***Self:-* "What are the ultimate answers to the basic questions on existence? "**

Supreme Self: "The ultimate answers emerge when we accept the fact that there is an intelligent energy underlying all existence in the universe. It creates all forms of matter through interactive intelligence in a suitable context. The exchange of intelligence might be taking place at some elementary level. The same process must be maintaining all kinds of structures including biological organisms. Every biological organism seems to be capable of interacting with the environment by exchanging information and developing according to some design evolved from the primordial state of energy. We cannot understand the causal relationships of all such phenomena, as they cannot be logically related to any specific origin.

The kind of causal relationships that can be traced in physical terms are mostly at the higher level of structures, but intelligent interaction probably takes place at the quantum level that is beyond our current capacity of comprehension. The undeniable fact is that the intelligent energy creates through self-organization all forms and varieties of matter and forces. When the mind is unattached, we get a glimpse of the immense presence of this energy. Acceptance of undifferentiated awareness gives us the correct answers to all ultimate questions about where we are, what we are and who we are. The questions of being and becoming are also settled when we realize that all our intellectual pursuits can only unravel the becoming as being is beyond our conceptual abilities. But the fact that it is an unknown form of energy should satisfy our curiosity."

***Self:-* "What is the objective of the activities of intelligent energy?"**

Supreme Self: "It is difficult to decipher any meaning or purpose, as all our thoughts, emotions and even the very existence is integrated with the primordial, intelligent energy. The main point is that the original energy contained all the intelligence including the basic designs to create various structures. The reality must have evolved from the primordial potential by the exchange of information in various contexts. The intelligent energy is the substrata of all matter and forces including the first live cell from which all complex life forms emerged through evolutionary changes. One possible message that we can deduce from this concept of energy is the unity of all types of matter that co-existed even before the big bang.

Further, it shows the utter senselessness of conflicts and divisions presumably for the survival of a particular manifestation of matter for a short duration. We are created from highly refined form of matter and our capability to understand most of the complexities of the universe and life itself is the greatest gift of nature. The intelligence that we possess should enable us to perceive the basic unity of all life in the initial conditions, in the first cell of life and in all its evolved variants. We should also humbly accept the fact that our intelligence is just a reflection of the original intelligence that pervades the entire universe in a timeless and inexplicable manner. This self-realization should make our life less complex, more honest and a highly enjoyable experience of coexistence. Lastly, it should make us more compassionate to all manifestations of energy in the universe."

***Self:-* " Finally, how do we demystify the mind after all the knowledge expeditions through the brain and mystic thoughts?"**

Supreme Self: "Well, after all our search we find that there is no separate entity called mind. Conscious perception creates memory with reference to the body, time and space. The smart molecules in the brain recycle memory to give us the illusion of an experiencing self. Actually, it could be the synchronized firings in the neural network that take the brain to some conscious level of quantum coherence to access its own identity and the external world. The process involved could be resonance or some such exotic exchange of energy. The mind is only an intelligent assumption that emerges from the purely physical processes in the brain. We fail to locate the mind anywhere in the brain simply because it does not exist. At best, the mind gives a useful reference point and identity for some neatly packed molecules.

It confirms the observation of Ashtavakra that the mind is just a reflection of universal consciousness. It may be some sort of quantum state of energy or electro-magnetic field that makes us aware of the outside world as well as our own body. What the mystic wisdom teaches us is to enrich the memory of self with extended awareness. It is possible to reach it only when we assimilate the truth of reality that all forms of matter is the manifestation of the same intelligent energy. With the realization of the real nature of self and universe, our perspective spontaneously changes into a compassionate mode. The mind ultimately gets the message to minimize body awareness to enjoy the enduring ecstasy of existence."

EPILOGUE

HUMANKIND IN THE THIRD MILLENNIUM

WITH HONEST EFFORTS AND
NO SENSE OF GUILT,
AND FULL FAITH IN CONSCIOUSNESS,
LET US ASCEND
TO
ETERNAL GLORY AND BLISS
[RIG VEDA]

THE WHEEL OF GOD TURNS,
WITH ALL FORMS OF LIFE ON ITS RIM
THEY GO ROUND AND ROUND
BIRTH AFTER BIRTH
UNTIL THE TRUE KNOWLEDGE
OF THE UNITY OF ALL EXISTENCE
MAKES THEM IMMORTALS.
[SHVETASHVATHARA UPANISHAD]

HE THAT SHALL ENDURE UNTO THE END
SHALL BE SAVED
[MATTHEW]

Future Perfect

In the preceding chapters, we examined the current level of scientific knowledge of nature at all levels. The tremendous progress made in the intellectual adventures made so far gives us the foretaste of the future possibilities for achieving more revolutionary discoveries. The incredible increase in computing power will give us highly advanced tools to acquire deeper knowledge and create new technologies. In fact, very soon, knowledge will become the global asset accessible of the entire humanity irrespective of divisive national or linguistic barriers. The conventional ideas about economic activities based on factors like capital and labor will soon be replaced by creative intelligence based on rational knowledge. When knowledge rather than inheritance becomes the genuine measure of wealth, literacy will spread like wildfire even in the most backward regions of the world. In the world of ideas, only rational knowledge will prevail and all our inherited ignorance will slowly wither away like the Marxian concept of state.

Rational knowledge acquired on different subjects will soon be integrated creating an interdisciplinary vision of the truth of reality. Super computers will give us the power to penetrate into all the mysteries of matter and life. It may even give us the capability to reengineer the mind. In the next few centuries, discoveries of a fundamental nature will be made particularly in biotechnology, molecular biology and cosmology. We will also have many new gadgets and appliances that will make life much more comfortable. We can now explore on some of the possibilities of knowledge breakthroughs in the very near future. An attempt is made to understand certain consequential problems that could even wipe out all the progress that we have so far achieved.

Adventure Unlimited

Space exploration is one area teeming with great potential for exciting discoveries. It can bring popular interest back into the unexciting reports on scientific enquiries. It is true that in the past few decades, material sciences suffered serious setbacks with environmental issues and new age fancies taking every new proposal to task for their ecological impact. Our space programs can simply ignore all such environmental and moralistic barriers and reveal many unknown fundamental secrets of nature. Moreover, the new knowledge about the real dangers hiding in space can easily scare humanity out of the complacency developed since the cold war days. We can hopefully reach out to other planets and stars without getting embroiled in domestic controversies.

The possibility of a meteor or even a comet colliding and eliminating life forever has been hanging over our planet all the time. We have evidence of several such calamities in the past and science holds out great hopes for effectively overcoming such challenges from the sky by intercepting and destroying the incoming heavenly bodies. If collision is imminent and inevitable, we may have to embark upon interplanetary migration or create space colonies to avoid the impact. Nothing will excite humanity more than the prospects of building new homes in the heavens without leaving our physical body. It is one sure way of accelerating the flow of funds to space programs presently abandoned for want of resources particularly after the initial euphoria of Star Wars subsided.

The threat of extinction of life from collision with a meteor cannot be ignored as mere science fiction. Our planet is undoubtedly a sitting duck in the middle of a cosmic shooting gallery. Thousands of near earth objects can suddenly spring a nasty surprise without any advance warning. Astronomers estimate that about 5,00,000 huge asteroids and hundreds of billions of small ones are always roaming about in the solar system. The big ones like those detected in 1993 and 1996 are real dangers. They appeared as if from nowhere but fortunately spared us from a major calamity. The small ones can be ignored, as they do not normally get past in tact beyond the upper atmosphere.

The most devastating collision our planet had was about 64 million years ago when a large meteor struck Yucatan in Mexico, creating a crater of about 180 miles in diameter. A much smaller collision took place about 15,000 years ago in Arizona in North America and the latest one was on 30 June 1908 in Siberia. According to astronomer Tom Gehries of the University of Arizona, an asteroid of 1 km across can release energy of one million watts of the type that fell on Hiroshima. Whether the collision occurs on land or sea, the damage will be immense to all forms of life on earth. It is estimated that there are about 400 asteroids larger than 1km across which are potential threats lurking in outer space. We can now meet the challenges from space by setting up more advanced observation centers to track down the potential killers.

Modern Noah's Ark

Another threat from the outer space is the possibility of deadly radiation from a supernova reaching earth and destroying all life. The supernova phenomenon occurs when an ageing star collapses under its own gravity. We cannot escape the radiation peril unless we make radiation-proof shelters for all forms of life. Assuming that we somehow manage to survive all these hidden cosmic perils, we still have to face the ultimate fate of earth. In about five billion years from now, the sun will turn into a red giant after using up all the hydrogen in the fusion reaction. The solar atmosphere will gradually reach up to the orbit of Mars and consequently the entire earth will vaporize and vanish forever. Humans can survive this eventuality only if they manage to migrate to other habitable planets. The idea of interplanetary migration is no more a simple story plot for an adventure film. It is something essential in the distant future for the very survival of all species. In fact, we may have to ensure that other species are also taken with us for new lease of life on another planet. The mythological Noah's Ark may have to be rebuilt during the last days of our planet.

Heavenly Abode?

The basic question is where in the vast cosmos can we go looking for a safe haven? In our own solar backyard, there is a promising candidate called "Europa" that is a moon of Jupiter. It looks like a frozen desert but astronomers see the possibility of vast oceans and volcanic activities underneath the desert that can be explored for possible human migration. Outside the solar system, astronomers have located about 28 extra solar planets capable of supporting life. They orbit their respective stars at the optimum distance and water is also likely to be available at least in a few of them. Some form of life may already exist in the moons of these extra-solar planets. Planet hunting is a very interesting scientific adventure to locate planets from the telltale wobble of the star that is evidently caused by the gravitational pull of the planet. Serious efforts are now on to zoom in on an earth-size planet with conditions that more or less match the parameters necessary for sustaining life. Several satellites and space stations will have to be set up for making launching pads for the innumerable space probes required to reach distant planets. Global co-operation will definitely ensure the discovery of new habitable planets well before the ultimate catastrophe puts an end to our mother earth.

Science has ambitious plans for creating space colonies and even terra forming of nearby planets. These alternatives can cut the huge cost involved in space travel. So far, other than Mars no planet in the solar system looks suitable for terra forming. Even an asteroid can be used as a space colony but for such ideas to take concrete shape we need great breakthroughs in rocket technology like laser engines or the use of anti-matter fuel. At the present level of technology, we can only say that it is not yet time to pack our bags for interplanetary migration. Maybe by the end of the next century, we will be in a position to identify suitable planets and plan for an exodus from the earth in the eventuality of an impending collision with an asteroid. We cannot postpone the trip indefinitely in view of the ultimate disaster that will vaporize the earth in a few billion years. Some scientists do not give more than 500 million years for life to enjoy its earthly existence before it becomes a desert.

Encounter With Aliens

Astronomers estimate that millions of planets in our Milky Way galaxy may have conditions somewhat conducive to life. At least in a few planets we cannot rule out the possibility of some sort of intelligent life. A project called "SETI" (Search for Extra Terrestrial Intelligence) has already been set up for detecting signs of alien intelligence. The electromagnetic radiations from our TV and radio signals might have already reached about 59 light years in radius surrounding us. So far, we have not received any response signal from alien intelligence to the overtures of our electronic beckons. One major constraint is that any alien civilization capable of contacting us should be several millenniums ahead of us in intelligence and technology. The presence of some simple form of life like bacteria alone cannot give us any positive indications of advanced forms of life in any distant planets.

Scientists hope to locate alien civilization when they achieve more advanced communication technology using new signal filtering devices. Another plan is to send thousands of

"Von Neumann's Probes" that will go into space and land on the moons of distance stars. Using the minerals and other materials available on the planets, they can make self-replicating factories to send several thousands of robotic copies into space. They can be equipped to detect and contact alien intelligence and, if possible, exchange useful information. The robots can incorporate the latest discoveries of artificial intelligence and biotechnology. They will be just like humans capable of taking independent decisions in all emergencies that might arise in space travel. These machines can even be self-conscious to experience feelings and emotions that can guide their decisions programmed to be in conformity with the needs of the masters at home.

Changing Lifestyle

We have already decoded the sequences in the three billion base pairs of nucleotides in the human DNA. The Human Genome Project will soon pin point the meaning of the specific messages recorded in the genes. Finally, the DNA sequences will reveal for our inspection the entire story of life including the details of instructions about the growth and functioning of various organs. The complete information about genetic sequences in all the 34,000 human genes will enable us to manipulate them to make marvelous changes in our destiny of existence. Genetic manipulations of animals and plants have already given us good results by creating high-yielding and disease-resistant varieties of life. Science can even create animals capable of photosynthesizing their own food and grow new strains of plants and trees that can automatically transplant from salty and desert lands to more congenial habitats. We can also make new strains of animal and plant species that can serve our needs without depleting the delicate planetary resources.

No Incurable Diseases

With the knowledge of the human genome being freely available, gene therapy and molecular medicine will effectively counter the genetic causes of certain incurable diseases. About 4000 genetic disorders and diseases can be more effectively controlled using the new knowledge available from Human Genome Project. Using the information of the genetic structure of the microbes, we can prevent infectious diseases spread by bacteria and viruses. Our immune system can be reviewed periodically and reinforced by identifying the vulnerable points. In fact, the DNA sequence of a patient will soon become the most accurate and reliable diagnostic tool. It can also indicate the susceptibility of a person to serious ailments much before the appearance of the symptoms of the disease. With the preventive steps taken well in advance, sudden heart attacks or strokes will become extremely rare in future. For every disease, gene therapy will become an efficient alternative particularly at the early stages of detection. In about 50 years, medical science can hope to eradicate all the major diseases with molecular remedies.

Cancer Can Be Checked

The well-known capacity of cancer cells for infinite cell division will be eventually checked by the new knowledge of genes. Normal cells stop division after a certain predetermined rounds but cancerous cells continue without any break until the victim is completely destroyed. Our genetic information now shows that cancer is actually caused by a major genetic disposition that is aggravated by certain environmental factors and lifestyles. Most of the common cancers are caused by mutation in a few genes particularly in P-53. It has been estimated that this particular gene is involved in about 52 common cancers. Science magazine called it "The Molecule of the Year" in 1994. Since it has a long molecular structure, mutation can occur at any of the weak points. Several environmental and lifestyle factors such as smoking, pollutants and diet can cause mutations. Science hopes to make cancer detection faster and more accurate by finding defective P-53 genes.

Similarly, the presence of "telomerase" that prevents the contraction of the biological clock in the genes can also indicate the existence of cancer cells. One way of fighting cancerous growths like tumors is by neutralizing or disabling telomerase. They extend the life of the cell by preventing fraying of the end of the chromosome during cell division. This enzyme is also known as the "elixir of youth" in view of its great potential to keep the cells alive forever. But a recent study shows that it is also capable of activating an oncogene that causes cancer. We can even create a cancer vaccine by making genetic modifications to get an effective immune response. The tumour can be injected with a gene to make it succumb to antibiotic or other drugs. The procedure will minimize the side effects of cancer treatment. We may not get a foolproof remedy for all the 200 or so varieties of cancer, but they can definitely be controlled by early detection and molecular intervention. Cancer will no longer be an incurable disease and the cost of treatment will be reduced considerably with freely available molecular alternatives.

Aids Will Be Eliminated

So far, we have not achieved any remarkable breakthrough in the relentless search for an effective cure for AIDS. The main hurdle is that when HIV enters the human body, they can mutate cleverly by disguising and misleading the immune system. They can also develop new mutant varieties that can render conventional medicines ineffective. HIV must have got into the human body from the animal kingdom and despite our earnest efforts to check the spread of infection, it has covered the entire planet in very little time. This virus has become the greatest global menace claiming millions of victims particularly in Third World countries.

Science hopes to get the ultimate defense against HIV by using gene therapy to alter the T-cells, which are the docking sites of the virus. Our knowledge of the HIV genome will eventually lead us to the genetic weak points of the virus for launching an effective molecular attack. The present strategy of controlling the key enzymes that sustain HIV is a combination therapy using three medicines. Although it has been found somewhat useful in controlling the virus, the cost of the cocktail is too prohibitive for the common man. In the USA alone, more than $20 billion had already been spent on AIDS research until 1996. But all that the research has produced so far is the expensive combination therapy that is out of the reach of the poor in developing countries. Molecular therapy will hopefully make treatment less expensive and affordable by all. In fact, we may be able to eradicate the HIV like small pox once we understand how they are genetically equipped to mutate more smartly than other viruses.

Biological Warfare

The ambitious plans of science for effectively controlling and even eradicating most of the diseases in a short while are also fraught with the prospects of deliberate misuse of genetic technology to launch deadly biological warfare. Historically, we find that many countries resorted to biological warfare, which affected the defenseless civilian population. Even the plague virus was used in ancient Greece for destroying large populations of hostile neighbors. There is also a possibility of accidental release of a deadly virus from one of the weapon centers. A mutated Ebola or some other virus can infect the entire planet and destroy millions of people within a few weeks. Yet another serious danger is the possibility of any lunatic getting the equipment from the market for large-scale manufacture of viruses capable of spreading incurable infections. If they hit densely populated areas, millions of people will be infected in no time. In addition to these real worries, viruses may also be developed to attack selectively certain ethnic groups or races. The genetic vulnerability of some races for particular types of diseases can become an effective biological weapon in modern warfare. Science cannot prevent the misuse of genetic knowledge and all countries will have to be extremely alert against ethnic groups or races with fanatics trying to target genetic weapons.

Ageless Wonders

There is worldwide concern for the problems of growing volumes of ageing population. This segment of vulnerable population has become the guinea pig for all sorts of alternative therapies that promise a return to eternal youth and vitality. The human propensity for keeping youthful looks at any cost has been sustaining several successful industries and services. With the new discoveries of the genetic origins of ageing, science will give humanity the much-awaited ultimate elixir of youth. Ageing is an inevitable universal process governed by the law of entropy or the increasing state of disorder. Any closed system, according to this law, would progressively deteriorate by the disorder. Nothing can escape the inevitable onslaught of entropy, which is a fundamental fact of the phenomenal world. The errors that accumulate in our DNA ultimately render cells irreparable and dysfunctional. The process steadily saps out the vitality of organs and in course of time they will cease to function effectively.

Studies now confirm that free radicals are the main culprits for the early ushering in of the ageing process. Anti-oxidants that can neutralize them have become the popular remedy for slowing down the ageing process. Some of the clinical studies on animals show that anti-oxidants can extend the life span by more than 300%. Hormones like estrogen also promise to restore youthful looks and useful years of life. Some select hormones are found to possess the ability to reduce damage to the genes by switching on the production of proteins like prolactin. But unchecked hormone therapy can also cause very serious side effects. Hormones are still not approved as anti-ageing remedy although they seem to temporarily arrest cell deterioration.

But, eventually, science hopes to find the anti-ageing genes that can automatically rectify mistakes in the DNA. Experiments with flies and worms show that gene therapy can considerably extend the life span. Some scientists claim that they have already isolated mortality genes in human cells and some retardation of ageing process has been noticed in clinical tests. The genes that can control the ageing process in yeast spores have also been recently identified. The nutritional processes that cause early ageing can be altered by gene therapy without imposing any strict regimen that curtails the culinary pleasures of life. Probably, the gene responsible for aging when finally found, may eliminate ageing process leaving us with the perennial problem of a planet full of senior citizens seeking discounted fare.

Even after we arrest the ageing process by modifying the genes, we will need lot of new organs to replace the worn-out old ones. Genetic technology can be used to grow artificial organs on polymer substrates. Skin grafts are now common but with the technology of tissue engineering complete organs will soon be available for transplantation. The advantage of this technology is that it does not create the problem of rejection that is rampant in conventional organ transplantations. In short, gene therapy can change our basic concept of life by extending the tenure of the existing ones and inventing new cures for sicknesses arising from the defective functioning of various organs. Creative human intelligence will find new avenues for the use of genetic knowledge to make life a more exciting experience.

Clones Galore

Scientists have successfully cloned animals from an adult cell by fusing the nucleus of a cell with an embryonic cell without nucleus. In these experiments the DNA in the undifferentiated mature cell must have been gently coaxed to revert to the embryonic state. But so far no one has declared a successful human cloning. Scientists are positive about the possibilities of human cloning within a few years. There are several serious legal and ethical issues in human cloning which will have to be resolved before permitting the creation of carbon copies of an adult individual. Ultimately, an effective international law will be required to control indiscriminate attempts to clone humans and even animals. Some countries have already declared human cloning as legal but many are not convinced about the morality of creating clones. In the animal kingdom we can surely preserve rare species by cloning but for humans, no such genetic emergency has arisen for resorting to unnatural ways of perpetuation.

Ethical considerations that discourage human cloning may not come in the way of gene manipulation for creating "designer children." The concept of designer children means elimination of all disease-causing genes and imparting the requisite level of intellectual and physical qualities. Growth hormones are already in use for improving the height and weight in children. Once the relevant DNA sequences are made available, it will be possible to create smarter and disease-free children. The state will find it difficult to deny parents the right to have a particular type of "designer child". There will be very wide commercial application of genetic technology that can be chosen by parents for maximizing desirable qualities in children.

However, the most controversial application of genetic technology will be in the field of behavior control. Science has already identified certain genes responsible for particular behavior patterns like aggression in animals. After mapping the human genome sequences, we can isolate the genes that induce alcoholism, improve memory and even for intensifying the feeling of pleasure. If used indiscriminately, specific genes can be manipulated to alter the behavior of large populations for ulterior political purposes. There is a clear possibility of influencing public opinion by using genetic technology without the knowledge of the victims. Instead of brainwashing, we may see gene washing to create a docile population that will not fight against exploitation or claim any right for freedom of life or expression.

In a few decades, it should be possible to create humans with flawless bodies, impeccable behavior and unlimited potential for the pursuit of dedicated tasks. They will try to achieve difficult objectives that require single-minded application. By manipulating the genes, some scientists even conceptualize the feasibility of creating human bodies capable of growing wings for carrying them anywhere. It shows that whatever fantasies humans nurtured in the past can now become genuine gene reality. After a few centuries, we may find winged traffic cops controlling sky routes and human beings with photosynthesized bodies living comfortably without bothering about food. We are likely to see more profound changes in lifestyles in about three to four generations.

Technology-Driven Life

Based on the new knowledge breakthroughs, this millennium will usher in many more innovative technologies. The most important technological innovation will be an efficient fuel for use in rocket engines and for meeting our increasing energy needs. An excellent fuel is anti-matter, which is the mirror image of matter with an opposite charge. Paul Dirac envisaged it in his conception of quantum theory. Anti-hydrogen has already been obtained but could not be held in a suitable container to prevent explosion. New age technologies will develop magnetic or other containers to hold anti-matter that can be used as the ultimate fuel for inter-galactic travel.

Like anti-matter, super conductors can also be a wonderful alternative energy source but they are too expensive to build and operate in practical situations. Super conductivity is a quantum phenomenon seen in several substances when the electrical resistance is lost at or near temperatures of absolute zero. Super conducting magnets can create powerful levitation to make trains float over the tracks. We can even create flying cars and other mobiles. The extremely low temperatures required can be achieved with innovative technologies using material having altered molecular structure. Super conductors will make energy much cheaper and it can particularly enhance computing speed and diversify the appliances. Interstellar travels will become less time consuming with the use of a new device called "ion thrusters". The idea is to extract electrons from gas atoms and accelerate them to very high velocity before forcing them out through a thruster. Ion thruster can give the spacecraft the high speed required to reach distant planets without wasting precious time.

Other Sources Of Energy

Most of our energy requirements are now met by fossil fuels, but all the known natural sources of such energy will dry up by the middle of this century. Our efforts to locate new supplies and make them more eco-friendly are not likely to fructify and the only way out of the muddle would be to seek alternative sources of energy. It has to be environment-friendly as well as affordable and available to meet the increasing demand for power for the new electronic gadgets.

Solar light is the universally available and cheapest source of energy, but its cost of conversion to usable forms of power is still prohibitive. Solar cells can be made of materials like silicon, which can absorb the energy and release electrons for generating power. We get clean and affordable energy, if the equipment for conversion would be less costly. But the great news is that the equipments are likely to become much cheaper very soon as silicon wafers will be mass-produced applying new technology.

Another excellent source of energy is seawater that can be converted into power through controlled fusion reaction. The basic reaction involved is fusion of hydrogen nuclei into helium nuclei at a very high temperature. The same reaction is what is going on in the core of the stars including our sun. If we can harness the energy released in this reaction, all our demands can be met at very low cost. The only problem is that fusion reaction requires a temperature of 10-100 million degrees Celsius. But scientists are hopeful of overcoming this problem by creating a magnetic field for the reaction.

Millions of dollars have already been spent to perfect the technology to create an affordable temperature for fusion. The Princeton Tawmon Laboratory has already achieved considerable progress in fusion technology, but the program seems to have been shelved for want of financial support. There are many claims of breakthrough in cold fusion technology, but no reliable data is available to verify them. It is likely to be revived soon when new tools are available to manipulate the various parameters for successful application of cold fusion in everyday life. Compared to fusion, fission is much more hazardous in view of the potential for accidental release of radiation. Immense damage has already been caused by several accidents in reprocessing the nuclear fuels. We also have the additional burden of the safe disposal of nuclear waste. Environmentalists oppose new nuclear plants coming up anywhere in the world and their concerns are fully justified from our experience with fission technology.

Compared to the different sources of energy so far discussed, the cheapest and most promising one appears to be fuel cells. Fuel cells use hydrogen to generate energy and the only byproduct is water. They can ultimately be the most effective source of motive power for automobiles and also function as micro power plants to serve domestic and industrial energy needs. The proton exchange membrane cell, which has already been developed, will be available for wide commercial application in a few years. Another technology called solid-oxide fuel cell is also about to enter the market and alkaline technology that claims much more cost effectiveness is waiting in the wings.

Some fuel cell powered cars are now being road-tested and once we sort out the storage and other allied problems, it will provide the cheapest and most environment friendly fuel. Before fuel cells become available for daily use, we will be using hybrid cars and electric cars that can meet the stringent emission standards. Within a decade, the highly polluting fossil fuels will be replaced by commercially viable and economically attractive, clean alternatives. But the tremendous impact of micro power will be felt, when they ultimately replace large power plants that presently supply all our energy needs. We will eventually get rid of all polluting giants who cause immense damage to life and property and make us pay for the transmission losses.

Molecular Machines

Nano technology is an attempt to combine biological concepts with the technological innovations of physical sciences. By manipulating atoms and molecules, scientists hope to create micro size molecular machines for various applications. In addition to the advantages of low-cost production and maintenance, molecular machines can replicate themselves using the unlimited supply of biological raw materials available in the environment. Using this new technology, we can make robots that will perform all the hazardous jobs, which endanger human lives. In medicine, molecular machine can be extremely useful in fighting infections and giving proper diagnosis. They can also be used in super computers and for sending space probes to distant planets. Even frozen bodies can be brought back to life by getting the damaged cells repaired by molecular robots.

Although scientists make many tall claims about the possibilities of nano technology, some people are skeptical about their capabilities and practical utility. It is true that to some extent miniaturization has already been achieved in making prototypes of sensors and motors called "MEMS" (Micro Electro Mechanical Systems). Such technology has already been applied successfully in medical diagnosis and chemical analysis replacing clumsy and expensive machines. It is, however, difficult to envisage too many applications for nano technology, as its size can become a constraint in certain critical areas.

Another technological innovation that science is contemplating is the creation of "Nano Tubes" of carbon to conduct electricity and connect parts of molecular machines. Nano tubes are hollow tubes made of carbon molecules. They are many hundred times stronger than steel and are of negligible weight. Once we succeed in manufacturing this ultimate fiber, the computer industry will act totally revolutionized.

Quantum Jump In Computing

The greatest achievement of 21st Century will be in computing technology. Within two decades, computers will become invisible so that they can be embedded almost everywhere. Spectacles or contact lenses may carry three-dimensional displays that create virtual visual environment over the real environment. In addition to the visual application of computing technology, there will be auditory gadgets for high-resolution sound in a three-dimensional environment. They can be implanted in the ear canal or even as jewellery. Electronic devices will replace rotating memories and other electromechanical computing devices. In education, most of the learning will be through software-based, robotic teachers instead of humans. Highly accomplished human teachers can also reach several learning environments through computer technology. Documents can be read on hand held displays or projected into virtual environment using direct-eye displays. Retinal and neural implants can remove blindness and deafness can be eliminated by cochlear and other implants. Computer-controlled nerve stimulations and robotic devices can also help disabled persons to function effectively and lead a normal life.

Another astonishing revolution will be in communication. Gadgets giving higher resolution three-dimensional displays projected through direct-eye implants and auditory lenses will replace conventional phones. Even three-dimensional phonographic images will be available to make users feel each other's proximity. The cable-based communication system will be replaced by the Web, which will not require any specific equipment to support. In business, transactions will be done with simulated persons having animated personality and two-way voice communication. They can be kept as personal assistants to conduct business with other automated persons. The automated office assistants will exchange appropriate knowledge structures instead of using language. Reliable robots using very little energy will perform all the household chores. Computerized cars and personal flying vehicles will be as common as household gadgets. Normally, no accidents can happen and life expectancy will reach a minimum of about 120 years with the use of molecular medicines and modern gadgets.

Integrated Intelligence

Probably, by the end of the next century, machine intelligence will be merged with human intelligence. The distinction between humans and machines will disappear gradually with virtual reality taking over objective reality in many real life situations. Ultimately, intelligence will not be tied down to any particular individual or machine as it becomes the freely available universal property of the entire humanity. Software-based intelligence of machines will become far more efficient than neuron-based intelligence of the humans.

Humans can also opt for specific neural implants to enhance the capacity of perception and comprehension. In fact, since neuron-based intelligence of humans has limited life and are inferior in speed of computation, it will be supplemented with implants to minimize individual differences in intellectual abilities less apparent. Eventually, biological matter may even lose its dominance as machine matter gain ascendancy over human intelligence. Quantum computing will ultimately take over from conventional parallel and serial computing. We may even manage to give the computers some sort of consciousness to take over many repetitive tasks.

Finally, Lucy The Great

Artificial Intelligence expert Steve Grand is reportedly creating history by making the first conscious robot called "Lucy". Unlike functional robots, Lucy will have to learn how to use her arms, legs and eyes without any specific program being fed into her computer. She will learn to live by responding to the stimulus from the environment through trial and error method and creating memories in her neural network to create consciousness. The only basic program that will be fed to her will be the motivation to survive and receive stimulus. Steve Grand is confident about the success of this machine in view of the fact that he has already created popular cyber pets.

If this experiment succeeds, we will have for the first time a machine capable of replicating conscious human functions. Initially the functions that the conscious machine can perform may be limited to somewhat adequate responses to the environment challenges. But in course of time, may be before the end of the third millennium, we may have fully conscious machines that can take over most of the human functions and leave us free for a totally relaxed and carefree life.

All the future scenarios discussed here may appear like wishful thinking when viewed from the present state of our technology. But looking at our wonderful record of scientific advancements, we cannot ignore them as simple daydreams of overheated brains. Rational knowledge will shortly spread like wildfire everywhere replacing all our inherited ignorance. Formal education will no longer be essential for any work as the on-line knowledge accessible to all can be tapped at any time, anywhere in the world. When knowledge becomes less expensive and more user-friendly, it would definitely usher in the greatest literacy revolution creating better standards of life all over the world.

GLOSSARY

ALGORITHMS- A sequence of rules to solve a problem. Computer programs are based on one or more algorithms.

AMINO ACIDS- are molecules having both basic and acidic properties. Proteins are made of long un-branched chains of amino acids. Proteins have a variety of properties acquired from their amino acids building blocks. Twenty different kinds of amino acids are found in the code for genes.

ANALOG- A continuous change in quantity as distinguished from the changes involving discrete steps. Most of the natural phenomena occur as analogs. In brain process have found both digital as well as analog computing.

ARTIFICIAL INTELLIGENCE (AI)- Uses knowledge based systems, expert recognition, learning and understanding to emulate human intelligence. It is based on the assumption that machines can imitate human intelligence more accurately to create the fields necessary for building comprehensive intelligence.

ASHTAVAKRA- The legend of Ashtavakra is found in the Hindu epic, the Mahabharata (Vanparva). His great contribution is the logical conclusion that universal consciousness is the Supreme Self. The style and composition of his verses belong to the epic period of about the 6th Century B.C. The mystic insights in the dialogues in Ashtavakra Geetha are closer to the later Upanishads like Shvetashutara, Mundaka and Mandukya. Ashtavakra Geetha probably heralded the advent of Buddhism. It does not make any reference to a supreme God as creator nor does it reposes faith in any scriptures or rituals. The monism of early Upanishads seems to have influenced the evolution of Ashtavakra's thoughts on consciousness.

ATTRACTOR- The last stage towards which a dynamic system eventually proceeds. The compulsive repetition of certain types of behavior in nonlinear systems indicates that they are in the grip of an attractor. Examples of attractors are the pendulum of a clock and the movement of water down the drain which are said to be experiencing limit-cycle attractor. Systems that never settle into a steady state are said to in the grip of strange attractor.

BLINDSIGHT- The phenomenon of large blind spots in the visual field. It is the outcome of some damage to the striate cortex in the back of the brain. People with blind sights are capable of locating objects in the blind spots although they are not aware of seeing them.

BRAHMAN- An all-inclusive term that means 'Grow' or 'Expand'. It is said to be beyond all distinctions of forms and is assumed to be the basic supreme reality that existed even before the beginning of the universe. It is the substrate that would have given rise to the phenomenal world of matter and forces.

BUTTERFLY EFFECT- A metaphorical term describing the effect of small systems interacting with large systems through a set of sensitive dependence on initial conditions. The fluttering of the wings of a butterfly in Japan can possibly create a hurricane in the Atlantic. Small differences can multiply upwards into larger systems which eventually cause strange consequences at a later stage.

CASTE SYSTEM- It was conceived originally in India in about B.C 1500 for the settlement of nomadic tribes into an agriculture community. The system assigned certain regulated positions for every individual in society. In the beginning, vocational apartheid was not rigidly enforced, but in course of time it was strictly observed to prevent any possibility of inter-caste movement. Later on, the system deteriorated to become the meanest tool developed by humans to keep large segments of population in perpetual slavery of the upper castes. The lower castes always remained the poor outcast of the society exploited economically by the cleaver coterie of upper castes.

The concept of caste in India differs from the Western system of different classes in the society. In the caste system, every caste is a watertight compartment, prevent inter-caste marriages and social mobility. The scholars, warriors and traders found the upper castes and agricultural laborers were at the lower position. But the lowest were the untouchables who removed the night soil and cremated the dead. In every caste several sub-castes were created to encourage a sense of separateness and identity. Even intra-caste marriages are not allowed if the families do not belong to the same sub-caste. The well-entrenched iron grip of the caste system in India is now slowly loosening with the adoption of universal adult franchise and increasing standard of education.

CHAOS THEORY- is the study of patterns and emergent behavior in complex systems like the weather that contain several unpredictable elements. It assumes that the quantity of the randomness is relevant to the emergence of new products. It is not complete disorder or randomness, but a kind of process based on the presumption that there is no accurate level of order for long-term predictions. Chaos is a useful concept for understanding non-linear processes and it provides logical support to the principle of self-organization.

CHROMOSOMES- Structures in the nucleus of the cell that carry DNA and other molecules. There are 23 pairs in human genome out of which 22 are identical and one that determines the sex. DNA is compressed into tight balls to make chromosomes.

COMPLEXITY- Assumes that the model of chaos and attractors can be applied to explain the evolution of order. Stuart Kauffman proposed complexity to explain the human genome system and also the immune system. He believes that the wonderful complexity of biological organisms could not have emerged from the process of random mutation leading to natural selection. Complexity scientists assume that they have found a unifying principle applicable to all systems. But the critics of complexity do not accept their assertions and consider its application limited to computer programs.

COSMOLIGICAL CONSTANT- Einstein's model universe contained matter in the form of dust. It was prevented from expanding by the introduction of what he called, "cosmological constant". The effect of the cosmological constant is a general repulsion between masses. When it was confirmed that the universe is expanding, Einstein considered that the formulation of the cosmological constant was his biggest blunder.

CEREBRAL CORTEX- The outermost layer of the cerebral hemispheres that looks like a crumpled blanket. It is presumably the seat of consciousness and intelligence.

CORPUS COLLOSUM- A bundle of nerve fibers which connects the left and right hemispheres of the cerebral cortex.

DEEP BLUE- A computer program created by IBM that defeated Gary Kasparov in 1997. He was the world chess champion and the fact that the machine could defeat him was to establish the superiority of machine intelligence over human intelligence.

DARWINIAN EVOLUTION- This concept explains the appearance of wide variety of life forms on the basis of random mutations of genetic materials. Most of the mutations are harmful but some beneficial ones enter the gene pool of the particular species. The potential for new varieties already present in the gene pool comes into existence in suitable contexts. It is an explanation of the process in which several organisms compete for the limited resources. The result of the evolutionary struggle is that more successful organisms survive and reproduce new generations that are better adapted to the environment. Over a period of time, the original design of the organism undergoes several adaptational changes with the sole purpose of survival. This explanation assumes that every organism has got its origin in an earlier form and evolutionary changes occur due to random mutations in the genetic instructions.

The main objection against the classical Darwinian concept of evolution is that chance mutations would have taken a very long time to create any tangible outcome. The wide variety of species on earth cannot be explained by evolution based on competition. In Neo-Darwinism several scientific discoveries are included along with other explanations like self-organization, negative and positive feedback etc.

DNA- (Deoxyribonucleic acid) is a macromolecule on which the instructions for unfolding life are encoded. It unwinds like a tape giving necessary instructions for the productions of proteins. DNA is organized into genes, which gives specific instructions to assemble a particular type of protein out of the chemical soup floating in the cell. The beginning and end of the genetic message are also indicated in the DNA and it has also got a mechanism for checking errors. It is something like a data warehouse of the genetic memory of a live cell. The special structure of the DNA (a double helix) enables the cell to reproduce by division. The curious fact is that the cell uses only about 1.5% of the genome while the rest appears to be redundant. The ultimate expression of the genetic instructions in the DNA however depends upon the cellular and environmental contexts.

When the cell replicates, DNA helix separates and the two separated strands attract corresponding nucleotides from the chemicals available in the cell nucleus. The cell begins to malfunction and die when the DNA message is incorrectly reproduced or chemical contamination, radiation, virus and so on damage it. Several secrets of the DNA like jumping genes, redundancy and DNA recombination are not yet clearly understood. The human genome project attempts to map the sequence in the genetic message.

ELECTROENCEPHALOGRAMS (EEGs)- is a device for amplification and recording of electric currents in the brain. It is used for medical diagnosis and for the study of the functioning of the brain.

THEORY OF RELATIVITY- Einstein's theory of relativity contains his two theories. His special theory of relativity postulates the speed of light as the fastest at which we can transmit information. His general theory relates to the effect of gravity on the geometry of space which includes the famous formula E=MC2 (Energy equals mass times the speed of light squared.) Implications of the theory of relativity are the equivalence of mass and energy, change in mass, dimension and time with increased velocity. These theories are the basis for the concept of nuclear power and even the big bang.

ENTROPY- Indicates the spontaneous movements of systems from order to disorder. The second law of thermodynamics postulates that isolated systems move towards maximum entropy. It increases a minimum force system close to equilibrium. Entropy is a concept that applies not only to machines, but also to the human body. It is also used in information theory to study the transmission of messages.

ENZYMES- are a kind of proteins that act as chemical catalysts regulating metabolic processes.

FRACTALS- are delicate patterns created by nonlinear systems, which capture all essentials of the system in the reproductions. In photography, fractals show repeated or self-similar patterns in the natural world. The repetitions in the patterns of ferns, is an example of fractal.

FREE WILL- It is the ultimate quality of the mind that is expressed in purposeful behavior and decision-making. Free will shows the non-physical nature of mind, as it does not follow the interaction of any known particles to create a predictable outcome. It is difficult to establish any causal link in the choices of free will.

GALILEO- is the first scientist who introduced scientific methodology to the study of natural phenomena. He established that acceleration creates force and also found that mass of an object measured by its weight on earth should be identical with the mass inferred when it collides with other objects anywhere in the universe. The equivalence principle discovered by Galileo gave the first insight into the natural phenomena of gravitational attraction. The modern theories of relativity have their foundations in the discoveries of Galileo.

GENOME- is the complete genetic material in a living cell. Human genome contains 3 billion units of DNA. It contains both genuine genes and junk genes. The active genes contain chemical instructions for making proteins. The gene is coupled to an m-RNA molecule to produce proteins in the cell. Each gene can make more than 10 protein.

GLIAL CELLS- are a kind of cells in the nervous system that perform several supporting functions. There are several types of glial cells but we are not aware of all their functions. They are supposed to contain the imprints of memory.

HOLOGRAM- is an interference pattern encoded by laser beams and read by means of laser beams. This pattern can reconstruct a three-dimensional image. An important property of hologram is that information is distributed in every part of the hologram. Some scientists presume that memory is distributed in the form of holograms in the brain.

HOMO SAPIENS- is a human species evolved about 400,000 years ago. The genetic heritage of homo sapiens is similar to the higher primates and it is believed that they evolved into homo sapiens about 90,000 years ago. Contemporary humans are believed to be the direct descendents of the homo sapiens.

HUMAN GENOME PROJECT- It is a research program for collecting more information about genomic maps and DNA sequence. The data collected by this project would give us information of the structure, organizations and characteristics of the DNA of humans and other animals.

JANAKA- The king of "Videha" who was, according to the epic "Ramayana", the father of "Sita", the wife of "Rama". He also figures in the epic "Mahabharata" and "Brihadaranyaka Upanishad". The king-seer was an avid learner and in his court he entertained several sages and philosophers. The vision of "Ashtavakra" unfolds in his dialogues with Janaka who gets fully convinced and enlightened with the realization of universal consciousness.

LEPTONS- are basic matter particles like quarks. Electrons and neutrinos are leptons. They also have their anti-particles. Leptons also have three different generations like the generations of quarks. The Grand Unified Theory states that leptons and quarks can be mutually transformed at high temperatures.

MAGNETIC RESONANCE IMAGING (MRI)- is a non-invasive diagnostic method for producing computerized images of body tissues. It is based on nuclear magnetic resonance of patterns within the body produced by applications of radio waves. For recording such images, a person is placed in a magnetic field about 30,000 times stronger than the normal magnetic field on earth. When the body is stimulated with radio waves it responds with its own electromagnetic transmissions, which are recorded and processed by a computer to generate the three-dimensional map of internal features like blood vessels.

MICROWAVE BACKGROUND RADIATION- is a thermal radiation detected in the1960s. It is one of the five fundamental observations of the universe. Scientists in Bell laboratories made the discovery. It is presumed that after the universe began with the big bang, it was originally filled with thermal radiation reacting with opaque matter. When the universe expanded and cooled to about 4000K, space became transparent to radiation and it has stretched the wavelength of the background radiation. It is uniform in all directions but there are some wrinkles also noticed in the radiation.

MULTIVERSE- The idea of Multiverse is that we co-exist with an infinite number of baby universes. Our universe is the most stable one having the largest probability of existence. Stephen Hawking proposed that all baby universes are connected by a network of thin worm holes. In the concept of multiverse, there is no need to find what existed before the big bang as the multiverse had always been there.

NANO TUBES- Are of the size of a billionth of a meter which is the width of five carbon atoms. Nano tubes are elongated carbon molecules that resemble long tubes. They are formed by pentagonal patterns of carbon atoms and they can perform the electronic functions of silicon-based components. Since they are extremely strong and heat resistant, they can be used for the creation of extremely powerful computers.

NEURAL IMPLANTS- A brain implant that presumably enhances our sensory capacity. It can be used to improve the memory and intelligence of a person far beyond the existing levels. Implants can also correct loss of faculties due to brain damage and even congenital disorders.

NATURAL SELECTION- The principle underlying Darwinian explanation of evolution of life. Briefly stated, it proposes that better adapted organisms have higher chances of survival and reproduction than their competitors.

NEANDERTHALS- Evolved from Homo erectus about 100,000 years ago in Europe. They were a very intelligent and highly civilized subspecies that observed elaborate funeral functions like burying the dead with ornaments and cared for old and sick persons. They knew the use of various kinds of tools and were said to be very articulate and artistic. The entire subspecies mysteriously disappeared about 34,000-40,000 years ago. It is now assumed that they were annihilated or assimilated by the more advanced Homo sapiens.

OMEGA- A density parameter signifying the average mass per cubic meter in the universe. Its range can be somewhere between 0.2 and 2. If only the omega was exactly 1, the universe would be a flat one, poised between a close and open scenario. If the omega were greater than 1, gravitational force would have been very weak to create any galaxies and stars.

PERCEPTION- is a biological function common to many forms of life. Human beings possess five well known perceptive senses in addition to about seven minor ones like the sense of balance, sense of tension and relaxation of the muscles and the fullness or emptiness in the stomach etc. Some animals have other senses to detect ultraviolet radiations and sonar. Most of the information collected by the sense organs is processed without the knowledge of the conscious self.

PLANCK AND GUT ERAS- After the big bang, the universe expanded and cooled which resulted in several phase transitions similar to steam condensing into water and water into ice. The phase transitions are said to have created seven eras. The first era, the Planck Era, lasted till 10 -43 seconds after the big bang. Out of the seven eras, only the last two are directly observable by telescope. About the first two eras, our ideas are only speculative.

PLANCK'S CONSTANT- is one of the two important constants in physics. Planck's constant is the ratio of particle energy to its frequency and it states that if the frequency increases, its energy must also increase. It is always constant and equal to one quantum. Planck length is the basic unit of length in a quantum theory of gravity and it is equal to appx. 10 -33 cms.

PUNCTUATED EQUIBRIUM- According to conventional evolutionary theory, evolution is a very slow and time-consuming process. Punctuated equilibrium is an explanation for the sudden jumps in the process of evolution that cannot be explained by the classical Darwinian concept. Stephen Jay Gould and co-workers proposed it to rectify the deficiencies in the evolutionary explanation of the variety of life. There is no convincing explanation for the sudden jumps in the evolutionary process, but it can be attributed to self-organization or feedback loops.

PRIMATES- Taxonomic classification of mammals that includes monkeys, lemurs, apes and humans.

PROTEINS- represents a large family of versatile molecules constructed by compiling amino acids to form long chains. They are the principle molecular basis of life carrying out almost all functions that sustain life. They are ordinarily folded, but some of them are also spherical in shape. All enzymes are proteins and their production is controlled by nucleic acids. Proteonics is the study of proteins in an organism. There are probably 5,00,000 to 1 million proteins in human body, which include haemoglobin, insulin, dopamine and countless enzymes.

QUANTUM- All constituents of the physical world at micro level are spinning like tiny tops. The amount of energy that would be required to stop the spin is its angular momentum. "Quantum" is a unit of spin or angular momentum. In quantum theory, the field for each kind of charge a particle carries is described as made up of "Bosons" that are the quanta of the field. In simple terms, quantum is the smallest amount of something that is capable of existing.

QUANTUM COMPUTING- A computing technology based on the mechanics of quantum physics. It uses the universal quality of elementary particles like electrons to exist in dual states. The program is based on quantum bit, which can exist both as zero and one at the same time, until observation causes each bit to collapse into a state of zero or one.

QUANTUM MECHANICS- relates to the interactions of subatomic particles and incorporate several discoveries of quantum phenomenon. It begins with Max Planck's discovery that energy is absorbed or radiated in discreet quantity called 'Quanta" followed by Werner Heisenberg's uncertainty principle, which states that both the exact position and momentum of an electron or other particles cannot be known at the same time. The electrons and other elementary particle simultaneously exist both as waves and particles. Their dual existence is resolved only when conscious observation collapses the wave function to create a particle of reality.

QUANTUM VACUUM- The quantum vaccum is assumed to be the lowest possible level of energy in the universe. In quantum vacuum there is no matter that can be perceived or measured. It seems to be totally empty, but filled with all potentialities for creating matter and forces. A substratum of quantum vacuum is created in the quantum field theory to understand the temporary transmission of the particles to waves and vice-versa. Waves and particles materialize in different forms of the potentialities of the underlying vacuum just like the undulating waves in an ocean. The assumption of vacuum does not mean that there was a vacuum before the beginning. It actually means that the universe emerged out of potentialities embedded in the initial conditions

QUARKS- are fundamental constituents of subatomic particles. There are now six known flavors (kinds) of quarks- up, down, strange, charmed, bottom and top. Each flavor of quark is in three colors and three anti-colors, which make a total of 36. They are the fundamental particles, which make protons, neutrons and other particles.

RED SHIFT- is the reddening of light from a star moving away from our planet. When the source is moving away, the frequency of the waves received will be lower like the stars shifting their spectra towards the red end of the spectrum.

RECOMBINATION GENETICS- is the process in which segments are exchanged between maternally derived and paternally derived chromosomes in each generation. Without recombination, all the genes on any chromosome would have been inherited as a single unit.

REDUCTIONISM- is the based on the principle that the properties of any system made of parts can be understood by knowing its components and their interaction with each other. In other words, it states that a system does not have any characteristics that is beyond the contribution of by its components.

REM- It stands for rapid eye movements, particularly occurring under the eyelids during dreams.

RESONANCE- When two structures vibrate in tune, they are said to be in resonance. There is a continuous exchange of energy between the two resonating objects. The molecules in super position is said to be in a state of resonance. Nuclear magnetic resonance is used in chemical analysis and magnetic resonance imaging is used in hospitals as a diagnostic tool. It is the same principle that is used in the making of microwave ovens.

SCHRODINGER'S CAT- is a thought experiment to prove Schrodinger's equation. The cat exists in superposition of the two possibilities of alive or dead before the box is opened. It is the wave function of two possibilities associated with a system at any given point of time. The experiment shows that two real and equal real possibilities do exist simultaneously before the observation collapses them into one cognizable event. The experiment gives ample proof of the dual state of matter at elementary level.

SCHRODINGER'S EQUATION- describes the dynamic unfolding of possibilities. It also gives the probabilities of materialization of any possibility in a given situation. We can predict the outcome of quantum events using this equation. The problem is that the equation is calculated on an undisturbed quantum system that exists only on probabilities. After materializing any one of the possibilities, the equation has to be recast with a new set of odds.

SERIAL COMPUTER- A computer that performs serial computation at the rate of one operation at a time. Parallel processing involves multiple operations that are be carried out simultaneously.

SUPERNOVA- is the explosion of massive stars after they burn out all the nuclear fuel available for reaction. It results in the creation of new stars and planets out of the products of nuclear reaction thrown into the interstellar medium.

SELF-ORGANIZATION- is a concept opposite of chaos. A complex and unpredictable substrate develops simple but large-scale patterns through the process of self-organization. Examples of self-organization are crystallization, living organisms, Bose-Einstein's condensations and even whirlpools. They always occur in open systems where matter or energy is allowed to flow through. The appearance of interesting patterns in computer simulations of the gene network is an example of self-organization.

SYMMETRY BREAKING- It assumes that nature evolves through the unpredictable breaking of its fundamental symmetries. After the big bang, the universe symmetric as all the forces had equal strength and masses of elementary particles were also identical. Now, we find that the universe is not uniform everywhere as clusters of stars and galaxies are unevenly distributed. The asymmetric distribution of the universe is said to be symmetry breaking. It is assumed that the very first instance of the creation of the universe involved a series of symmetry breakings. The universe started evolving when the color codes between quarks broke away from the electronic force and the electronic force fragmented into electromagnetism and the weak force.

THE STEADY STATE- It is based on the assumptions that the universe looks almost the same at all places and at all times. This is the basic view of all cultures and religions. In fact, even Newton, Einstein and many other prominent scientists accepted the steady state view of the universe. It was only when Edwin Abel discovered in 1929 with the evidence of astronomical observations that the universe is expanding, the steady state theory was finally abandoned. Fred Hoyle tried to redeem it with by stating that the expansion of the visible universe is compensated by the continuous creation of new matter in the consequence phases. The steady state hypothesis stands falsified with the observational evidence of the cosmic background radiation in 1965.

UPANISHADS- are mystical insights attached to the four major Vedas. Vedas are the collection of sacred hymns of the Indo-Aryans, which are four in number called "Rig", "Yajur", "Sam" and "Atharva". Many Upanishads existed at one time, but presently about 10 of them are considered to be more important. They are called Isha, Kena, Katha and Krashna, Mundaka, Mandukya, Taitreya, Aitreya, Chandodya, Brihadaranyaka. In addition to the 10 major Upanishads, Shvetashvatara, Kausitaki and the Maitri are also considered to be important ones.

VEDA- It means revealed wisdom or mystical revelation of ultimate truth. Rigveda is the oldest one followed by Sama, Atharva and Yajurvedas. Veda is considered to be the most ancient collection of Hindu scriptures. They are inspired hymns directed to the various Gods of the Indo-Aryan pantheon.

WORLD WIDE WEB (WWW)- A communication network allowing instantaneous connectivity for sharing of texts, images, sounds, videos and other forms of information. The user interface is based on hypertexts connected by links. It is a system of data and message service linked by communication networks.

YOGA- A system comprising of several disciplines that presumably leading to the ultimate realization of self or union with the God. It is one of the six basic systems of Hindu philosophy.

ZYGOTE- A fertilized egg containing all genetic instructions for the growth of an organism.

SUGGESTED READING

Alexander, Richard (1987) The Biology of Moral Systems. Hawthorne, NY: Aldine de Gruyter

Allport., Gordon, The Individual and His Religion, Macmillan, New York;1950

Andrei Linde, The Self Reproducing inflationary Universe, Scientific American, ,November 1994, pp.48-55.

Aristotle: Metaphysics - in the Basic Works of Aristotle, eds. R. Mec Keon, Random House, New York. 1941.

Armstrong, Este, A. Schleicher, and K. Zilles(1995) Cortical folding and the evolution of the human brain, Journal of Human Evolution 25, 387-392.

Asimov, Isaac, Robot Dreams, Ace Books, New York. 1986.

Atkinson D., Radical Urban Solutions, London: Cassell, 1994.

Baheall J. & Ostriker J.P., Unsolved Problems in Astrophysics, "Princeton University press, Princeton". 1996.

Barkow J.H., L. Cosmides & J., True Bytes, Eds., The Adapted Mind: Evolutionary Pschychology and the Generation of Culture, Oxford University Press, New York. 1992.

Barrow John D. & Frank J. Tipler, The Anthropic Cosmological Principle, Oxford University Press, New York. 1986.

Bateson Gregory, Mind and Nature- A Necessary Unity, Bantom Books, New York. 1980.

Bateson Gregory, (1972) Steps to an Ecology of Mind. New York: Ballantine Books.

_______(1979) Mind and Nature. New York: E.P. Dutton.

Beardsly, T. Weird Wonders: Was the Combustion explosion a Big Bang or a Whisper, Scientific American, June 1992 pp-30-31.

Bickerton, Derek, Language & Human Behavior, University of Washington Press, CIT. 1995.

Bohm,David, Quantum Theory, Constable, London:1951

Bohm David, Wholeness & The Implicate Orders, Rouledge, New York. 1980.

__________ & Mark Edwards,Changing Consciousness, Harper, San Francisco. 1991.

Bohr, Neils, Atomic Physics & Human Knowledge, John Willey & Sons, New York. 1958.

Brockman, John, The Third Culture: Beyond the scientific revolution, 'Simon & Schuster', New York. 1995.

Brown, Lester R., State of the World, 'W.W. Norton', New York, 1996.

Buss, David, The Evolution of Desire, "Basic Books", New York. 1994.

Caird, Rod (1994) Ape Man: The Story of Human Evolution. Edited by Robert Foley. New York: Simon & Schuster.

Calvin, William (1996) The Cerebral Code. Cambridge, MA: MIT Press

Campbell Francis A. & Craig Grimey, 1994 , Effects of Early Intervention on Intellectual & Academic Achievements: A follow-up study of children from low income families, Child Development, 65: pp. 684-98, 1994.

Capra, Fritjof , Uncommon Wisdom, 'Simon & Schuster', New York. 1988.

______, The Turning Point, Flamingo, London. 1983.

__________ , The Web of Life, 'Anchor Book', New York. 1996.

__________, The Tao of Physics, 'Shombhala, Boston, 3rd ed. 1991.

Cavalle, Sforza, Luise Lucur & Francesco Cavalle Sforza, "The Great Human

Diasporas , The History of Diversity & Evolution, 'Addison - Wesley Reading Hall', 1995.

Chalmers, David, The Conscious Mind", 'Oxford University Press', New York. 1996.

Chalmers, David (1996), The Conscious Mind: In Search of a Fundamental Theory. Oxford: Oxford University Press.

Chomsky, Noam, Language & Problems of Knowledge, 'MIT Press', Cambridge. 1988.

____________, Knowledge of Language, Praeger, New York. 1986.

____________, Rules & Representations, Columbia University Press, New York. 1980.

Chomsky, Noam, (1972) Language and Mind. New York: Harcourt Brace Jovanovich.

Chopra D. , Quantum Healing, Bandom-Double Day, New York. 1990.

_______, Ageless Body Timeless Mind, Harmony Books, New York. 1993.

Christiansen, Morton (in press), Language as an Organism- Implications for the evolution and acquisition of language. Cognition.

Cohen, Jack & Ian Stewart, The Collapse of Chaos: Discovery of Simplicity in a Complex World, Viking Penguin, New York. 1994.

Cook,C.M and Persinger, M.A., 'Experimental Induction of a "Sensed Presence" in Normal Subjects and an Excepted Subject', Perceptual and Motor Skills,85 (2), pp.683-93: October 1985.

Cook- Deegan, Robert, The Gene Wars: Science, Politics and the Human Genome, W.W. Norton, New York. 1994.

Coren, Stanley (1995) The Intelligence of Dogs. New York: Oxford University Press.

Coveny, Pelter & Roger Highfield, Frontiers of Complexity: The Search for Order in a Chaotic World, "Ballantine Books", New York. 1995.

Crick, Francis, The Astonishing Hypothesis, Simon & Schuster, New York. 1994.

____________ & Christof Koch, Towards a Neurological Theory of Conscious, Seminars in the Neurosciences 2 (1990): 263-75. 1990.

Damasio, Antonio,Descarte's, Error, Avon Books, New York. 1994.

__________(1994) Cortical systems for retrieval of concrete knowledge: The convergence zone framework. In C. Koch, ed., Large-Scale Neuronal Theories of the Brain. Cambridge, MA: MIT Press.

Darwin Choles, The Origin of the Species by Means of Natural Selection or the

David Neel, Buddhism : Its Doctrines & its Methods, Avon Books, New York. 1979.

Davis Paule, The Mind of God, "Simon & Schuster", New York. 1992.

__________, About Time-Einstein's Unfinished Revolution, Touchstone, New York. 1995.

__________, The Last Three Minutes: Conjuctures about the ultimate fate of the Universe, Basic Books, New York. 1994.

Dawkins, Richard, The Blind Watchmaker, W.W. Norton, New York. 1986.

_______________, The River Out of Eden, Basic Books, New York. 1995.

_______________, The Selfish Gene, II nd edn. Oxford University Press, New York. 1989.

__________, Preservation of Favored Races in the Struggle for Life, "Penguin Classics". 1986.

______________, The Variation of Animals and Plants under Domestication, Organe Judd, New York. 1868.

Dennet Daniel C., Consciousness Explained, Little Brown, Boston, 1991.

___________, Darvins Dangerous Idea, Simon & Schuster, New York. 1995.

Descartes, Rene, Meditations, Bobbs-Merill, New York: 1960

Descartes, Rene (1637) The Philosophical Works of Descartes, rendered into English by Elizabeth S.Haldane and G.R.T.Ross(1970). New York: Cambridge University Press.

Dixon, Bernard, Power Unseen : How Microbes Rule the World, W. H. Freeman, New York. 1994.

Donald Merlin (1991) Origins of the Modern Mind. Cambridge, MA; Harvard University Press.

Drilica, Karl, A. Double Edged Sword: The Promises and Risks of Genetic Revolution, Addison-Wesley, Readers Hall. 1994.

Dunbar, Robin (1992b) Neocortex size as a constraint on group size in primates. Journal of Human Evolution 20, 469-493.

Edelman, Gerald (1987) Neural Darwinism: The Theory of Neuronal Group Selection. New York: Basic Books.

Eccles J. , How the Self controls its Brain, Springer Verlag, New York. 1994.

Edelman,G. Topobiology, "Basic books", New York. 1988.

___________, Neural Darwinism, "Basic Books", New York. 1987.

_____________, The Remembered Present, "Basic Books", New York. 1989.

_____________, Bright Air, Brilliant Fire, "Basic Books", New York. 1992.

Eldredge N., Timeframes: The Rethinking of Darvinian Evolution & The Theory of Punctuated Equilibria, Simon & Schuster, New York. 1985.

Feynman R.P., The meaning of it all, Allen Lane, Penguin, New York. 1998.

Flamagan, Owen, The Science of the Mind, 2nd ed., "MIT Press", Cambridge. 1991.

___________, Consciousness Re-considered, "MIT Press", Cambridge. 1991.

Fodor, J.A (1983) The Modularity of Mind. Cambridge, MA:MIT Press/ Bradford Books
Frank-Kammenetskii, Maxim, Unraveling DNA, "VCH Publications", New York. 1993.
Freedman David H, Brain Makers, Simon & Schuster, New York. 1994.
Freud Sigmund, The Ego and the Id, standard edition, Collected Works, Vol.19, Hogarth Press, London: 1923
Freud,Sigmund, The Interpretation of Dreams, "Avon Books", New York. 1965.
Frisch, Karl von (1967) The Dance Language and Orientation of Bees. Cambridge, MA: Harvard University Press.
Fuster, J. (1980) The Prefrontal Cortex: Anatomy, Physiology and Neuropsychology of the Frontal Lobe. New York: Raven Press.
Futiyoma D., Science on Trail, "Pantheon Books", New York. 1982.

Gallup, G.J., Self-Awareness & The Emergence of Minds in Primates, American Journal of Primatology-2, pp. 237-248, 1992.
Gardner, Harward, Extraordinary Minds, "Basic Books", New York. 1991.
___________(1983) Frames of Mind: The Theory of Multiple Intelligences, New York: Basic Books.
Gates, Bill, The Road Ahead, "Viking" New York. 1995.
Gell-Mann, Murray, The Quark and the Jaguar, W.H.Freeman, New York. 1994.
Gibson K.R. & T. Ingold, eds. Tools, Language & Cognition in Human Evolution, Cambridge University Press, Cambridge ,U.K. 1993.
Goodall, Jane (1986) The Chimpanzees of Gombe: Patterns of Behavior. Cambridge, MA: Harvard University Press.
Goodsill, David S. Bar, Molecular Nature: The Body's Motors, Machines and Messages, Springer - "Verlag", New York. 1996.
Gould S.J., The Pandas Thumb, W.W.Norton, New York. 1980.
Gould, Stephen, Jay, The Mismeasure of Man, W.W. Norton, New York. 1996.
Gray, John, Men Are from Mars, Women Are from Venus, HarperCollins, London: 1992
Grof S. , The Holotropic Mind, Harper, San Francisco. 1992.
Grof, Christina and Grof, Stanislav, The Stormy Search for the Self, Thorsons, London: 1991
Grubber, J. In Search of Schrondiger's Cat, "Banston Books", New York. 1989.

Hafhee, Kathe and Mathew Lyon, Where Wizards Stay Up Late, The Origins of the Internet, Simon and Schuster, New York. 1996.

Harvey, Andrew, The Essential Mystics, Castle Books, New Jersey: 1996.

Hawking, Stephen, A Brief History of Time, "Banston Books",New York. 1988.

Heisenberg, Weiver, Physics and Beyond, Harper & Row, New York. 1971.

Henderson, H., Paradigms in Progress, Adamantin Press, London. 1993.

Hillman James, The Souls Code, Random House, New York. 1996.

Horgan, John, The End of Science, Broadway Books, New York. 1996.

_____________, The Undiscovered Mind, The Free Press, New York. 1999.

Houston, Jean, A Passion for the Possible, Thorsons, London: 1998.

Hoyle, Fred, Home is where the Wind Blows, University Science Books, Mill Valley, Calif. 1994.

Huxley, Aldous, The Doors of Perception and Heaven and Hell, "Harper & Row", New York. 1990.

Jamison, Kay, An Unquiet Mind, "Vintage Books", New York. 1995.

Jerison, Harry (1973) The Evolution of the Brain and Intelligence. New York

Johnson P.E., Darwin on Trial, December 1992.

Joyce, G.F., "Directed Molecular Evolution", Scientific American,

Jung C.G., On the Nature of the Psyche, Vol.8, Collected Works, Vol 8, Routledge & Kegan Paul, London: 1954

Jung, C.G. Memories, Dreams, Reflections, Collins and Routledge & Kegan Paul, London: 1954.

Kagan, Jerome, Three Seductive Ideas, "Harward University Press", Cambridge. 1999.

Kaku,Michio Visions, "Anchor Books", New York. 1997.

_______________, Introduction to Super strings - Sponger-Verlag, New York. 1988.

Karmiloff-Smith, Annette (1992) Beyond Modularity. Cambridge, MA: MIT Press.

Kauffman, Stuart, At Home in the Universe, "Oxford University Press", New York. 1995.

______________, The Organs of Order, "Oxford University Press", Oxford, England.

Kimbrell, Andrew, The Human Body Shop: The Engineering and Marketing of Life, Harper Collins, San Francisco. 1993.

Kinura M., The Neural Theory of Evolution, "Cambridge University Press", New York. 1983.

Kitener, Philip, The Levels to come: The Genetic Revolution and Human Possibilities, Simon and Schuster, New York. 1996.

Kolb, Brain, and Ian Whishaw (1990 Fundamentals of Human Neuropsychology. 3d ed. New York: W.H. Freeman & Co.

Kuhn T. H. , The Structure of Scientific Revolutions, University of Chicago Press, Chicago. 1970.

Laing, R.D., The Divided Self, Penguin, London: 1959 (1990)

Lassen, N.A., and B. Larsen (1980) Cortical activity in the left and right hemispheres during language-related brain functions. Phonetica 37, 27-37

Le Doux, Joseph, The Emotional Brain, "Simon & Schuster", New York. 1996.

Levy, Steven, Artificial Life, "Vintage", New York. 1992.

Lewin Roger, Complexity, Mac Milan Publishers, New York. 1992.

Lewis, John S. Minning the Sky : Untold riche from the Asteroids, Commets and Planets, Addison -Wesley, Reading March, 1996.

Libet B., 'Unconscious Cerebral Initiative and the role of Conscious Will in voluntary action'., The behavioral and brain sciences, Vol.8pp. 529-66. 1985.

Lindley, David, The End of Physics, Basic Books, New York. 1993.

Lovelock, James, Ages of Gaia, W.W. Norton, New York. 1988.

Lovelock J.E., Geia- A New look at Life on Earth, Oxford University Press, Oxford. 1982.

Luria, A.R. (1980) Higher Cortical Functions in Man (2nd edn., English translation). New York: Basic Books (original Russian text published by Moscow University Press, 1962)

Margulis, Lynn and Dorion Sagan, What is Life? Peter Neuranmont, Inc., New York. 1995.

Maturana, Humberto D. & Francisco J. Varela, Auto Poiesis & Cognition: The Realization of the Living, D. Reidel, Boston. 1980.

Mayor E., One Long Argument, "Harward University Press", Cambridge. 1991.

Mc Donald J.F., "The Molecular Basis of Adaptation" Annual Review of Ecology and Systematics 14, 1993.

McKinney, Micheal, and K.J. MacNamara (1991) Heterochrony: The Evolution of Ontogeny. New York: Plenum Press.

Meginn, Colin, The Problem of Consciousness, Black well, Cambridge Mass. 1988.

Morse, Stephen, S. Ed., Emerging Viruses, "Oxford University Press", Oxford. 1997.

Mukherjee, Radhakamal, Astavakragitha, "Motilal Banarasidas Publishers, Delhi". 1971.

Myss, Caroline, Anatomy of the Spirit, Bantam Books, New York: 1997

Neher, A., The Psychology of Transcendence, Dover, New York. 1990.

Nikhilananda S., The Upanishads, Arthur & Row, New York. 1964.

Olivier, Richard, Shadow of the Stone Heart: A Search for Manhood, Pan Books, London: 1995.

Ornstein, Robert (1973) The Nature of Human Consciousness. San Francisco: W.H. Freeman.

Pais Abraham, Einstein Lived Here, Oxford University Press, New York. 1994.

Passingham, Richard E. (1979) Brain size and intelligence in man. Brain Behavior and Evolution 16, 253-270

__________(1985) Memory of monkeys (Macaca mulatta) with lesions in prefrontal cortex. Behavioral Neuroscience 99, 3-21.

Penrose Roger, The Emperor's New Mind, "Oxford University Press", New York. 1989.

______________, Shadows of the Mind, "Oxford University Press", New York. 1994.

Persinger, M.A., 'Feelings of Past Lives as Expected Perturbations Within the Neurocognitive Processes That Generate the Sense of Self: Contributions from Limbic Lability and Vectorial Hemisphericity', Perceptual and Motor Skills, 83 (3 Pt. 2), pp. 1107-21: December 1996.

Peterson John L., The Road to 2015: Profiles of the Future, "Waite Group Press", Carte Madera, Calif. 1994.

Pinker Steven, How the Mind Works, Norton, New York. 1997.
______________, The Language Instruct, Harper Perennial, 1994.
___________, The Language Instinct: How the Mind Creates Language. New York: William Morrow.
Pinker, Steven, and P. Bloom (1990) Natural language and natural selection. Behavioral and Brain Sciences 13, 707-784.
Popper, K.R. and Eccles, J.C., The Self and its Brain, Springer-Verlag, Berlin: 1977
Porter Eliot, James Gleick, Natures Chaos, Viking, New York. 1990.
Pratt, Annis, Dancing with Goddesses, Indiana University Press: Bloomington and Indianapolis, 1994.
Priogogine Ilya, from Being to Becoming, Freeman, New York. 1980.
Putnam, Hilary (1975) Mind, Language and Reality. Cambridge, UK: Cambridge University Press.

Ramachandran, V.S. and Blakeslee, Sandra, Phantoms in the Brain, Fourth Estate, London: 1998.
Raup David M., Extinction: Bad Genes or Bad Luck, Norton, New York. 1991.
Rees M., Before the Beginning, Pergens Books, Reading, Massachusetts. 1997.
Reges, Ed., Nano: The Emerging Science of Nanotechnology, Little, Brown, Boston. 1995.
Reps, Paul, Zen Flesh, Zen Bones, Penguin, London: 1971.
Rescher,Nicholas, The Limits of Sciences, "University of California Press", Berkeley. 1984.
Restak, Richard Brainscapes, Hyperjon, New York. 1995.
Richards, Robert (1987) Darwin and the Emergence of Evolutionary Theories of Mind and Behavior: Chicago: University of Chicago Press.
Roth, Michael, editor, Freud : Conflict and Culture, Knopf, New York. 1998.
Ruelle David, Chance & Chaos, Princeton University Press, Princeton. 1991.
Russell, Bertrand, The Analysis of Matter, Kegan Paul, London and Boston: 1985
Russo, Enzo and David Cove, Genetic Engineering, Dreams and Nightmares, W.H. Freeman, New York. 1995.

Sagan, Carl, The Dragons of Eden : Speculations on the Evolution of Human Intelligence, "Ballentine Books", New York. 1977.

Savage-Rumbaugh, E.Sue, and Roger Lewin (1994) Kanzi: The Ape at the Brink of the Human Mind. New York: John Wiley.

Scientific American, Mysteries of the Mind, Special Issue, 1997.

Searle ,John(1980) Minds, brains, and programs. Behavioral and Brain Sciences 3, 417-458.

Searle J. R. , The Rediscovery of the Mind, The MIT Press, Cambridge M.A. 1994.

Shapiro, R., Origins: A Skeptic's Guide to the Creation of Life on Earth, "Summit Books", New York. 1986.

Simmon, Geoff, Robots, The Quest for Living Machines, Cassel, London. 1992.

Simon, Herbert, The Science of the Artificial, 3rd Ed., "MIT Press", Cambridge. 1996.

Singer, W. and Gray, C.M., 'Visual Feature Integration and the Temporal Correlation Hypothesis', Annual Reviews of Neuroscience, 18, pp.555-586: 1995.

Singer, W. 'Striving for Coherence', Nature, Vol.397, pp.391-393: 4 February 1999.

Sirag S., In Mishlove, J., The Roots of Consciousness, Council Ox Books, Oklahoma. 1993.

Skarda, C.A. and Freeman, W.J., 'How Brains Make Chaos in Order to Make Sense of the World', Behavioural and Brain Sciences, 10(2), pp.161-173: 1987.

Smith, J.H., "Life at the Edge of Chaos", New York Review, March 22, 1995, pp.28-30.

Smolin L., The Life of the Cosmos, Phoenix, London. 1997.

Stanley Steven N., Children of the Ice Age, Crown Publishers, New York. 1995.

Stapp, H. P., Mind, Matter and Quantum Mechanics, Springer, New York. 1993.

Steen, R.Grant, DNA and Destiny: Nature and Nurture in Human Behaviour, "Plenum Press", New York. 1996.

Stewart Ian, Natures Numbers, Basic Books, New York. 1995.

__________& M.Goluviesky, Fearful Symmetry: Is God a Geometer, Blackwell, Oxford. 1993.

Sulloway, Frank, Born to Rebel, "Pantheon Books" , New York. 1996.

Talbot Michael, The Holographic Universe, Harper Collins, New York. 1991.

Tarnas, Richard, The Passion of the Western Mind, Pimlico, London: 1996.
Terrace, Herbert (1979) Nim: A Chimpanzee Who Learned Sign Language. New York: Knopf.
Thurow Lester C., The Future of Capitalism: How Today's Economic Foress shape
Tilley, D.R. and Tilley, J., Superfluidity and Superconductivity, Adam Hilger Ltd, Bristol and Boston: 1986
Tipler, Franch, The Physics of Immortality, Double day, New York. 1944.
Tomorrow's World, Willium Morrow, New York. 1996.
Treffert, Darold A. (1989) Extraordinary People: Understanding Savant Syndrome. New York: Ballantine Books.
Trefil, James, Are We Unique ? John Wiley & Sons, Inc., New York. 1997.

Varela F. J., Thommpson E. & Rosch E., The Embodied Mind, The MIT Press, Cambridge M.A. 1991.
Veggeberg, Scott, Medication of Mind, Henry Holt & Co., New York. 1996.

Waldrop M.M., Complexity: The Emerging Science at the edge of Order and Chaos, Simon & Schuster, New York. 1992.
Walker, Alan (1996) The Wisdom of Bones: In Search of Human Origins. New York: Alfred Knopf.
Walsch, Neale Donald, Conversations with God, Hodder and Stoughton, London: 1995.
Webster, Richard, Why Freud Was Wrong?, "Basic Books", New York. 1998.
Weimer J., The Break of the Finch, "Vintage Books", New York. 1994.
Weinberg Steven, Dreams of a Final Theory, "Pantheon", New York. 1992.
_______________, The First Three Minutes, "Banston Books", New York.1977.
West Thomas, In the Mind's Eye, Prometheus Books, Buffalo. 1991.
Wilber, Ken, ed., The Holographic Paradigm and other Paradoxes, New Science Library, Boulder, USA: 1982.
Wilber, Ken, Sex, Ecology and Spirituality, Shambala, Boston and London: 1995.
Willis, C. (1993) The Runaway Brain: The Evolution

Wilson, Edward O., Naturalist, "Strand Press", Washington D.C. 1994.

________________, The Diversity of Life, Harward University Press, Cambridge. 1992.

Wingerson, Lois, Mapping our Genes: The Genome Project and the Future of Medicine, "Penguin Books", New York. 1990.

Winson, Jonathon, The Measuring of Dreams, Scientific American, November, 1990.

Wolf, Fred Alan, The Dreaming Universe, "Simon & Schuster", New York. 1995.

______________, Parallel Universes: The Search of another World, "Simon & Schuster", New York. 1989.

______________, Conscience,

______________, The Body Quantum, Mac Millan, New York. 1986.

________________, Consilience, Alfred A.Knoff, New York. 1998.

Wolpert Lewis, The Tramp of the Embryo, Oxford University Press, New York. 1991.

Zohar, Danah, Through the Timer Barrier, "Paladium Books", London. 1982.

Zohar, Danah and Marshall, I.N., The Quantum Society, Bloomsbury, London and William Morrow, New York: 1990.

Zohar, Danah and Ian Marshall, Spiritual Intelligence, The Ultimate Intelligence, Bloomsbury, London: 2000.

Zukav Gary, The Dancing Wuly Masters, Bantom Book, New York. 1979.

__________, The Seat of the Soul, Simon & Schuster, New York. 1990.

Zukirman, Ben and Hart Michael, edn. Extraterrestrials, where are they? Second ed. "Cambridge University Press", Cambridge. 1955.

INDEX